COOPERATIVE LEGAL SYSTEM

By

Dr. R. Karunakaran

Assistant Professor

Department of Cooperatives

Faculty of Business Economics

Hawassa University, Awassa

Ethiopia

Mail: ramakaruna2004@yahoo.com

&

Dr. M. Karthikeyan

Assistant Professor

Department of Cooperatives

Faculty of Business & Economics

Hawassa University

Hawassa

Email: mkeya2003@gmail.com

mkeya2003@yahoo.com

DPH

DISCOVERY PUBLISHING HOUSE PVT. LTD.

NEW DELHI-110 002

Published by:
Tilak Wasan

DISCOVERY PUBLISHING HOUSE PVT. LTD.
4383/4A, Ansari Road, Darya Ganj
New Delhi-110 002 (India)
Phone : +91-11-23279245, 43596064-65
Fax : +91-11-23253475
E-mail : parul.wasan@gmail.com
discoverypublishinghouse@gmail.com
web : www.discoverypublishinggroup.com

***First Edition:* 2012**
ISBN: 978-93-5056-070-9

Cooperative Legal System

Printed at:
Shree Balaji Art Press
Delhi

Preface

Dear Readers! We are very much glad to present a textbook on "Cooperative Legal System", which is an important course for a Cooperative Degree programme. This work is based on our experience as teachers, trainers and researchers in the field of cooperatives for more than 15 years, of which 6 years in Ethiopia. The present work is based on Undergraduate programme and outcome of our teaching and research experience, and many articles published in reputed journals. This book is first of its kind in the field of cooperatives. This book will be very much useful to the student of undergraduate, and also to professionals and managers involved in cooperative movement, the trainers and policy-makers in the field of cooperatives. We have drawn inputs from official documents, various materials— papers, journals, books and we have consulted several of our friends, colleagues and field experts. We are ever grateful and thankful to them for their immense support and healthy criticism. We hope that the readers of this book will get knowledge on cooperative legal systems. Any useful comments, suggestions to improve the present version are welcome and solicited from the readers. We are thankful and grateful to Parul Wasan, Discovery Publishing House Pvt. Ltd., New Delhi for publishing the book neatly under his renowned label for the knowledge community.

R. KARUNAKARAN

M. KARTHIKEYAN

Contents

Part-II
Development of Cooperative Law in Ethiopia during the Periods of Imperial Government and DERG Regime

Part-III
Development of Cooperative Law in Ethiopia During Transitional Government (At Present)

Part - I
General Framework and Cooperative Legislation

1 Preliminary Considerations of Law

Cooperative Law — A Reflection of Economic Social and Political Circumstances

Over the past twenty years employment has decreased in number and its nature has been transformed fundamentally. Population patterns and demographic structures have changed. Economic decision-making processes have been concentrating. Rapidly accelerating urbanization has aggravated the ensuing social problems. These developments have occurred amidst a reciprocal process of globalization and technological innovations and amidst growing concern for sustainable modes of production and consumption.

For various ideological and structural reasons, the prevalent state model prior to the 1980s catered for a gamut of social and economic needs. Since the early 1980s this model has been questioned. Internal budget constraints, external debt burdens and the end of the ideological world-divide led, as a first reaction, governments, international donor organizations and nongovernmental organizations to advocate a minimalist state model. Today, they agree that development requires an effective state – everywhere – limited in its powers to creating market-enabling political and legal frameworks and concentrating government action on those public goods which the market cannot or does not provide effectively or efficiently.

More and more governments understand that structural adjustment measures, which are implied by these changes, compel them to reduce their role in the economic and social sphere, to decentralize and liberalize administrative, political and economic structures, to move from planned to market economies and to balance the development of the different sectors of the economy. These measures will fall short of success if not complemented by the development and strengthening of institutions based on self-help and self-responsibility. Thus, cooperatives are increasingly being rediscovered as a means in their members' hands to achieve goals which companies do not find profitable and which governments are no longer able or willing to achieve.

At the same time, this rediscovery has been shedding light on the fact that the gap between cooperative values and principles, on the one hand, and legal reality on the other, leaves cooperative self-help potential under-utilized, if not unutilized. Current cooperative law reforms are to rectify this state of affairs and thus provide institutional support to structural adjustment measures.

The challenge for the national legislator is two-fold:

- reinstate, based on the universally recognized cooperative values and principles, the distinctive features of cooperatives whilst;
- responding to appeals by the international community for more cultural diversity in legislation, as legal reforms are marked by a harmonization within and across the boundaries of economically defined regions.

The international community supports these legal reform initiatives.

Why a Cooperative Law?

In certain countries, such as Denmark and Norway, cooperative movements prosper without being ruled by their own law.

But there are no cooperative movements prospering without any legal rules applicable to them. Some of the main reasons for this are:

1. The existence of a cooperative law is a necessary, though not a sufficient condition for getting a cooperative policy to work.
2. The rule of law is a fundamental element in the new approach to development, which emphasizes the respect for human rights. This presupposes that the legal relationship between citizens and the state is founded on acts of parliament.
3. International cooperation and global economic agents use law in an ever increasing manner as a means of information and communication. Law is a reference point and a guide mark.
4. In complex societies, where social control can no longer be based on close personal relationships, regularization of social relationships has proved to be the most adequate means of regulating the activities of economic agents who are not personally linked to one another. By definition, this is especially true where economic relations are not entertained by physical persons only but also by legal persons. In order to provide for legal security, the law has to establish the criteria for the definition of these persons, the power of their organs and their liability in lieu of that of the members or the individual shareholders.

5. Law is a suitable and tested means to represent and maintain a just balance between the autonomy of the cooperators and the cooperatives, on the one hand, and the powers of the state, on the other.
6. Law adds to stabilizing the political system.
7. National laws are a necessary means to implement the public international cooperative law.

Cooperative Principles

The United Nations (UN), the International Labor Organization (ILO) and the International Cooperative Alliance (ICA), i.e. those universal organizations which have a mandate to further the development of cooperatives, promote the following cooperative values and principles:

❖ voluntary, open membership within the limits of the social objective defined in the bylaws/statutes of the cooperative in question, and the right to freely withdraw.

The interpretation of this open-door principle – i.e. negative and positive non-discrimination as regards gender, social origin, race, political affiliation or religion – must take into account the associative character of cooperatives. The free will of the members to work together constitutes one of the keys of their motivation. This is incompatible with any attempt to impose certain persons as members.

❖ self-help, self-determination, self-administration, self-control and self-responsibility through democratic means ("one member/one vote"). This principle embraces that of cooperative autonomy, meaning that cooperatives should be allowed to regulate their internal affairs free of outside influence, be it by government or any other agent.

The matter is also linked to that of positive discrimination of cooperatives by the state. It is now commonly accepted that negative discrimination of cooperatives violates basic rights and rules on fair competition and thus distorts market conditions. More and more, it is also held that positive discrimination, i.e. the granting of privileges and advantages, prevents cooperatives from becoming competitive. Competitors are not willing to enter into business relations with entities which are known to be fed by the state. Regional and universal economic organizations, like the European Union and the World Trade Organization, increasingly insist on states abiding by international competition law. In addition, positive discrimination is often the justificatory basis for infringing upon the autonomy of cooperatives and it bears the risk of false cooperatives being created

❖ economic contribution by the members to the activities of their cooperative;

- ❖ information to the members by the cooperative's officers;
- ❖ inter-cooperative cooperation; and
- ❖ concern for the community. The ICA added the principle of "concern for the community" during its Centennial Congress in Manchester in 1995. The long-standing debate on the question whether cooperatives should exclusively serve their members or whether they should also serve their communities was, however, not re-opened. Nothing prevented the members of a cooperative in the past from working in a voluntary manner in favour of their community. As specified by the 7th ICA principle, they may continue to do so "through policies approved by their members", i.e. on a voluntary basis. By design, cooperatives are to further their members' interests. This design is not suited to further the interests of society at large. According to the cooperative ideal, the well-being of the members of cooperatives should contribute to that of the community. Questions linked to finding sustainable modes of life, i.e. modes which care for ecological balance, economic security, social justice, and participation in the political decision-making processes require that the interests of the members of cooperatives be constantly redefined.

Summary

- ❖ Cooperative law is a reflection of economic, social and political circumstances.
- ❖ Over the past twenty years, lot of changes occurred in the spheres of socio-economic, political, legal, government, and technology.
- ❖ Owing to the change in the above spheres, Cooperatives are increasingly being rediscovered as a means in their members' hands to achieve goals which companies do not find profitable and which governments are no longer able or willing to achieve.

Self-Learning Activity

1. State any three reasons for having a separate cooperative law.
2. What do you think of the challenge ahead for the national legislator as for legal reform initiatives?

2 Public International Cooperative Law

Core of Public International Cooperative Law

The ICA Statement, the UN Guidelines and ILO Recommendation No. 193, containing the cooperative values and principles, form the core of the public international cooperative law. This law has to be respected when legislating.

The binding force of these instruments for national legislators has long been questioned. The ICA is a non-governmental body whose decisions do not bind states. UN Guidelines do not have the binding force of treaties or conventions. An ILO recommendation, as the name implies, serves as a guide for Member States and compliance cannot be enforced in the same way as ILO conventions can. However, governments are accountable to the ILO Committee of Experts on the Application of Conventions and Recommendations.

It is to be noted, in addition, that ILO Recommendation No. 193 was adopted by an overwhelming majority (two abstentions only) and that the UN Guidelines were adopted by consensus. If it ever were, the view that these instruments are not legally binding is not tenable anymore, because:

- the ICA definition of a cooperative and the cooperative values and principles, as laid down in the ICA statement, form an integral part of ILO Recommendation No. 193; the UN Guidelines make reference to "cooperative values and principles"; and
- ILO Recommendation No. 193 is a concretization of cooperative-relevant binding Human Rights instruments, which contain all the basic prerequisites for cooperative legislation.

Those who are not convinced that these instruments form the core of the public international cooperative law must at least recognize that the cooperative values and principles constitute a public international customary cooperative law. The cooperative values and principles have a long history of being applied by cooperators and of being considered by those who have to decide whether certain facts are to be recognized as reflecting cooperative values and principles. The ICA, as the guardian of these values and principles, is the largest non-governmental organization worldwide. Its non-ideological and apolitical approach to cooperative development over a period of 110 years has contributed to its being recognized and respected by all quarters.

Summary

- The challenge for the national legislator is two fold: reinstate, based on the universally recognized cooperative values and principles, the distinctive features of cooperatives whilst responding to appeals by the international community for more cultural diversity in legislation, as legal reforms are marked by a harmonization within and across the boundaries of economically defined regions.
- In certain countries, such as Denmark and Norway, cooperative movements prosper without being ruled by their own law. But there are no cooperative movements prospering without any legal rules applicable to them.
- The United Nations (UN), the International Labor Organization (ILO) and the International Cooperative Alliance (ICA), i.e. those universal organizations which have a mandate to further the development of cooperatives, promote the cooperative values and principles.
- The ICA Statement, the UN Guidelines and ILO Recommendation No. 193, containing the cooperative values and principles, form the core of the public international cooperative law. This law has to be respected when legislating.

Self-Learning Activity

1. What does form the core of public international cooperative law?
2. What is the binding force of the core of public international cooperative law?

3 Socio-economic, Political and Administrative Factors and Systemic Nature of Cooperative Law

Socio-economic, Political and Administrative Factors

In order to thrive cooperatives need a favourable socio-economic, political and administrative framework. The current development model is based on political and economic freedom. The state must ensure respect for human rights, including the rule of law, the freedom to choose one's economic activity, free access to national and international markets, private property as well as a clear distinction between the public and the private sector based on the principle of subsidiarity. Apart from exercising the functions of legislation, registration, deregistration, and general normative control, the state in a market economy must not interfere in the economic affairs of cooperatives.

This statement needs three clarifications:

1. This type of relationship between the state and economic organizations is not cooperative-specific. It determines the legal nature of the cooperative law and it is the foundation of the non-discriminatory treatment of cooperatives and their members, be it to their advantage or to their disadvantage (prohibition of positive and negative discrimination).
2. After decades of interference in the affairs of cooperatives, and in times when the living conditions of disadvantaged people in a number of countries are further deteriorating, the state must not withdraw instantly and/or completely from economic affairs. Under such circumstances the legal policy on genuine cooperatives might have to be accompanied during a specified period of time by a policy of disengagement of the state and of promotion of cooperatives.
3. It would be an illusion to think that the modern market economy needs only a simple political and legal structure. Quite to the contrary, it

functions because of its highly complex political and legal structure. The balance between non-intervention and a policy of laissez-faire, which would be destructive in the long term to the cooperative system as a whole, can only be maintained by a complex legal system. The law must provide for the existence of the greatest possible number of different private agents and induce their participation in the decision-making in economic matters. With regard to cooperatives, and given past experiences, this implies the prohibition for governments to convert cooperatives into transmission belts for national policies and, in particular, for policies accompanying structural adjustment programmes. The private character of cooperatives should prevent their being used as instruments for political, developmental, social or other goals. Any such use of cooperatives endangers their economic efficiency. State administration related to cooperatives must thus be as restrained as that related to the private sector in general. Thus, for example, one single, possibly decentralized, register for companies and cooperatives could be envisaged. For the rest, government should be concerned with providing a well-functioning business environment at all levels, for example effective and efficient tax administration, an independent judiciary, an efficient banking and insurance systems, and with promoting chambers of commerce, industry and agriculture as well as professional organizations (trade associations). In addition, it should include cooperative issues in the learning curricula at all levels and in its extension services and it should encourage business advisors to make cooperatives part of their expertise.

This necessary (re)distribution of roles between the state, the cooperatives, their movement and other private actors might be facilitated by setting up a national council for cooperatives, which could reconcile state sovereignty with the independence of the cooperatives. Conceived as a discussion forum and as a consultative body, this council should in no case take on a mission of tutelage.

The application of a policy of non-intervention in the economic activities of the private sector depends essentially on the organization of the politico-administrative system and the willingness of its office-holders. Thus, to the extent the constitutional system permits it, decentralization and de-concentration of power should be favoured, so that decisions can be taken and applied at the local level where cooperatives mainly operate. This could also mean entrusting local administration with the application of the cooperative law, even if it is a so-called "traditional" administration.

In theory, the administration is only an instrument in the hands of the government. Frequently, however, administrators acquire such independence as to be able to effectively oppose changes in policy orientation. The passage to a market economy brings about the transition from a more or less direct intervention in the management of dependent cooperatives to the recognition of cooperatives as independent structures. Administrators are required to apply more subtle rules. They might not always have the necessary qualifications and/or they might not be prepared to exercise the necessary flexibility to do that.

The Systemic (Universal) Nature of Law

Cooperative legislation is part of cooperative law. Cooperative law is constituted by all national, supranational and international normative, administrative and judicial acts and the praxis commonly accepted among cooperators as they bear on the formation, the structure, the operations and the dissolution of cooperatives.

Thus, the rule on the non-discretional and non-discriminatory exercise of administrative power and on the justifiability of all public acts, constitutional and administrative norms, rules on local and regional administration, real estate and private law in general, irrigation, water, investment, commercial law, company, tax, competition, labour, bankruptcy, and credit laws, regulations on imports, exports and pricing, on contracts, inheritance, accountancy, banking, consumer protection and social security, transport and marketing, etc. must all be severally and jointly conducive to and supportive of genuine cooperatives if cooperative legislation is to be effective.

When drafting the law the legislator must therefore make sure that other legal provisions do not run counter to his project. It will be particularly important to be vigilant regarding the provisions contained in competition law and in social and labour laws. The latter two are marked by the wish to guarantee minimum social protection and to establish a balance between unequal partners, and they are at times incompatible with the right to self-determination of cooperatives and their members. These aspects require resorting to a general legal expert who looks after the compatibility of the different texts. The ministry of justice is normally the guardian of the harmony of the legal system.

Summary

- ❖ In order to thrive cooperatives need a favourable socio-economic, political and administrative framework. The current development model is based on political and economic freedom.
- ❖ The state must ensure respect for human rights, including the rule of law, the freedom to choose one's economic activity, free access to national

and international markets, private property as well as a clear distinction between the public and the private sector based on the principle of subsidiarity.

- ❖ Apart from exercising the functions of legislation, registration, de-registration, and general normative control, the state in a market economy must not interfere in the economic affairs of cooperatives.
- ❖ Cooperative legislation is part of cooperative law. Cooperative law is constituted by all national, supranational and international normative, administrative and judicial acts and the praxis commonly accepted among cooperators as they bear on the formation, the structure, the operations and the dissolution of cooperatives.
- ❖ These aspects require resorting to a general legal expert who looks after the compatibility of the different texts. The ministry of justice is normally the guardian of the harmony of the legal system.

Self-Learning Activity

1. What do cooperatives need from the state in framing the law?
2. What does a cooperative law constitute?

4 Scope and Nature of the Cooperative Law

Scope of the Cooperative law

Before elaborating the law, the legislator will have to consider its scope.

It is suggested that the scope of the cooperative law be limited to one specific, organized type of self-help.

State structures do not allow for the reproduction of knowledge necessary to administer unorganized self-help groups, let alone a combination of these and organized groups on the basis of one single law. In addition, legislation on all forms of self-help in one law would necessarily tend to neglect the informal, non-organized in favour of the formal sector. Besides, the administration of a comprehensive law on all forms of self-help would be extremely costly.

When distinguishing between organized and non-organized self-help groups it is important to differentiate between cooperatives as voluntary associations of persons, i.e. a mode of organizing a group, and communities, i.e. a way of life. Cooperatives may only prosper if their members are autonomous in their economic activities and if economic life in general is kept separate from other social activities.

Societies where the community is considered as an indivisible entity find it difficult to integrate the concept of legal personality, which allows for abstract bodies to exist independently of their members. They find it, for example, difficult to understand that the financial liability of cooperators may be limited to their shares.

Where the concepts of association and community are confused, it may happen that the implementation of the cooperative law will be hampered by community-type mechanisms. This mixture tends to be harmful to both the cooperative and the community-type group in which cooperative members often continue living.

The distinction between associations and communities must not be confused with that between cooperatives and simplified cooperative structures, as proposed in these Guidelines. With the latter distinction the Guidelines draw on a trend to be observed in recent cooperative laws. These include chapters on "simplified cooperative structures", i.e. organizations that function according to cooperative principles without fulfilling all the requirements of a fully-fledged cooperative. Other laws do exempt such structures from a number of otherwise compulsory requirements. Such structures might not need, for example, a supervisory committee (where required), a full-time manager, an elaborate accounting system or a chartered accountant as an auditor. The distinguishing criteria might be the turnover, the membership size or the degree of interrelatedness with third parties. This concept is gradually replacing that of "pre-cooperatives" according to which these entities had to either convert into "full" cooperatives or to dissolve after an unsuccessful probationary period of time. Some countries do discuss in this context the appropriateness of having separate legislation for so-called new (generation) cooperatives.

There is an interesting parallel in legal history. In the past, legislation on companies with limited liability was introduced because stock companies proved to be organizations too complex for many entrepreneurs.

Nature of the Cooperative Law

Public or Private Law?

The legal nature of the cooperative law depends on the definition of its objective. If it is to regulate the activity of the cooperative sector, it will be part of public economic law and should include, besides rules on the formation, structure, operations and dissolution of cooperatives, also rules on the establishment, the set-up and the powers of a supervisory authority. If, on the other hand, it is to only propose to potential cooperators a mode of organization which will permit them to develop their activities in an autonomous manner, then it will be part of private law.

The insertion of the cooperative law in one or other of these fields reflects a political choice. In the context of structural adjustment to the requirements of human rights, democracy and the rule of law, private law is the logical choice since the legislator is not seeking public involvement in the activities of cooperatives.

Development Law

The history of cooperatives has been frequently marked by their being used as instruments to serve the goals of the state, more often than not synonymous with one political party, a family or even a single person. In the context of development the end of this instrumentalization allows for a more genuine reflection of the special legislative needs of the countries of the South. Their mainly externally geared, accelerated socio-economic change suggests a specific, development enhancing and this change accommodating law. The legislators of these countries might have to define the kind and the scope of issues to be dealt with in a cooperative law in a different way than legislators in other countries.

In the past, development efforts of states often ended up in managing cooperatives on a day-to-day basis in order to make them fit modern, mostly imported law. What was originally meant to be provisional often became institutionalized. Public funding brought about tight control, thus closing the vicious circle of government involvement and a growing dependence of the cooperative system on the state. Not masters of their destiny, cooperatives saw state officials survey their formation and operations, define their activities or organize their vertical integration and use the cooperative law to shape society at large.

On the other hand, cooperatives were granted tax privileges, they had easy access to credit or state controlled support. In so far as these privileges violate the equal treatment principle or are granted because of the mere sake of the cooperatives being cooperatives, these privileges should not be granted anymore. The 4th ICA principle indicates which shape the relationship between government and cooperatives ought to take in this context.

Such constraints and privileges can no longer be part of cooperative law. Not only are they incompatible with the fact of cooperatives belonging to the private sector; they are also incompatible with development requirements.

The proponents of the transplantations of so-called modern law which was to secure this kind of "development" were, if at all, guided by the theory of the "development of law". Law was seen as a technique apt to be developed. They ignored the theory of "development law", which is rather concerned with finding out how development could be induced and supported by law. Law is not to create social reality but to structure it.

The widely ignored "development law" theory pre-shaped the current human rights approach to development, at least as far as law is concerned. The Human Right to Development replaces the classical notion of development with that of development through cultural diversity.

Mistakenly, the challenge of designing a development enhancing law is frequently thought to be solvable by allowing for deviations from the cooperative principles through government decrees on key areas of cooperative development.

Development law is a body of law which not only shapes socio-economic activities. It must at the same time bear the features of development by channeling rapid socio-economic change into a direction which is beneficial for those concerned by the change. A number of key rules must therefore be in the form of graduation clauses, i.e. clauses whose application ceases once the aim which was to be reached through that rule is reached.

Summary

- Before elaborating the law, the legislator will have to consider its scope.
- It is suggested that the scope of the cooperative law be limited to one specific, organized type of self-help.
- State structures do not allow for the reproduction of knowledge necessary to administer unorganized self-help groups, let alone a combination of these and organized groups on the basis of one single law.
- In addition, legislation on all forms of self-help in one law would necessarily tend to neglect the informal, non-organized in favour of the formal sector. Besides, the administration of a comprehensive law on all forms of self-help would be extremely costly.
- Cooperative structure is also one of the areas to be considered while framing the law for cooperatives.
- The legal nature of the cooperative law depends on the definition of its objective. If it is to regulate the activity of the cooperative sector, it will be part of public economic law and should include, besides rules on the formation, structure, operations and dissolution of cooperatives, also rules on the establishment, the set-up and the powers of a supervisory authority.
- If, on the other hand, it is to only propose to potential cooperators a mode of organization which will permit them to develop their activities in an autonomous manner, then it will be part of private law.
- Development law is a body of law which not only shapes socio-economic activities. It must at the same time bear the features of development by channeling rapid socio-economic change into a direction which is beneficial for those concerned by the change.

Self-Learning Activity

1. Is the law to apply to all forms of self-help or to organized forms of self-help only?
2. What do you think of public or private law?
3. What do you think of development law?

5 Choice of the Adequate Legal Instrument

Introduction

The choice between the different legal instruments, i.e. the constitution, laws, ordinances, decrees, regulations, government orders, (government) model bylaws etc., is not a free one.

The principle of cooperative autonomy and the rule of law determine the choice.

The autonomy of cooperatives will only be achieved and/or maintained by respecting the principle of subsidiarity. Only matters which surpass the competence of an individual cooperative, which are of a democratically defined public concern or involve third party interests may be regulated through public norms, while everything else must be left to be determined through bylaws/statutes. This notwithstanding, the cooperative law should be sufficiently detailed to avoid its character being altered through government rules. This is of particular importance in countries where laws take effect only once the relevant government decree of application is issued.

According to the rule of law, questions relating to cooperative principles must be regulated by law, whereas decrees or other administrative acts are limited to operationalizing the law, especially in matters that are of a temporary nature or which are subject to frequent changes, such as for example rules on fees and fixed interest rates.

Once inscribed in the law, a rule cannot be overturned unless a competent court of law so requires or the law is revised. However, rules of whatever legal nature cannot nullify those contained in other texts having the same or a higher legal ranking. This is an additional reason for the importance of taking into account the systemic character of cooperative law.

One Cooperative Law or Several Laws?

In view of the wide range of self-help organizations with differing activities, needs, membership bases, stages of development, sizes, degrees of complexity and inter-relatedness with competitors, it must be decided whether there shall be one law for all types of cooperatives (for example, service, workers, consumer), all types of activities (for example, agriculture, housing, fishery, cattle raising, savings and credit, transport, supply, marketing etc.), all types of professions (for example, fishermen, craftspeople, medical doctors, lawyers etc.), single-purpose and/or multi-purpose cooperatives and all levels of cooperative organizations, one law with separate parts for all or some types of cooperatives/activities or several distinct laws. It might even be that there is no need for a separate cooperative law at all if the civil code, commercial or other laws provide for the regulation of cooperatives.

For the legislative procedure this choice has an immediate incidence, for example, on the designation of the lead ministry in charge of the formulation of the law or the amendments to the law.

Worldwide one finds any thinkable combination, from many laws to no law. The trend is towards having one single general law covering all types of cooperatives because it is believed that:

- one law for all types of cooperatives, possibly with specific parts for specific types of cooperatives/activities, for example, housing or savings and credit cooperatives, best guarantees the autonomy of cooperatives, i.e. their power to regulate their own affairs as far as possible through bylaws/statutes, since the degree of detail in such a law will be lower than in a multitude of laws.
- this low degree of detail diminishes bureaucracy.
- one single law avoids the fragmentation of the cooperative movement that might occur where different types of cooperatives were registered under different acts and placed under the supervision of different public authorities with, perhaps, heterogeneous policies.
- one single law creates legal security for those dealing with cooperatives. Legal security relates rather to structural and liability aspects than to a specific type of cooperative or activity.
- in the context of development constraints, one single law is the most adequate tool to reach congruency between development-oriented, member-oriented and self-sufficiency goals of cooperatives.

However, in the light of the recent discussions on how to restore cooperative distinctiveness, it is being considered, especially in the industrialized countries, to have different laws.

Summary

- The choice between the different legal instruments, i.e. the constitution, laws, ordinances, decrees, regulations, government orders, (government) model bylaws etc., is not a free one. The principle of cooperative autonomy and the rule of law determine the choice.
- In view of the wide range of self-help organizations with differing activities, needs, membership bases, stages of development, sizes, degrees of complexity and inter-relatedness with competitors, it must be decided whether there shall be one law for all types of cooperatives or no need for a separate cooperative law at all if the civil code, commercial or other laws provide for the regulation of cooperatives.

Self-Learning Activity

1. What determines the choice between different legal instruments?
2. What is your opinion on having one single general law covering all types of cooperatives?

6 Language and Format of Cooperative Law and Sequence of Matters to be Contained in the Law

Language of the Cooperative Law

Understanding the law is a prerequisite of its implementation. It is not unusual that the primary addressees of the cooperative law neither master the official language in which the text is written nor understand the legal terminology. The promulgation of the law in vernacular languages, the use of an accessible style or the adoption of a law that one can understand as far as possible without having to resort to other texts are some of the means to improve access to the cooperative law.

But the cooperative law cannot and must not be an exception within its legal system. Its language must be consistent with that of the other legal texts so as to ensure the cohesiveness of the legal system.

Format of the Cooperative Law

The format of the cooperative law might seem of secondary importance. Nevertheless, it must be noted that form and content are one. The degree of detail should therefore be reflected upon.

A brief law, only defining an organizational framework for cooperatives, necessarily refers to other provisions, making it less intelligible and therefore relatively difficult to understand. From a practical point of view, a detailed law thus seems preferable. However, in reality detailed texts, while avoiding cross references to other texts, develop a degree of detail which risks impeding the autonomy of cooperatives by limiting notably the space they may fill with their bylaws/statutes.

On the other hand, detailed laws prevent an excessive resort to government instruments. The time dimension has to be taken into consideration as well when deciding on the format. Often, details in the cooperative law pertain to time-bound political, social and economic issues which change more or less rapidly over time, thus requiring adaptations of the law. Frequent changes of the law not only consume resources but they also affect public opinion about the value of a law. They do not match the long-term perspective of cooperative development, for which legal stability/ continuity is vital, and they meet the inertia of administrators.

Sequence of the Matters to be Contained in the Law

There are many ways to present the sequence of the different sections of a law. They have no influence on the legal value of the sections. However, the "life" of a cooperative or the subject matters may predetermine to a certain extent this sequence. On the other hand, one may also think about the sequence of the different sections from the point of view of those who shall apply the law, i.e. the members, the organs or their representatives. These Guidelines try to marry these two approaches by suggesting a sequence which follows the phases of a cooperative from its formation to its dissolution, on the one hand, while regrouping those sections which pertain to either single members or to the organs, on the other. This results at times in repetitions.

Summary

- The language of the cooperative law must be consistent with that of the other legal texts so as to ensure the cohesiveness of the legal system.
- The format of the cooperative law should be in detail and the time dimension has to be taken in to consideration as well when deciding on the format.
- There are many ways to present the sequence of the different sections of a law. They have no influence on the legal value of the sections. However, the "life" of a cooperative or the subject matters may predetermine to a certain extent this sequence. On the other hand, one may also think about the sequence of the different sections from the point of view of those who shall apply the law, i.e. the members, the organs or their representatives.

Self-Learning Activity

1. Comment on the language of the cooperative law?
2. What do you know about sequence of the matters to be contained in the law?

7 ABC of Cooperative Law

As legal entities cooperatives have to be subject to legislation. Their structure, functioning and especially their position vis-à-vis third parties have to be regulated.

The following main topics of a cooperative law will be presented here:

- Preamble
- General provisions
- Formation and registration
- Obligations and rights of the members
- Organs/bodies and management
- Capital formation, accounts, surplus distribution and loss coverage
- Audit
- Dissolution
- Simplified cooperative structures
- Horizontal and vertical integration
- Dispute settlement
- Miscellaneous, transitory and final provisions

Preamble

If the legal system of the country permits it, and by clearly stating the legal nature thereof, the cooperative law could start with a preamble.

The preamble will guide the interpretation of the law, which is all the more important where genuine cooperatives are not yet solidly implanted. The preamble could indicate the following matters:

- The role and the function of cooperatives in society in general and in the economy of the country in particular.

- The character of cooperatives as private and autonomous organizations having access to all lawful activity.
- The involvement of the government which will be limited to the formation, dissolution and promotion of cooperatives and to general normative control.
- Equal treatment of cooperatives and their members with regard to other business organizations; i.e. they will not be discriminated against, either negatively nor positively, in order to avoid distortions between competitors and the formation of bogus cooperatives.

Equal treatment in the legal sense means identical treatment with other business organizations, where possible, but different whenever the specific nature of the cooperatives sc requires. For example, one might point to the taxation of two items which are typical for cooperatives— surplus and patronage refunds. Surplus produced on transactions with the members is the result of a cooperative specific way of calculating costs (near costs) and patronage refund, paid pro-rata of the business of the members with their cooperative, is a deferred price reduction or a correction of the price calculation at the end of the financial year, should the economic risk included in the original cost calculation not have materialized. If surplus may therefore not be compared with profit, it should not be taxed as such.

General Provisions

Definition of terms used in the law

A glossary of key legal terms used in the law could be included in the text, annexed to it or contained in a separate document. This is all the more necessary where this kind of law is new or marks a change of policy, or where a single general text replaces several more detailed ones. Such a glossary would also have the merit of facilitating communication at the international level.

Application of other norms

Because of a widespread false assumption the law must clearly indicate that the registration under the cooperative law does not exempt cooperatives from abiding by the rest of the legal order. Cooperatives are not exempt from obeying other legal norms, especially not from obeying those regulating their activity.

Definition of cooperatives

The universally recognized definition of cooperatives as contained in the ICA Statement and in ILO Recommendation No. 193 reads as follows: "A co-operative is an autonomous association of persons united voluntarily to meet their common economic, social and cultural needs and aspirations through a jointly owned and democratically controlled enterprise." In addition to uniting voluntarily the potential members should also come together on their own initiative. Rather than copying this or another definition, it is advisable to formulate their own one where the local context so requires, whilst paying respect to the universally recognized cooperative values and principles. The definition will also depend on the legislator's choice between a single law governing all types of cooperatives and several specific laws.

The definition and the subsequent rules must reflect those features which best distinguish cooperatives from other forms of business organizations, namely the cooperative identity principle and the principle of member promotion. The identity principle means that members were the co-founders and that the members are co-financing the cooperative of which they are the co-owners, co-managers, co-controllers, co-users and co-beneficiaries and for the debts of which they have co-liability. The principle of member promotion means that the betterment of the situation of the members is preferred over producing high returns on invested capital. The combination of these two principles constitutes the dual nature of cooperatives. They are groups of persons (associations) and economic enterprises at the same time or, more precisely, they are a group of persons who have an enterprise, i.e. cooperatives are not investor controlled enterprises, but associations of persons who work towards common objectives through a joint enterprise. Although this enterprise must be run in a profit-oriented way, it is distinct from capitalist enterprises in that it is oriented towards its members' interests and not towards its own interests.

The definition of cooperatives is not only to differentiate them from capital-centred organizations but also from non-profit organizations, from charity organizations and from other possible forms of self-help organizations.

The definition should be written into the law as this helps:

- ❖ the government to carry out the normative functions of the state;
- ❖ to distinguish genuine cooperatives from false ones;
- ❖ to determine the rights and obligations of the members, as well as those of the organs of the cooperative;
- ❖ to specify the qualifications and duties of cooperative officers concerning capital management and serving the interests of the members;
- ❖ to state minimum rules concerning accountancy and audit in order to further the efficient use of financial and human resources;
- ❖ to resolve the conflicts that might arise between cooperative law and labour law or between cooperative law and competition law;
- ❖ to adequately assess the tax status of cooperatives and their members;

- to justify equal treatment of cooperatives, in the sense explained earlier;
- to regulate the relationship between private and public entities;
- to facilitate the evaluation of the economic, social and political impact of cooperatives; and
- to promote international cooperation for the development of cooperatives.

The definition of cooperatives is not limited to primary cooperatives. It also applies to secondary and tertiary cooperatives if they are allowed to carry out an economic activity. Finally, considering the number of groups and organizations based on self-help, mutual aid or solidarity, those structures which do not come under the cooperative law could be listed in the law by way of so-called negative definition, especially if they are regulated by other laws of the country.

Cooperative Principles

The universally recognized cooperative principles may be included in the preamble or in the definition of the cooperative, by listing them or by making reference thereto. A reference has the merit of being more flexible and of not imposing a revision of the law should the principles change, but it makes the application of the law more complicated because it refers to external texts. Another solution is to draw up a list of the cooperative principles, taking care not to give this list a limiting and definite character. This could be translated by the use of expressions such as "among others ..." or "in particular ...". Thus the reference would include possible changes and allow for additional principles.

Whatever the solution, it is important that the nature of the referred to or cited cooperative principles be expressly stated and that the cooperative principles not be written as if they were legal norms, because that would limit the legislator in making adaptations of these principles to the national circumstances and, in fact, respect for these principles would be rather improbable. It would also limit the autonomy of cooperatives.

Likewise, legal rules must not be written in the form of principles because in that form they are not applicable and will most likely call on government to replace the legislator by issuing norms where it should limit itself to issuing regulations, which make legal norms operational, where necessary.

Formation of Cooperatives

Registration

The recognition, and thus the protection, of cooperatives by the state manifest itself in the registration of their name and all other information justifying their status as a legal person in a public register. Noting what has happened during the last decades in a number of countries, it appears that the law must foresee severe sanctions against any abuse of the name "cooperative".

The granting of the status of legal entity is, as a rule, motivated by the wish to favour the participation of private persons in joint economic activities since these are judged to be more viable. The fact that their personal responsibility and, in particular, their financial liability, is not committed beyond the amount of the shares subscribed, unless decided otherwise in the bylaws/statutes, is certainly an encouraging factor for people to become members of legal entities. One might object that the distinction made between the organization and its members contradicts the cooperative principle according to which the cooperative may not be dissociated from its members. But if members are not to bear personal liability for the activities of their cooperative, then only such a distinction will allow for a shift of liability to an independent entity with legal person status.

Types of Registration

There are two basic types of registration:

- the quasi-automatic registration; and
- the registration after approval by a public authority.

According to the first option, which complies best with the rule of law, a cooperative must be registered once the conditions laid down in the law are fulfilled. If, for whatever reason, prior approval is necessary, the discretionary power of the approving authority must be strictly and effectively limited by law.

Registration Authority

The separation of state powers, the legal nature of the cooperative law, the definition of cooperatives and the use of the registration procedure as a means of an *a priori* control are elements to consider when choosing the registration authority.

Recognition of cooperatives as economic organizations of the private sector would permit having all types of enterprises registered in one single register. Even though registration is an administrative task, it could be exercised by the judiciary. But experience has also shown that an authority specialized in cooperative matters, and possibly helped by personnel seconded by the cooperative movement, is more apt to handle registration issues properly.

The legislator has to ensure that the registration be conceived as a local service and that the potential cooperators have to deal preferably with a single authority only when applying for registration. Where different authorities are involved, these should communicate amongst themselves and vest the power to deal with the potential cooperators with one of them.

Registration Procedure

In no case must the registration procedure hinder citizens from forming groups in the way that suits them best. No registration will be made without a request from an elected representative of the nascent cooperative. This request must be filed within a brief time limit, fixed by law, after the constitutive general assembly.

Documents to be attached

❖ the minutes of the constitutive general assembly, with the signatures or finger prints of all founder members. If the bylaws/statutes were adopted on the basis of model bylaws/statutes, the minutes must document a detailed discussion of these model bylaws/statutes;

❖ a sample of the signatures of the persons with the right to represent the cooperative;

❖ several copies of the bylaws/statutes with the signatures or the finger prints of all founder members;

❖ the report of an economic feasibility study concerning the planned activities of the cooperative and a statement as to the qualifications of the board members. This study should be carried out by a cooperative apex organization or another recognized structure. Where there are no such structures yet government may temporarily carry out this task. The task must not be given to the registration authority in order to avoid it being judge and party at the same time.

The objective of this requirement, which is not imposed on the founders of other business organizations, is not to hamper the freedom of potential cooperators, but to see to the interests of the members of the future cooperative and potential business partners, since the risks these are running are greater than those usually permitted for other types of enterprises, because cooperatives have no minimum capital requirement and, generally, their capital base is weak. The legislator must, however, refrain from such preventive measures if it cannot exclude abuses of power in connection with this study:

❖ a list of the persons entitled to file the application for registration and to notify all subsequent changes to be made to the registry;

❖ a document showing that an adequate portion of the total amount of the member's shares has been paid up and stating the period of time within which the remainder must be paid.

The implementation of a speedy and impartial registration procedure is a first step by the state towards facilitating the development of a genuine cooperative movement.

To this effect, the following procedure is proposed:

- ❖ A deposit receipt stating the application for registration and listing the documents presented, duly signed and dated, will be given upon presentation of the above-mentioned documents.
- ❖ Registration will be concluded within a short time period. One certified copy of the bylaws/statutes, mentioning the number and date of registration will be given to the cooperative. It will be proof of the official recognition of the cooperative as a legal person.
- ❖ A refusal to register must be justified in writing and notified to the group that requested registration.
- ❖ In the case of such a refusal, the founders may appeal before a court (to be specified) which should give a decision within a brief time period.
- ❖ If within the required time limit, no refusal has been notified, or if the court has not given its decision, registration will be presumed. The registration authority will also in this case, within a fixed and brief time period, send a certified copy of the bylaws/statutes, indicating the number and date of the presumed registration to the cooperative.
- ❖ Whichever its type, the registration should be published within a fixed and brief time period by means of an easily accessible medium, generally used by the local authorities. In case the registration is not published within the time limit set, the cooperative will be presumed registered and the person not having fulfilled his duties will be financially liable for the consequences;
- ❖ The fees for the registration and publication must in no case be prohibitive.

Where the registration becomes effective with its publication only, cooperatives must have the right to demand that the time periods mentioned be brief and respected by the registration authority.

Only registered, in some cases registered and published, or known information is binding on third parties. After registration, cooperatives must therefore make sure that any subsequent changes in the registered data be notified to the registration authority, failing which, the persons not having fulfilled this duty will be held financially liable for the consequences.

Nature and Effects of the Registration

By registering (and publishing the registration, where necessary), the state confers legal person status to the cooperative. The status signifies that the cooperative is responsible and liable as a legal entity, independently of its members and with perpetual succession. The members will not be, for example, individually responsible for any acts performed in the name of the neither cooperative, nor will they be liable beyond the amount of the subscribed shares for the debts of the cooperative, unless otherwise decided through the bylaws/statutes.

As a legal entity, the cooperative has rights and duties. It can acquire property rights, contract debts, develop an economic activity and be party to law suits. As with companies and in accord with the legal system in question, this legal capacity will be infinite or limited by the objective of the cooperative concerned.

The legal person status includes the right to own subsidiaries in another legal form than a cooperative. The establishment of such independent bodies should not, however, discard members from the decision-making.

The frequently used formula according to which cooperatives were "the mandatory of their members" does not adequately portray the legal status of cooperatives. On the one hand, they are legal persons. Once registered, acts performed on their behalf exclusively commit them, i.e. cooperatives are independent of their members. On the other hand, because of the close involvement of the members in the decision-making processes of the cooperative, a feature which distinguishes cooperatives from other business organizations, cooperatives may not act beyond the mandate which the members may modify at any time.

The status of acts performed on behalf of the cooperative during the period from its constitution until its registration (and the publication thereof, where necessary) must be clearly defined.

In order to favour the rapid development of cooperatives as part of overall public development programmes, most of the legislations adopted during the 1960s in the countries of the south provided for the possibility of provisional registration of mainly "pre-cooperatives". After thirty years of experience one must, however, admit that most of these pre-cooperatives, often preferred because of their light structure and their exemption from a number of constraints, have not evolved towards autonomous cooperatives. On the contrary, their dependence on external support increased with the intention of turning them into cooperatives. The control which had to follow this support has discredited government as a promoter of cooperatives in many a country.

In addition, provisional registration gave birth to considerable confusion, especially among banks and other creditors with whom it was supposed to facilitate relations, because the legal nature of a provisional registration remained unclear.

Membership

Membership issues are the single most important ones to be dealt with by the law as cooperatives are member-centered organizations.

Membership qualifications

The universally recognized definition of cooperatives allows for both physical/natural and legal persons to be members of a cooperative. With the exception of rules for service cooperatives, much legislation does however exclude legal persons from membership in primary cooperatives. As long as the democratic principle of "one member/one vote" is respected in real terms, such limitations should not be included in the law. To ensure this respect one might consider limiting the total voting power of legal person members in those primary cooperatives which also have natural person members, so as not to allow these legal person members to outnumber the votes of the natural person members or to take decisions by themselves.

According to western legal concepts, physical/natural and legal persons only may hold rights and hence be members of a cooperative. This definition is based on a cultural assumption which individualizes physical persons. Other societies are organized on the basis of extended families, or even larger groups, as the smallest entity. These entities may be admitted as members in cooperatives, provided they are stable. One would have to make certain, however, that the decision-making procedure within the cooperative is not affected by admitting such groups as members and that the democratic rights of individual members are not infringed upon. The admission of such groups as members might even facilitate the functioning of the cooperative in certain circumstances by permitting it to respect the decision-making procedures of the existing social environment, notably in matters concerning the management of natural resources.

Restrictions concerning age

The admission of legal minors is generally an exception to the civil law of the country concerned. Without preventing economically active minors from membership, the possibility of minors to affiliate themselves to a cooperative needs careful studying of the implications in terms of responsibility and financial liability, the right to vote and the eligibility to posts of responsibility. In order to avoid joining a cooperative becoming a means of access to a position which would not legally be accorded to minors individually, their number and rights must be limited. Notably, minors must be prevented from being able to control the cooperative. Exceptions might be made for school and student cooperatives.

Minimum number of members in primary cooperatives

To respect the freedom of association, restrictions on the number of members of a cooperative should be limited. The economic viability of cooperatives with too few members is, however, generally speaking, precarious. Under such conditions, granting them legal personality might go against the interest of their potential partners and creditors. This is why most legislation does require a minimum number of members, at least three.

The experiences of a country might require that different minimum numbers be fixed according to the type of cooperative. Thus the number might be higher for consumer cooperatives than for producer cooperatives, the number for service cooperatives falling in between.

Maximum number of members in primary cooperatives

In theory, the "open-door principle", a shorthand term for the 1st ICA principle, does not authorize any restriction on the number of members. In practice, the number of members must be compatible with the objective of the cooperative in question. Just as with the minimum number of members, it is difficult to define absolute upper or relative limits for the different types of cooperatives.

One might note that, in general, the problems of administration grow with the size of membership. The more members, the more difficult it is to maintain a democratic mode of administration, and the fewer members identify with their cooperative. Decentralization by means of regional assemblies and/or assemblies by sections, combined with a more effective administration, may make up for some of the negative consequences of large memberships, but they may not make them disappear.

The problems vary also with the type of cooperative. Thus, a high number of members in a consumer cooperative have little influence on the decision making processes, whereas the necessarily high number of members in a savings and credit cooperative requires rather complex work mechanisms. Producer cooperatives will most likely suffer if the size of membership outgrows certain limits. The question will have to be left to the members for decision, if necessary.

Admission of Members

Principle

Within the limits of the objective of the cooperative in question and according to the open-door principle, all persons who request membership should be admitted. The associative character of the cooperative must, however, permit the members to have a say. Mutual acceptance by the members is a condition sine qua non for the success of the cooperative.

The policy adopted by cooperatives in matters of capital distribution has an influence on the number and quality of the members. The risk of membership applications motivated by the search for a lucrative investment may be avoided by not distributing the profit gained on transactions with non-member users and/or by reimbursing shares in the event of termination of membership or liquidation at nominal value only.

The residence of the applicant should not be decisive for admission unless the objective of the cooperative has it as one of the keys for its success, in which case the bylaws/statutes should foresee the necessary clause.

A good number of cooperative laws permit the exclusion from membership of persons who do not have a clean police record. Unless the punished behaviour is likely to harm the cooperative, the members should assume their general social obligations by helping to reintegrate such persons into society.

Admission Procedure

Given the associative character of cooperatives, the admission of new members must be decided by the general assembly. For practical reasons, the board of directors may decide, but the general assembly will keep, if it wishes, a right of confirmation or veto, to be exercised during the first general assembly following the decision taken by the board. In order to be able to determine with certainty the rights and obligations of the members, it is important to specify in the law that final act which constitutes membership.

Applications for membership must be dated and confirmed upon receipt. A refusal must be justified in writing and the applicant must be notified immediately. The applicant must have the right to appeal to a court of law (to be defined). If the cooperative has not met the time limit set by the law, membership is presumed.

Resignation/withdrawal of Members

The right of the members to resign or withdraw must be guaranteed by the law which must see to it that administrative acts or the bylaws/statutes of the cooperative do not have an adverse effect. Withdrawal may be restricted until a minimum period of membership has expired, or be subject to discharging the mainly financial obligations incurred towards the cooperative or third parties. These conditions must in no case be excessive, and the required time period (for notification, reimbursement of shares, etc.) must be reasonable.

The effect of the resignation/withdrawal is the postponement or immediate termination of the rights and obligations of the resigning member. Remaining under certain conditions financially liable, the resigning/withdrawing member has a right to have his shares reimbursed, in principle at nominal value. However, the cooperative must have the possibility to temporarily (term to be specified) withhold the reimbursement if an immediate reimbursement would seriously affect its functioning. In this case, the cooperative will pay a limited interest on the sum to be reimbursed.

Exclusion and suspension of Members

Given the open-door principle, exclusion must be an exceptional measure. It can take place when members do not withdraw voluntarily even though they no longer fulfill the conditions of membership, if they seriously violate the bylaws/statutes or if their behaviour is detrimental to the cooperative. Depending on the kind of misconduct, the cooperative might also decide a partial or total suspension of the rights of a member for a certain period of time.

In both cases, the member concerned must be heard and, at his request, the motives for the decision of the cooperative must be communicated to the member in writing. The member may appeal before the general assembly of the cooperative, use the dispute settlement procedures provided for in the law or in the bylaws/statutes and/or he has the right to appeal to a court of law (to be defined). The terms and effects of an exclusion or suspension are the same as those for resignation.

Obligations and Rights of Members

Principle

Again, the sequence by which the matters are dealt with in the law is not indicative of any ranking. It does however at times reflect the weight given to a specific item. Thus, emphasis is put here on the members' obligations which are far less discussed than members' rights. Membership is linked to rights. These are conditioned by the discharge of obligations. The cooperative law and subsidiary legislation must ensure that this rule be respected, even in cases where general social rules tend to override these rights and obligations. In no case must family ties, race, age, religion or any other affiliation to a group affect the independence and the equality of the members.

Obligations

Personal Obligations

By belonging to a cooperative, members commit themselves:

- to respect the bylaws/statutes as well as the decisions taken by the general assembly, whether they voted for their adoption or not.
- to abstain from any activity detrimental to the objective of their cooperative. Membership in several cooperatives having the same objective and territory of activity must not automatically be considered as harming the cooperative(s).

- ❖ to participate actively in the life of the cooperative. This obligation may not, however, be enforced.

Financial Obligations

Membership in a cooperative implies the following financial obligations:

- ❖ Each member must subscribe to and pay for the minimum number of shares fixed in the bylaws/statutes.
- ❖ Each member is financially liable for the debts of the cooperative, at a minimum with the amount of money to be paid for the shares subscribed by him.
- ❖ Each member might have to purchase additional shares or make supplementary financial contributions to the cooperative.

In order to compensate, at least in part, for the inherent financial weakness of most cooperatives, and in order to incite the members to actively contribute to the success of their cooperative, the law or the bylaws/statutes may impose an obligation on the members to make supplementary payments in case the cooperative is unable to pay its debts. This may result in an unlimited financial liability of the members. The amount of these supplementary payments may be the same for each member, it may be proportional to the transactions made by each of the members with the cooperative over a specified period of time, according to the method used for surplus distribution, or it may be determined according to the number of shares held by each member.

If not specified in the law, the type of financial liability of the members must be dealt with in the bylaws/statutes in order to protect the interests of third parties. Because of the legal person status of cooperatives, the financial liability of members commits the members towards their cooperative only, and not towards the creditors of the cooperative. It extends beyond the termination of membership, for a period of time to be specified in the law or in the bylaws/statutes. As a rule, a member must contribute to the discharge of only those debts which are on the balance sheet at the time of the end of his membership.

Other Obligations

One might envisage obliging the members to use, to a certain extent at least, the services or installations of their cooperative. Although favoring the development of the cooperative in the short run, such a rule would in time have a negative influence on the competitiveness of the cooperative and it might violate competition law in those cases where the members themselves run a business. Therefore, rather than reasoning in terms of legal obligations, one might consider that the members have the moral duty to work with their cooperative. Furthermore, it is up to the cooperative to offer sufficiently attractive services to its members. Exceptions are possible, particularly in the case where the members decide to make an important investment, the success of which depends on the members using that facility. Members could then temporarily be forbidden to look elsewhere for the rendered services. In order to guarantee certain stability in specific cases, the cooperative might have to conclude individual contracts with each of its members.

Rights

Personal Rights

Each member has the right to:

- ask for those services which form the objective of the cooperative.
- ask for education and training by the cooperative according to the bylaws/statutes or the decisions of the general assembly.
- use the installations and services of the cooperative.
- participate in the general assembly, propose a motion therein, and vote.
- elect or be elected for an office in the cooperative or in that of a higher level structure of which his cooperative is a member.
- obtain at all reasonable times, from the elected bodies of the cooperative, information on the situation of the cooperative.
- have the books and registers inspected by the supervisory committee, if any.

Jointly (necessary number to be determined) the members can also:

- convene a general assembly and/or have a question inscribed on the agenda of a general assembly; or
- ask for an additional audit.

Financial Rights

The members have the right to:

- receive a share of the surplus at economically reasonable intervals in the form of a patronage refund, paid pro-rata of their transactions with the cooperative, and/or a limited interest on the paid up shares;
- ask, when terminating their membership, that the paid-up shares be reimbursed at nominal value. Losses or devaluations may be deducted from this amount. The limitation to the nominal value is to prevent members from withdrawing for speculative reasons. As mentioned above, the reimbursement may be deferred in case it would otherwise endanger the viability of the cooperative. However, this deferment must not undermine the right to withdraw.

- receive, in the case of liquidation, a share of the remaining sum, if any, unless these funds were declared indivisible by the bylaws/statutes and as required by strict cooperative principles (*cf.* 3rd ICA principle). In this case, the remaining money must be credited to another cooperative, a vertical cooperative structure or to a charitable organization.

Provisions Relating to Member Employees

The employer/employee relationship in cooperatives is a complex issue when the employees are members of the cooperative and, consequently, their own employers. These members might find contradictory interests in terms of working hours, salary, trade union rights etc. The problem presents itself at varying degrees of intensity in the different types of cooperatives:

- In service cooperatives, it is seldom that members are employees of their cooperative.
- In consumer cooperatives, the employees are frequently members of their cooperative. However, the substance of the cooperative is not identical with that of the labour contract. To prevent the interests of member employees from dominating, the voting rights of these members must be limited in cases relating to work conditions, or the general assembly must delegate its decision-making power in these matters to the board of directors. Besides, member employees will refrain from encroaching upon the interests of the employer since they are themselves their own employer.
- In producer cooperatives the conflict is obvious. Here, the substance of the labour contract is cooperatized. It is identical to the substance of the cooperative. With the exception of the rules on social protection, workplace and product safety, the labour law must not normally be applied to these relationships because the members freely consented to organize their work according to cooperative principles instead of seeking a work relation. Some legislations do see, however, the cooperative — a separate legal person — as the employer and the individual members as employees with an employment contract with the cooperative while, as members, they have a separate contract with it, concluded with the acceptance of the bylaws/statutes when becoming a member.

Organs and Management

Principle

The functioning of cooperatives, as opposed to that of companies, depends on the participation of the members who must be able to exert an effective influence on the affairs of the cooperative.

Nevertheless, as a legal entity, the latter must be able to keep certain independence. The law must therefore provide for the principle of democracy and the principle of economic efficiency to be applied simultaneously, i.e. it must cater for the two elements of the definition of cooperatives— the association element and the enterprise element. Therefore, the internal organization, the sharing of powers between the different organs, the elections to offices as well as all important decisions must reflect the will of all members, regardless of their financial contribution. Broadly speaking, matters relating to the associative character of the cooperative are to be dealt with by the general assembly; matters pertaining to the enterprise of the cooperative are to be dealt with by a board of directors, whereas the day-to-day running of the enterprise should be delegated by the board of directors to a (professional) manager who works under the supervision of the board of directors. This demarcation of powers is to avoid inefficiencies that arise where a non-informed membership retains too much of the management powers and it is to prevent a loss of cooperative identity where the membership loses its effective control because the management uses its information without properly consulting with the membership.

A clear power-sharing allows also to more easily establishing civil liability and penal responsibility of those in charge of running the cooperative. Every cooperative must at least have:

- a general assembly; and
- a board of directors, which is sometimes also called "management committee".

Although the formation of a cooperative does not require the existence of a control unit, it is advisable to at least provide for the possibility of its nomination and leave the decision to the members. Cooperatives which have such an independent organ, a "supervisory committee", "supervisory commission" or "control commission", which acts on behalf of the members as a mini general assembly so to speak, seem to function better than those without it because the members often lack the necessary qualifications to exercise an effective and continuous control over the board of directors and the management, if any.

This dual system does not replace internal control mechanisms of the board of directors, such as internal auditors, nor does it replace the obligatory external audit of the cooperative. As for the optional post of manager, it is not an organ of the cooperative since its powers are delegated by the board of directors.

General Assembly

Composition

The ordinary and the extraordinary general assembly, composed exclusively of the members of the cooperative, is the supreme decision- taking body of the cooperative. Third parties, who have invested in the enterprise, may possibly participate in the general assemblies, but they should not have voting rights.

An ordinary general assembly must convene at least once a year; an extraordinary general assembly may take place at the request of the persons entitled to do so according to the law or the bylaws/statutes.

If the size of a cooperative in terms of territorial coverage or the number of members is such that the necessary quorum is difficult to attain or the proceedings of the general assembly become too cumbersome, or where in a multi-purpose cooperative diverse interests so require, regional assemblies and/or assemblies by sections may be formed. These decentralized assemblies elect their representatives to a delegates' assembly which replaces the general assembly. The agenda of these meetings as well as the mode of deliberations and voting will be decided at central level so as to ensure the same standards throughout the cooperative. In order to reinforce communication between the different parts, members of the board of directors and of the supervisory committee, if any, should participate in the meetings of these decentralized assemblies.

These basic rules about the general assembly fit with the reality of most cooperatives. Generally, cooperatives are locally rooted, in the physical sense of the term. While this is a safeguard against quick shifts of their activities in search for comparative business advantages, one must not exclude the cooperatives from being run without a physical centre. New ways of communication and production neither require a stable physical production unit or an administrative centre, nor the physical presence of the members in order to hold a general assembly. Where this is required, the members may decide so in their bylaws/statutes. Otherwise, they should be free to discuss and vote via, for example, the internet. What matters is the democratic control by the members, not their physical presence at meetings, although this may still help to generate and regenerate the necessary reciprocal confidence.

Powers

As already mentioned, the dual character of cooperatives as associations and enterprises is indicative of the way in which powers must be shared amongst the general assembly and the board of directors. According to the definition of cooperatives, the members use the cooperative enterprise to attain certain economic, social or cultural objectives. The board of directors/management must have the necessary working margin which is indispensable for efficient management, whereas all decisions concerning the cooperative as an association must be taken by the general assembly.

Starting from this basic distinction, one may draw a list of exclusive powers of the general assembly. These powers may not be transferred to any other body or person, not even by a unanimous decision of all the members.

Among these powers the most prominent one is the right and obligation to adopt and to modify the bylaws/statutes within the limits of the law and the universally recognized cooperative values and principles. This is why the bylaws/statutes are dealt with in a separate paragraph.

Bylaws/Statutes

Principle

The general assembly, or the constitutive first meeting of the founder members, may stipulate on a matter through its bylaws/statutes where the law is silent, where the legislator leaves it a choice amongst several options, invites it to specify legal provisions or when the members decide to rewrite certain clauses of the law in order to make them easier to understand and/or more easily operational.

What has been said concerning model laws is *mutatis mutandis,* equally valid for the bylaws/statutes? Although the adoption of model bylaws/statutes, recognized by the authorities, makes registration of organizations easier because of their supposed conformity with the law, their adoption should not be made compulsory.

Contents of the bylaws

Minimum obligatory content of the bylaws

The bylaws must deal with the following items:

- The name and the trade name of the cooperative, which may be freely chosen as long as there is no confusion possible with the name of another legal entity already registered and as long as the public is not left in doubt about the limited financial liability of the cooperative and the type of financial liability of the members.
- The locality of the head office, if any, its postal address and, possibly, the conditions for its transfer to another locality.
- The definition of the objectives of the cooperative, including the indication of whether the cooperative is a single-purpose or a multi-purpose cooperative.
- The conditions and procedures for admission, resignation, exclusion and suspension of members as well as eligibility criteria of membership. These criteria must reflect the particular character of the cooperative in question, as also its being a primary, a secondary or a cooperative of an even higher level.

- The value and minimum and maximum number of the shares to be subscribed by each member. The general assembly ensures that the economic means of the least affluent members form the basis for the decision and that the share value is high enough to support the envisaged objectives of the cooperative and to incite the members to exercise their control rights.
- The procedure and conditions for the subscription and payment of the shares. Shares may be contributed in cash, kind, labour, service or by leaving a part of the surplus, to which a member is entitled, with the cooperative.
- The type of financial liability of the members for the debts of the cooperative.
- The administration of the cooperative registers and the documents to be kept.
- The conditions and procedures for convening and holding general assemblies (form of notice, fixing and notifying the agenda, election of the president of the session, preferably not a member of the board of directors, quorum and voting, etc.).
- The limited size of the board of directors, the conditions of eligibility to the various offices, the duration of the mandates and the reimbursement of their expenses and the expenditures of the manager, if any. The rights and obligations of officers, mode of decision taking.
- The conditions and procedures for convening the board of directors and, if any, the supervisory committee (quorum, voting etc.).
- Financing: capital formation, constitution of the legal reserve and of the statutory funds.
- Surplus distribution and contribution to cover losses.
- The distribution of the capital in case of resignation, exclusion or liquidation.
- Definition of the financial year.
- Auditing (cooperative-specific financial, management and social audit and advice).
- Conditions and procedures for voluntary dissolution.
- Dispute settlement procedures.
- Specification of any other legal matter.
- The procedure for modifying the bylaws/statutes.

Additional, Non-obligatory content of the bylaws

Without being compulsory, the bylaws may also include rules on:

- the duration of the cooperative.
- its geographical area of activity.
- its affiliation to one or several secondary or higher-level cooperative organizations.
- the nomination of a supervisory committee.
- the nature and volume of transactions possible with nonmember users. A balance must be found between the efficiency and the autonomy of the cooperative. This may translate into a definition of a threshold (percentage of total turnover which the transactions with non-member users must not exceed). These transactions must be kept separately in the accounts of the cooperative.
- the remuneration of office-holders. While it is true that according to cooperative principles office holders should not be remunerated, it is also true that thus financially weaker members may not be able to afford to take office. Remuneration should not be paid as a function of the turnover or the profit/surplus of the cooperative.
- the number of additional or supplementary shares per member and the conditions of their subscription and payment.
- the acceptance of non-member investments and the rights attached thereto.
- the formation of regional and/or assemblies by sections, their decision-making, voting and number of delegates to represent the regional or sectional assemblies at the central level.
- voting by proxy.
- the establishment of education and other statutory funds.
- the establishment of commissions/committees, their tasks, their term, the qualifications of their members.
- any other matter falling within the autonomy of cooperatives.

Other powers

In addition to drafting and modifying the bylaws/statutes the general assembly has the power to decide the following matters:

- Keeping of minutes of its meetings.
- Distribution of powers between the different organs according to the above-mentioned principles, and the adoption for each of them of internal regulations.

- Election and dismissal of the members of the supervisory committee (if any) and the board of directors unless the latter is to be chosen by the supervisory committee. The more powers the board/management has, the easier it must be to remove it from office.
- Surplus distribution and loss coverage.
- Amalgamation, scission, conversion of the cooperative into another legal entity or dissolution of the cooperative.
- Decisions concerning the possible limitation of loans, deposits or investments.
- Nomination of auditors, the duration of their mandate and their remuneration.
- Examination of the auditor's report as well as of the annual report (including the yearly activity plan).
- Giving or refusing the final discharge of board members.
- Adoption of the annual budget.
- Final admission, expulsion or suspension of members.
- Education and training of members and employees.
- Extension of the duration of the cooperative.
- The decision on whether the board of directors may appoint a professional manager, member or not of the cooperative.
- The possible creation of sub-committees with specific tasks, and the duration of their mandate.

Decision Making

Quorum

The mode of decision making must respect the principles of democracy and economic efficiency. Fixing a quorum, i.e. the minimum number of members who must be present or represented for the general assembly to validly sit, deliberate and vote, constitutes a compromise between these two principles.

This quorum most often expressed either in a percentage of the number of members at the time of convening the general assembly or in an absolute figure, or in a combination of the two, may vary according to the topic on the agenda of the general assembly. Provision must be made for cases where the general assembly repeatedly fails to gather the required quorum. As a rule, a second meeting with the same agenda may decide regardless of the number of members present or represented.

Voting

The basic rule for primary cooperatives is 'one member/one vote'. This also applies to members being legal persons.

Exceptionally, (a limited number of) plural voting rights may be granted through the bylaws/statutes. The volume of transactions with the cooperative or other criteria might be used when allocating these rights. In no case, however, may plural voting rights be granted on the basis of the amount of capital invested by a member. The plural voting rights may not be exercised when taking decisions on important matters, as specified by the law. In no case must one single member be in a position to take decisions by virtue of the number of voting rights he is holding or representing.

In secondary and higher-level cooperative organizations, a system of plural voting rights may be applied without the above mentioned restrictions, but in line with democratic principles. The law must regulate the criteria for granting voting rights to delegates, i.e. members elected by regional or sectional assemblies, if any, to the assembly of delegates.

The participation of non-member investors in the general assembly, should they have voting rights at all, must be regulated in such a way as to ensure that they cannot outweigh regular members. It must, however, be emphasized that voting by non-members constitutes a severe deviation from cooperative principles. For the above-mentioned reasons, the voting rights of member employees will also have to be restricted to exclude them from voting on issues related to their employment.

If voting by proxy is to be allowed, the proxy must be a member of the cooperative and should not represent more than two or three members, himself included. Voting by mail or via the internet might be a way to involve the greatest possible number of members in the decision making process, whenever the physical presence of the members is not necessary. At least important decisions should be taken by ballot in order to limit the influence of certain members, mainly the president of the assembly. Elections should always be held by ballot.

Majority

Generally, decisions may be taken by simple majority if the required quorum of members is present or represented. Resolutions concerning the "association contract", be it a modification of the bylaws/statutes or a decision on merging/amalgamating, dividing, dissolving, converting or on affiliating the cooperative with an apex organization, must be taken by a qualified majority, generally at least a two-thirds majority.

Board of Directors

Composition

As the executive organ of the cooperative, the board of directors must function according to precise legal rules. The board members are not only the representatives of the current cooperative but they are also under the obligation to preserve its assets for the members to come.

Provisions relating to the board of directors

The law must contain rules on:

- the eligibility criteria and on the question whether or not all board members must be members of the cooperative. In cases where non-member investors sit on the board of directors, one must ensure that they are not able to neither take decisions on their own nor constitute a blocking minority.
- incompatibilities, be they of an economic, personal, political or other nature; for example, incompatibilities between belonging to the supervisory committee, if any, and the board of directors of the current or that financial year which is subject to control by the supervisory committee, if any. Also, members of the same family (to be defined) must not sit on the supervisory committee and the board of directors of the current or that financial year which is subject to control by the supervisory committee.
- the duration of the mandate and the possibility to be reelected.
- the quorum and the mode of voting.
- the qualifications of the members of the board of directors. These qualifications must be technical and personal. The board members may compensate a deficit in the first case by hiring a professional (non-member) manager, but nothing will replace a lack of confidence of the members in their representatives. Independently of whether the cooperative has a professional manager or not the board must be professional, i.e. the board members must have those qualifications which are necessary for their specific cooperative. One of the differences between cooperatives and capital-centered companies is that the responsible persons must be able to manage the capital of the cooperative, while at the same time provide services to the members, within the limits set by the bylaws/statutes and the decisions of the general assembly.
- liability of the board members. This liability may be excluded where it relates to a decision of the board concerning which a board member expressed his dissenting opinion immediately after he knew about the decision. The liability may be stricter where the board or single board members receive a salary from the cooperative.

Powers

The list of powers/obligations of the board of directors covers, by default, all the matters which do not explicitly come under the authority of the general assembly. It includes the power/obligation to:

- represent the cooperative in all acts of civil life and to administer and manage the cooperative. This power is limited by the legal capacity of the cooperative and the decisions taken by the general assembly. Thus, the latter may for example fix a financial ceiling above which the board of directors cannot by itself commit the cooperative, or decide that certain decisions of the board of directors must be taken unanimously.
- keep the registers and books of the cooperative and the minutes of its own meetings.
- make certain that the accounts and the balance sheet are drawn up according to the rules in force, always keeping in mind the specific character of cooperatives.
- verify that the audit is conducted regularly and within the prescribed time limits before discussing the conclusions with the supervisory committee, if any, and/or the general assembly.
- convene the ordinary and extraordinary general assemblies and prepare their agenda according to the bylaws/statutes.
- prepare the management report (including an activity plan for the following year) and the annual budget.
- admit, exclude or suspend, possibly provisionally, members.
- co-opt in the case of a vacancy new members unless this power is explicitly given to the general assembly.
- facilitate the exercise of the rights of the members and make certain that they assume their obligations.
- facilitate the work of the auditors.
- nominate, if necessary, a manager or director, member or not of the cooperative, and ensure that the manager or director carries out the assigned duties correctly. In practice, this employee must assume the management functions which are not explicitly reserved to be performed by the board. He may employ and direct the necessary number of personnel. Where the work of the board of directors requires making use of the professional knowledge or know-how of the manager, he may be integrated into the board of directors as a member.
- file, if necessary, an application for the opening of bankruptcy procedures.

- ❖ make certain that its functioning be transparent by adopting internal regulations, unless drawn up by the general assembly.
- ❖ assume several and joint responsibility/liability in case of wrongdoings and finally.
- ❖ take on any other right or obligation, assigned by the general assembly or contained in the bylaws/statutes.

Supervisory Committee

Composition

Where the law provides for the possibility of nominating a supervisory committee and where the statutes/bylaws so stipulate, this supervisory committee carries out the control function in the interest of the members. Consequently, it is exclusively composed of members of the cooperative.

Provisions Relating to the supervisory committee

Just as for the board of directors, the supervisory committee must be directed by a certain number of provisions, in particular on:

- ❖ the eligibility criteria and the prohibition to sit at the same time on the board of directors of the current or a financial year which may be subject to control by the supervisory committee. The presence of several members of a family (to be defined) in one or several organs must be avoided.
- ❖ the qualifications of the members of the supervisory committee. In order to be able to effectively control the board of directors and the management, if any, the members of the supervisory committee must have the necessary time and skills.
- ❖ the duration of the mandate.
- ❖ the quorum and the mode of voting.
- ❖ the financial liability.

Powers

The supervisory committee's principal task is to control the activities of the board of directors, of the management, if any, and those of any commission. In order to be able to carry out this task, it will have access to all information at all times. Since it is only answerable to the general assembly, it may only take orders from that organ.

Besides these broad rights it can have a number of particular ones. For example, should the board of directors fail to properly convene a general assembly, the supervisory committee could do so and it might elect the members of the board of directors in cases where they are not elected by the general assembly or in the case of a vacancy, if it is impossible for the general assembly to take a rapid decision, subject to confirmation by the latter.

Capital Formation, Accounts, Surplus Distribution and Loss coverage

Financial resources

Principle

The autonomy of cooperatives will not become reality unless they have the necessary economic independence and, in particular, financial independence. The general withdrawal of public funds from the private sector and growing competition put cooperatives in a difficult situation in many a country. Today's markets are global, dominated by capital, through which the main means of production, i.e. knowledge, is/will be accessed. Competitiveness presupposes a capital base that is difficult for most cooperatives to constitute, given the nature and the structure of their capital. The capital varies with the number of members. As a rule, cooperative members have only limited financial or other resources. As additional contributions do not increase their voting power, and as interest payments are limited, members are generally not inclined to invest more than their obligatory share.

The difficulties in raising a sufficient amount of capital are seen by many as the principal drawback of cooperatives. If governments want to avoid cooperatives being restricted to low productivity, easy to imitate activities, they must see to it that the inherent weak capital base of cooperatives be raised to a level where they may stand the harsh winds of national, regional, international and indeed global competition. Especially in industrialized countries, legislators have therefore opened the way to capital formation similar to that of stock companies, putting however the cooperative identity at risk.

The autonomy of cooperatives flows mainly from a system of carefully balanced internal and external financing, the latter, for example, through non-member business, non-patronizing member investments, and non-member investments. The conflict between user and investor interests, which is to be avoided by the cooperative model, is likely to emerge through any such external financing mechanism.

Internal Financial Rcsources

(a) Member shares

The member shares do not constitute a gainful investment. The paid-up shares constitute money which the members put at the disposal of their cooperative for the time of their membership in order for the cooperative to attain the jointly fixed objective(/)s. Shares are nominative, indivisible, non-transferable (unless decided otherwise by the general assembly), not attachable and non-negotiable.

In primary cooperatives the amount of capital held by one member must be limited so that the principle of equality of the members in real terms is not endangered. When this balance becomes disturbed through the termination of a membership, the cooperative must redistribute the shares. In order to rebalance the relationship between the overall economic situation and the nominal value of the shares, cooperatives should be allowed to re-evaluate their shares under strict supervision of the competent authorities.

(b) Additional member shares

It may be advantageous to encourage members to subscribe to additional or supplementary shares. These may be conceived in such a way as to not entail an additional financial liability, as to grant the right to fixed interest payments, as to be reimbursable upon request, and/or as to grant a right of participation in the reserves upon withdrawal from membership where the reserves are otherwise indivisible.

(c) Further means to improve the internal financing

To counterbalance the inherent financial weakness of cooperatives, the legislator might fix a limit below which the share capital must not fall, even if this means that a withdrawing member is not immediately reimbursed his share, or that the remaining members are obliged to contribute to the recapitalization by making supplementary payments. Such a system of separating the amount of share capital from the number of members brings cooperatives closer to the financial structure of capitalist enterprises.

On the contrary, the constitution of a reserve fund is a genuine cooperative way to at least partly overcome the inherent financial weakness. It must be obligatory. If indivisible, at least until liquidation, such a fund assures minimum stability and limits the risk of voluntary liquidation driven by speculation. The reserve fund cushions both against a lack of liquidity and against the loss of value of the obligatory shares. The reserve fund must not sit idle, but be used.

The legal reserve fund could be supplied by:

- ❖ the transfer of a minimum percentage of the surplus gained on transactions with the members until the fund reaches at least an amount equivalent to the share capital. This use of the positive results is all the more interesting if the sums transferred to the reserve fund are not taxed, as opposed to that part of the surplus a member may receive, even when that part is transformed into a credit, a deposit or an additional funding by that member. This should at least apply as far as the reserve fund is indivisible.
- ❖ the transfer of the total profit gained on transactions with non-member users.

- the transfer of the results of activities not related to the objective of the cooperative, such as, for example, the sale of fixed assets.

Furthermore, the legislator should encourage the establishment through the bylaws/statutes of education, training or any other funds. The designated use of these funds should be made compulsory.

External Financial Resources

Debentures and negotiable subordinated bonds have been allowed by a number of legislations for quite some time already. Provided some rather technical precautions are taken and the amount of external investment does not create a factual dependence of the cooperative on that capital, these do not influence the members' autonomy since no voting and/or participatory rights are attached to them.

Another way of attracting external financing is the issuance of transferable investment certificates for members and non-members, granting a right to participate in the distribution of the surplus and in the distribution of the assets in case of liquidation. Where these certificates do not grant any decision-making power or, in the case of members, any additional decision-making power, they might represent a still acceptable case of deviation from cooperative principles. Where, however, these certificates do grant voting rights, even to a limited extent only, the cooperative principle of identity is in danger.

When it comes to external financing, the distinctive features of cooperatives are easily at risk. Ideally, cooperative members are the sole investors and users (cooperative principle of identity). Non-user members and non-member users have been accepted as deviations from the identity principle. The admission of investment members and non-member investors is a further step away from this identity principle. Where, as some legislations provide for, cooperative shares may be traded at the stock exchange and members' shares have a symbolic value only, capital holders become anonymous and the (capital) structure of the cooperatives may not be distinguished any more from that of stock companies. In addition to violating the identity principle, these developments put the cooperative principle of the promotion of the members at risk.

Surplus Distribution at the End of the Financial Year

As already mentioned, it is important to distinguish between profit and surplus. By definition, cooperatives ought to calculate the prices for transactions with their members' near costs. In order to cover market related risks, a small profit margin must be included which will, however, be returned to the members at the end of the financial year, should the risk not have materialized, and should the balance sheet show a profit. This redistribution, in the form of patronage refunds, calculated pro-rata of the transactions with the cooperative, thus constitutes a deferred price calculation/reduction. Therefore, instead of speaking of "profit" in this connection, one should speak of temporary surpluses. Where there is no profit, such "profit" may not be taxed.

The surplus will be distributed in the following manner:

- Transfer to the legal reserve fund.
- Transfer to the statutory funds, if any.
- Interest payments on the paid-up shares and the investments, at a rate not higher than that paid by commercial banks for certain kinds of deposits.
- Patronage refunds to the members calculated pro-rata of their transactions with the cooperative.
- Possibly premium payments to employees.

Any payment to members is conditional on their having fulfilled their obligations, especially the obligation to pay up their shares.

Reimbursement of Capital

In the case of resignation/withdrawal or exclusion, the shares are reimbursed at their nominal value, in order to avoid membership motivated by speculation. Where the economic interests of the cooperative are seriously threatened by an immediate reimbursement or where it would lead to reducing a minimum capital requirement, it may (temporarily) be withheld. As a rule, the same type of reimbursement of shares applies in the case of liquidation. The remaining liquidated assets are transferred to the cooperative movement, to a charity organization or, in the exceptional case where the legal reserve fund is divisible; they are distributed among the members according to the method used in distributing a surplus at the end of the financial year, whereby seniority of membership might be considered as an additional criterion.

Transactions with Non-member Users

Depending on its objectives and its situation, each cooperative must decide whether it wants to offer its services to non-members as well. In cases where membership comes from a pre-existing group, for example, savings and credit cooperatives founded within an enterprise or a district, non-members of such groups might not be admitted as users. If non-member business is admitted, it is important not to let it jeopardize the independence of the cooperative.

As already mentioned, the volume of transactions with non-members must consequently be limited so as not to restrain the autonomy of cooperative members. This might be done by fixing a percentage of the total turnover, above which no transactions may be made with non-members. For the purpose of taxation, distribution of the surplus and supplying the legal reserve fund, book keeping must distinguish between the transactions made with members and those made with non-members.

Audit

The implementation of a system of internal and external, timely and regular audit of the financial, management and social standing of the cooperatives by qualified and independent auditors, combined with advice on how to improve operations, is a condition *sine qua non* for the existence of any cooperative system.

As it becomes difficult to involve the members directly in the running of the cooperative enterprise, it becomes ever more important to provide for transparency of the management in order to preserve the democratic nature of the cooperatives. The establishment of a supervisory committee, as suggested above and an extended audit are means employed to this end.

The establishment of an effective audit system, independent from the state and the cooperatives, whose services will be accessible by all cooperatives, should be made an obligation. An audit fund might be created to allow those cooperatives which need auditing most to be able to afford it. The purpose of the audit is to check that everyone respects the rules of the game. It is a periodical control of whether the attribution of the legal person status continues to be justified. It helps to monitor the interests of third parties, managers and members. As such, it is a general tool for any kind of enterprise.

The specificity of cooperatives requires the auditor to make additional investigations to ensure that cooperatives comply with their task of promoting their members. Especially where economic developments require a management system of cooperatives that does not allow for direct participation of the membership, the audit must also include a control of whether the democratic rights of the members were respected. The fact that the objectives of cooperators differ from the purely financial interests of company stockholders must especially be taken into account by the auditors who have to be trained accordingly.

The audit of a cooperative can thus not be made only on the basis of accountancy documents. The auditors have to verify whether the overall objectives, which the members set, were reached or at least furthered, and that the decisions of the management were taken in conformity thereto (management audit in order to establish a social balance alongside the financial or economic one). Scrutiny of minutes of the meetings of board of directors might give useful information. The members must be consulted and their opinion used in drawing up the final report. Generally speaking, the auditor must have access to all material, premises and persons able to inform him about the operations of the cooperative. The external auditor will also have access to the findings of the internal auditors.

The auditors should not limit their activity to that of an ex post control but they should also give advice on how to improve the management and administration of the cooperative. Whereas internal audit is to be performed permanently, the frequency of the external audit might be decided on the basis of the turnover, the kind of activities, the size of the capital, the volume of non-member business or other criteria.

The internal audit will be carried out by a group of members. Their number, the duration of their mandate, the required qualifications, powers, duties and salary as well as their civil and penal responsibility must be determined by the general assembly. Internal auditors may not be or have been a member of a cooperative organ which is or may be subject to their control.

The external audit will be carried out by a higher-level cooperative organization or by private, preferably chartered, auditors. If the cooperative movement is not yet able to provide this service and if private services are not affordable, a public authority may temporarily audit cooperatives. In no case must an administrative unit in charge of the promotion or the registration of cooperatives audit cooperatives.

The auditor's report is to be submitted to the board of directors and to the supervisory committee, if any, with a view to them explaining it to the general assembly. It must be made available for inspection by the members. The auditors must have the right to participate in the general assembly and, should the board of directors or the supervisory committees not has convened the general assembly, or not have (sufficiently) explained the contents of the auditor's report, the auditors have the right to do so. The conclusions drawn from the audit must be communicated to the competent authority.

Dissolution: Dissolution without Liquidation: Amalgamation, Scission and Conversion

Principle

The autonomy of cooperatives permits them to dissolve without any restriction, provided the interests of third parties are preserved. Thus, creditors may object to the dissolution as long as they have not been satisfied. The law must lay down the steps to be followed, from the quorum and the majority required for such a decision to the modifications to be entered into the public register. According to the freedom of association principle, members opposing the dissolution must have the right to resign.

Amalgamation

There are two types of amalgamation:

1. One or several cooperatives are absorbed by another one, something which is at times psychologically difficult for the members of the absorbed cooperatives.
2. A new cooperative is born by merging two or more cooperatives. In this case, new bylaws/statutes will have to be adopted.

Often, expectations as to the economic effects (rationalization of management and administration, economies of scale, etc.) are not met because of identification problems related to the enlargement, which in turn entails demotivation and difficulties in decision-making, etc. Before deciding to amalgamate the cooperatives should therefore considers integrating horizontally.

Scission

Only those cooperatives that have a divisible legal reserve fund may split. The others have to dissolve, after which the members may set up two or more new cooperatives. In the case of a scission, members, assets and debts have to be split.

Conversion

Only those cooperatives that have a divisible legal reserve fund may be converted into another form of business, within the limits of the provisions relating to the new organization. In the case where the legal reserve fund is indivisible, the members have the possibility of dissolving their cooperative and constituting a new organization.

Dissolution with liquidation

In the case of dissolution with liquidation, too, the decision may freely be taken by the members. A special quorum and a qualified majority are, however, required due to the importance of the decision. Several legislations require that at least two consecutive general assemblies are held and decide on the question. The dissolution may also be pronounced by an authority, ex officio at its own initiative or upon request by an interested person.

Such a decision can in particular intervene when the general assembly has not pronounced its dissolution, despite the fact that

- ❖ the duration of the cooperative, laid down in the bylaws/statutes, has come to term;

- the objective of the cooperative has been attained or is impossible to attain;
- the conditions for registering the cooperative are no longer given, for example, when the number of members remains below the required minimum during a specified period of time;
- the cooperative has repeatedly violated laws, regulations and/or its own bylaws/statutes;
- the cooperative is bankrupt, after having taken into consideration the possible obligation of the members to make supplementary payments. If there is no legislation concerning bankruptcy or if it turns out to be insufficient, it will be necessary to include provisions in the cooperative law;
- the cooperative has not had any activity during a given period of time; or
- there is any other reason, to be specified by law in order to avoid arbitrariness.

The liquidation procedure, from its official beginning, the nomination of the liquidators, the establishment of the opening and closing balances, the transactions with the creditors, the distribution of assets or the attribution of liabilities etc., to the public action of the deletion of the cooperative from the register, must be regulated. The liquidation process should not be allowed to go on forever thus preventing the cooperative from being wound up finally and cancelled from the register.

Simplified Cooperative Structures

As already mentioned, even though the experiences with pre-cooperatives can be criticized, this does not mean that the provision for a less complex form of organization than cooperatives is not necessary. The French groupement d'intérêt économique (GIE) and the Cameroonian common initiative groups may serve as models.

Unlike with pre-cooperatives, it is not a question of granting a temporary status to organizations which should eventually become cooperatives, but to recognize the diversity of needs and organizational capacities. The state might, in a simplified procedure, recognize such groups, taking into account their reduced size, turnover, share capital, degree of inter-relatedness with third parties etc., which might require less strict rules on accountancy, audit and internal administration (number of organs, number of members of the organs, documents to be kept etc.).

Horizontal and Vertical Integration

The freedom of association includes the right of cooperatives to unite horizontally and to form apex organizations, i.e. unions, federations and/or confederations. Joining forces horizontally is to avoid concentration and a way to preserve the independence of the individual cooperatives whilst creating the advantages of economies of scale.

As for vertical integration, the number of tiers should be decided by the cooperatives, keeping in mind the cost/benefit relation of the structures. The state should refrain from any intervention, except monitoring these organizations' compliance with their obligation to support and represent their members. Especially, cooperatives should not be forced to integrate on the lines of administrative subdivisions or on the lines of activities if they freely choose otherwise.

Consequently the cooperative law must define the legal form of the different levels of this cooperative pyramid and specify the activities which each level should exercise. The rights and obligations of the higher-level cooperative organizations include:

- representation of the members at national, regional and international level;
- promotion, education and training;
- advice, financial, insurance and economic services (marketing, supplies, exports, imports, etc.);
- development of inter-cooperative relations;
- research and development;
- arbitration;
- control and audit, and finally;
- dissemination of the cooperative law.

The very idea of the vertical structures defines also their functions as being subsidiary to those of their members, i.e. the activities of the higher-level cooperatives should complement those of their affiliates.

In order to establish a system of partnership between the state and cooperatives, in full respect of the freedom of association, the state should promote an independent and competent cooperative movement.

Dispute Settlement

Disputes within the cooperative movement, i.e. disputes involving exclusively members, the organs of the cooperatives, the cooperatives themselves or their apex organizations, should be subject to reconciliation, mediation and/or general or special arbitration procedures before the parties may access a general or a special court of law.

Because of the importance of good personal relations for the success of cooperatives, most legislation therefore provide for the obligation to resort to such out-of-court procedures before submitting a dispute to a court of law. This is stipulated either by law or through the bylaws/statutes of the cooperatives.

Generally, the parties prefer these procedures to official ones because they are cheaper, more expedient and also because they allow for the consideration of local human and social issues. Especially because of the latter, the legislator should recognize such procedures and attempt to preserve traditional modes of dispute settlement. The rule of law out-rules any obligation to submit disputes to government authorities for final solution. In no case may access to court as a last remedy be prohibited.

Miscellaneous

Government decrees of application

The statutory powers of the government must be limited to setting rules for the application of the law only. Each section of the government decree should state that clause of the law on which it is based.

Sanctions

The cooperative law must establish a list of acts liable to penal sanctions, indicating the articles of the penal code. This should prevent cooperatives from taking on the role of a judge, a duty which is not within their competence. Their own sanctions are those foreseen by the bylaws/statutes and by individual contracts. The daily functioning of cooperatives is guaranteed by the possibility of dismissing the members of the board of directors and of the supervisory committee and by applying sanctions to those who do not fulfill their obligations.

Summary

- ❖ As legal entities cooperatives have to be subject to legislation. Their structure, functioning and especially their position vis-à-vis third parties have to be regulated.
- ❖ The preamble will guide the interpretation of the law, which is all the more important where genuine cooperatives are not yet solidly implanted.
- ❖ A glossary of key legal terms used in the law could be included in the text, annexed to it or contained in a separate document.
- ❖ The universally recognized cooperative principles may be included in the preamble or in the definition of the cooperative, by listing them or by making reference thereto.
- ❖ As for formation of cooperatives, the guidelines suggested to incorporate provisions relating to registration, types of registration, registration authority, registration procedure, and nature and effects of registration.

- As for membership, provisions relating to membership qualifications, restrictions concerning age, minimum and maximum number of members in primary cooperatives, admission of members, admission procedure, registration/withdrawal of members, expulsion and suspension of members, obligations and rights of members and member employees are to be incorporated.
- As for organs and management of cooperatives, provisions relating to general assembly and its powers, bylaws/statutes, decision- making, voting, majorities, board of directors and their powers, and supervisory committee and their powers should be included in the cooperative law.
- Provisions should also be included in the law on capital formation, accounts, surplus distribution and loss coverage. Provision of audit, inquiry and supervision should be incorporated in the cooperative law.
- As for dissolution, provisions should be made on dissolution without liquidation, amalgamation, scission, and conversion and dissolution with liquidation.
- Provisions should also be made on dispute settlement and miscellaneous aspects in the cooperative law.

Self-learning Activity

1. What does legal person status include?
2. What do you know about restrictions concerning age for admission of legal minors in cooperatives?
3. What do you know about the personal obligations of members in a cooperative?
4. What do you think of the composition of general assembly?

8 Legislative Procedure, Dissemination and Implementation of Cooperative Law

Legislative Procedure

Since the very idea of cooperation is based on participation, it is suggested that a participatory approach to cooperative law-making be adopted.

This method constitutes the organic link between the generation, dissemination and implementation of the law. The right to participate in the definition and design of law, the right to share ideas of justice to create legal structures, and the right to use law to change law is an undeniable human right. This participatory approach must, however, be embedded in the procedures laid down in the respective national constitution in order to ensure that the text fits into the legal system and is respected by non-cooperators as well.

After having been suggested for some time,[24] participatory law making is now being practised. The procedures followed in Cameroon in 1992, in the Indian State of Punjab in the 1990s and in Canada during the same period stand out as examples. Several countries (e.g. Belgium, Burkina Faso, France, Hungary, Mali and Namibia) have even institutionalized this participatory approach by establishing a national council for cooperatives or a similar organization.

The difference between legislating for member-based entities, like cooperatives, and that for other entities must also be considered in the legal procedure. This procedure also requires to identify the real law makers in today's world and to take into account the functional notion of law. The term "law" includes all legal norms (acts of parliament, government regulations) judicial and administrative praxis and the praxis of the cooperators as they bear on the operational environment of cooperatives.

Special attention must be paid to an adequate relationship between the law and government instruments. Not only do these instruments tend to be too detailed, thus exceeding their function to make the law operational, but they are also being used to circumvent the rigidities of the law in a situation which requires flexibility and quick adjustment to the necessities of development. Together, the law and the decree of application must leave the necessary space for the cooperatives to be able to express their autonomy through their bylaws/statutes.

Dissemination of the Cooperative Law

The cooperative law, by and of itself, does not change anything. Besides the many other conditions to be fulfilled in order for an effective and efficient cooperative movement to emerge and/or to thrive, the law must be applied. In order to be applied the law must be understood. Knowing that in a good many countries the official language and, a fortiori, the legal vocabulary are not mastered by the addressees of the law, who are often even illiterate, and knowing that the difficulties related to the implementation of the law are not limited to language issues, one understands that maximum attention must be focused on the dissemination of the cooperative law. This task rests as much with the state as with the cooperative movement.

Some countries have started to develop laypersons' guides in the main vernacular languages and to organize nationwide popularization campaigns. In a similar move, cooperative apex organizations of most industrialized countries have produced guides to or commented versions of the legislation, and the internet is increasingly being used to popularize and explain the legal provisions.

Implementation of the Law

The successful implementation of the law depends mainly on an adequate institutional back-up, like efficient registration, audit and promotional services with qualified manpower. Where these requirements are not given and cannot be created within a reasonable time frame, the legislation might be premature.

Summary

- ❖ It is suggested that a participatory approach to cooperative law- making be adopted which constitutes the organic link between the generation, dissemination and implementation of the law.
- ❖ The cooperative law should be disseminated through proper publicity and propaganda mechanism. To facilitate this, cooperative apex organizations of most industrialized countries have produced guides to or commented versions of the legislation, and the internet is increasingly being used to popularize and explain the legal provisions.

❖ The successful implementation of the law depends mainly on an adequate institutional back-up, like efficient registration, audit and promotional services with qualified manpower. Where these requirements are not given and cannot be created within a reasonable time frame, the legislation might be premature.

Self-Learning Activity

1. What are the ways and means of dissemination of the cooperative law?
2. Examine the ways and means of dissemination of cooperative law.

9 International Dimension of Cooperative Legislation

Introduction

Just like any other law reform, especially in the field of economic law, the reform of cooperative legislations has become a field of international cooperation. Governments feel more and more bound by the public international cooperative law and the locus of legislation is shifting from national parliaments to supranational and international mechanisms, which leads to the harmonization of cooperative laws at regional levels and even worldwide.

As a rule, international cooperation in the field of legislation favors the transfer of Western legal know-how which has been on numerous occasions of little use outside its own cultural context. It is somehow paradoxical that at the very moment when lawyers start to take an active role in the process of development and when appeals for respect for cultural diversity multiply, the confusion between the Concepts of Law and laws reaches a climax.

Ways to Surmount the Problems Associated with Adoption of Cooperative Law

On the other hand there are numerous obstacles on the way that could lead to the adoption of cooperative laws which are better adapted to their cultural context. In order to surmount these problems one must start to:

- ❖ redefine the role of lawyers in development cooperation by rejecting the widespread conception according to which law is a technique without technology.
- ❖ reject the idea of Western law being universal. Its merits, as well as those of the other laws, must be uncovered by using available comparative legal methods.
- ❖ formulate and apply a theory of the Human Right to Development as

- ❖ recognize each country as the agent of its own development and thus cease to treat countries as objects of development.
- ❖ universalize the process of public international law making.
- ❖ cease to consider cooperative law as a means of development aid.
- ❖ search for ways of resolving the conflict between different legal systems within and between states.

The search for a cooperative law which better reflects the cultural particularities of a given country is a challenge that the international community must accept. It is a delicate task because it could be conceived as going against the present globalization of economies, and it could bear the risk of disintegrating the cooperative movements by giving away too much of their common features. But, as suggested throughout the text, the choice is not between a unitary system and cultural diversity. The choice is cultural diversity in human unity.

Summary

- ❖ International cooperation in the field of legislation favors the transfer of Western legal know-how which has been on numerous occasions of little use outside its own cultural context. It is somehow paradoxical that at the very moment when lawyers start to take an active role in the process of development and when appeals for respect for cultural diversity multiply, the confusion between the Concepts of Law and laws reaches a climax.

Self-Learning Activity

1. What does international cooperation in the field of legislation favour?
2. How do you overcome the obstacles in the adoption of cooperative law?

10 Policy, Resolutions and Recommendations of UN Guidelines *Aimed at Creating a Supportive Environment for the Development of Cooperatives*

Objectives

Within the General Assembly and the Economic and Social Council, and at major recent international conferences, governments have acknowledged the significance of cooperatives as associations and enterprises through which citizens can effectively improve their lives while contributing to the economic, social, cultural and political advancement of their community and nation. They have recognized the cooperative movement as a distinct and major stakeholder in both national and international affairs.

Governments recognize that the cooperatives movement is highly democratic, locally autonomous but internationally integrated, and a form of organization of associations and enterprises whereby citizens themselves rely on self-help and their own responsibility to meet goals that include not only economic but social and environmental objectives, such as overcoming poverty, securing productive employment and encouraging social integration.

Consequently, governments seek to create an environment in which cooperatives can participate on an equal footing with other forms of enterprise and develop an effective partnership to achieve their respective goals. Policies should protect and advance the potential of cooperatives to help members achieve their individual goals and, by so doing, to contribute to society's broader aspiration.

However, such policies can be effective only if they take into account the special character of cooperatives and the cooperative movement, which differs significantly from that of associations and enterprises that are not organized according to cooperative values and principles.

The objective of the present guidelines is to provide advice to governments and set out broad principles on which national cooperative policy might best be based, recognizing that more specific and detailed national policies fall within the responsibility of each government. Because of the governmental expectations regarding the cooperative movement and the rapidly changing global conditions and changes in the cooperative movement itself, many policies in most of the members states of the United Nations might benefit from review and in some cases from substantial revision.

Policy Regarding Cooperatives and Cooperative Movement

The objective of the policy is to enable recognition of cooperatives as legal entities and to assure them and all organizations and institutions, set up by the cooperatives movement, real equality with other associations and entities. In order to ensure equality, the special values and principles of cooperatives must receive full recognition as being desirable and beneficial to society and that appropriate measure are taken to ensure that their special qualities and practices are not the cause of discrimination and advantage of any kind.

To achieve this objective, governments are concerned with creating, and with maintaining as conditions change, an enabling environment for cooperative development. As part of such an environment, an effective participation between governments and the cooperative movement could be sought.

Public Recognition

It is appropriate and useful for government to acknowledge publicly the special contribution, in both quantitative and qualitative terms, made by the cooperative movement to the national economy and society. The joint observance of the International Day of Cooperatives and the International Cooperatives Day organized by the International Cooperative Alliance, pursuant to General Assembly resolutions 47/90, 49/155 and 51/58, may provide an occasion on which information on the cooperative movement is publicly disseminated.

Legal, Judicial and Administrative Provisions

Appropriate provision is necessary within legal, judicial and administrative practice if cooperatives are to contribute positively to improving the lives of their members and the communities in which they operate. Legal provisions may take various forms appropriate to individual national legal systems. The status, rights and responsibilities of cooperatives, the cooperative movement in general, and, if appropriate special categories of cooperatives or distinct aspects of cooperation should be addressed.

National Constitutions

The legitimacy of cooperatives and the cooperative movement could be acknowledged in these instruments, if appropriate. Provisions that limit the establishment and operations of cooperatives should be appropriately amended.

General Law or the General Section of a Single Law on Cooperatives

A general law on cooperatives or laws specific to cooperatives or under which cooperatives fall should ensure that cooperatives enjoy real equality with other types of associations and enterprise and not be discriminated against because of their special character. Laws should include the following basic set of acknowledgements, definitions and provisions:

- acknowledgement that the organization of associations and enterprises on the basis of cooperative values and principles is legitimate; acknowledgement of the utility of the cooperatives approach to association and enterprise, its contribution to national life and the status of the cooperative movement as a significant stakeholder within society, acknowledgement that intervention by Governments in the internal affairs of the movement should be strictly limited to measures applied generally to all associations and enterprises equally in order to ensure their conformity with the law.
- definition of cooperatives, using the "Statement on the cooperatives identity", adopted by the International Cooperatives Alliance in 1995; recognition of the unique nature of the values and principles of cooperation, and hence the need for their separate and distinct treatment in law and practice; commitment that neither their unique nature nor their separate and distinct treatment in law and practice should be the cause of discrimination, intended or not; undertaking that no law or practice should restrict the rights of citizens to full participation in the cooperative movement in any capacity consistent with its values and principles and should not restrict the operation of that movement;
- provision that a general law apply to all categories of cooperatives but that, in order to respond to the situation of certain categories of cooperatives, special laws might be enacted, consistent with the general law; stipulation that all judicial and administrative regulations and practices be based only on the general or special laws on cooperatives; that all regulations clearly identify the provision of the law on which they are based and the purpose for which they are made; recognition of the full autonomy and capacity for self-regulation of the cooperative movement; Adjustments may be made only to ensure: real equality in treatment; definition of the responsibilities of the cooperative movement for self-regulation in all matters distinctive to it; provision that the texts of laws and regulations be made available to all cooperative members and employees; provision that representatives of the cooperative movement participate fully in drafting special laws or judicial or administrative regulations and guidelines concerning practice; provision for the maintenance of a public register of cooperatives as a part of

procedures for registration of all associations and enterprises; provision for procedures for continuous monitoring and regular review of law and practice which would include the full and equal participation of representatives of the cooperative movement and for encouragement of research on the effect of law and practice on the environment for cooperative; establishment of the responsibility of governments to formulate and carry out a policy in respect to cooperatives that would seek to establish a supportive and enabling environment while avoiding any infringement of the autonomy of the movement and any diminution of its capacity for responsible self-regulation and would seek also to engage in an effective and equal partnership with the movement in all matters where it is able to contribute significantly to the formulation and carrying out of public policy; recognition of the value of governmental support for the international cooperative movement, including through inter-governmental activities; and definition of the responsibilities of the cooperatives movement as a major stakeholder in society, to the extent these responsibilities are consistent with its full autonomy.

Special Laws on Certain Categories of Cooperatives

Consistent with the basic provisions of general cooperative legislation, and recognizing the distinctive nature of the business of some cooperatives, it may be appropriate to make special provisions in law for certain types of categories of cooperatives to safeguard their ability to enjoy real equality with other types of associations and enterprises and not be discriminated against because of their special character.

Judicial and Administrative Practice Concerned with Cooperatives

These must be consistent with the general law on cooperatives and, specifically, with its provisions concerning such practice.

Other Laws and Practices that may have Effect on Cooperatives

Governments should seek to exclude or eliminate provisions of any law that discriminate against, or are specifically prejudicial to cooperatives. Governments should create an environment that enables cooperatives to identify and communicate cases needing revision.

Monitoring, Review and Revision of Laws and Judicial and Administrative Practices

This is necessary to ensure that the impact of laws and judicial and administrative practices on the cooperative movement is entirely positive. If identified, discriminatory provisions should be rendered inoperative as quickly as possible pending enactment of revised laws or the issuance of revised regulations and guidelines concerning practice. This process should have, as its purpose, the early and complete disengagement by governments from the internal affairs of cooperatives and the cooperative movement, where this still exists, and full operational realization of the principles that cooperatives, although different, are equal to other business enterprises and civil associations.

For these purposes, formal procedures for consultation and collaboration should be set up and should include regular and full participation by the cooperative movement. Advantage may be taken also of the special programmes and guidelines offered by specialized international cooperative organizations and inter-governmental organizations.

Research, Statistics and Information

Research

Given the significance of the cooperative movement, it may be appropriate to envisage collaboration between governmental and cooperative movement research on matters relevant to public policy; publication and wide diffusion of research results, including those produced by the international cooperative movement, inter-governmental organizations and the United Nations. Emphasis should be on applied research of immediate utility in improving the efficiency of cooperatives, extending benefits to society and improving partnerships between the cooperative movement and governments.

Statistics

Several measures may be undertaken to improve statistics for and about cooperatives in view of integrating statistics on cooperatives in regular programmes of the national statistics service and participate in international efforts to improve cooperative statistics, including the establishment of a uniform set of definitions for use by national statistical services.

Information

Given that governments regulate and broadly influence information diffusion, a number of measures may be useful in expanding knowledge of the cooperative movement and overcoming prejudices and misconceptions; extension of technical and financial assistance to an extent equal to that made available to other stakeholders; ensuring that no discrimination exists because of the distinctive nature of cooperatives; equal and non-discriminatory access by the cooperative movement to all public media commensurate with its contribution to national life; use of affirmative action to overcome prejudice and misinformation where the term cooperative is associated with a previous and inappropriate usage; diffusion through public media of material on inter-governmental activities undertaken in partnership with or in support of cooperatives; dissemination of printed and computer-based information prepared by governmental or inter-governmental bodies with the same priority and resources as allocated to information on other stakeholders.

Education

Given the important contributions of the cooperative movement to education, a number of enabling measures might be useful including the provision of public funds if they are made available to other forms of enterprise for educational programmes. Governments may also consider the inclusion within the national curricula at all levels of the study of the values, principles, history, current and potential contribution of the cooperative movement to national society; and encouragement and support of specialized studies in cooperatives at the tertiary level.

Provision of Public Funds

Financial self-reliance, total responsibility and full independence are vital for an effective cooperative enterprise. The best policy approach is one where cooperatives receive the same treatment as any other form of enterprise. A number of other measures are valuable: acknowledgement and protection of the special character of cooperatives and avoidance in law or practice of any discrimination arising from the special financial status, organization and management of cooperatives; avoidance of any direct or indirect engagement in the internal financial affairs of cooperatives or of the cooperative movement and recognition of the full responsibility of the movement for its own financial affairs; and the development of partnerships with cooperative financial institutions in such matters as community and regional development, drawing on their experience of mobilizing and managing capital in a manner and for purposes conducive to the public good.

Institutional Arrangements for Collaboration and Partnership

All government departments and bodies that have contact with the cooperative movement should be aware of, and act consistently with, national policy on cooperatives. In order to ensure consistency, certain coordinating functions within government, as well as with the cooperative movement, will be useful.

It is advisable that a single department or office assume central coordinating, focal and liaison functions, of which the following might be most important:

- elaboration of a single national comprehensive policy in respect of cooperatives, formulation of guidelines for consistent execution throughout government, including monitoring and review of that execution;

❖ collaboration with legal departments in drafting the general and any special laws; and

❖ liaison, consultation and collaboration with the cooperative movement.

The most effective organizational location for the responsible entity would be within a department already charged with broad strategic and coordinating functions, such as the office of a prime minister or president, or that responsible for economic management of development planning.

An institutional arrangement which enables regular consultation and effective collaboration between Governments and the cooperative movement would be valuable. Liaison between inter-governmental programmes and the international cooperative movement should be supported.

Summary

❖ Within the General Assembly of UN and the Economic and Social Council, and at major recent international conferences, Governments have recognized the cooperative movement as a distinct and major stakeholder in both national and international affairs.

❖ Consequently, Governments seek to create an environment in which cooperatives can participate on an equal footing with other forms of enterprise and develop an effective partnership to achieve their respective goals. Policies should protect and advance the potential of cooperatives to help members achieve their individual goals and, by so doing, to contribute to society's broader aspiration.

❖ The objective of the UN guidelines is to provide advice to Governments and set out broad principles on which national cooperative policy might best be based, recognizing that more specific and detailed national policies fall within the responsibility of each Government.

❖ The objective of the policy is to enable recognition of cooperatives as legal entities and to assure them and all organizations and institutions set up by the cooperatives movement real equality with other associations and entities

❖ It is appropriate and useful for Government to acknowledge publicly the special contribution, in both quantitative and qualitative terms, made by the cooperative movement to the national economy and society.

❖ Appropriate provision is necessary within legal, judicial and administrative practice if cooperatives are to contribute positively to improving the lives of their members and the communities in which they operate. Legal provisions may take various forms appropriate to individual national legal systems. The status, rights and responsibilities of cooperatives, the cooperative movement in general, and, if appropriate special categories of cooperatives or distinct aspects of cooperation should be addressed.

- Given the significance of the cooperative movement, it may be appropriate to envisage collaboration between governmental and cooperative movement research on matters relevant to public policy; publication and wide diffusion of research results, including those produced by the international cooperative movement, inter-governmental organizations and the United Nations.
- Several measures may be undertaken to improve statistics for and about cooperatives in view of integrating statistics on cooperatives in regular programmes of the national statistics service and participate in international efforts to improve cooperative statistics, including the establishment of a uniform set of definitions for use by national statistical services.
- Given that Governments regulate and broadly influence information diffusion, a number of measures may be useful in expanding knowledge of the cooperative movement and overcoming prejudices and misconceptions.
- Governments may also consider the inclusion within the national curricula at all levels of the study of the values, principles, history, current and potential contribution of the cooperative movement to national society; and encouragement and support of specialized studies in cooperatives at the tertiary level.
- Financial self-reliance, total responsibility and full independence are vital for an effective cooperative enterprise. The best policy approach is one where cooperatives receive the same treatment as any other form of enterprise.
- All government departments and bodies that have contact with the cooperative movement should be aware of, and act consistently with, national policy on cooperatives. In order to ensure consistency, certain coordinating functions within government, as well as with the cooperative movement, will be useful.

Self-Learning Activity

1. What would be the government's policy regarding cooperatives and the cooperative movement as per the guidelines?
2. What do the guidelines insist as for making special laws on certain categories of cooperatives?

11 International Labour Conference Recommendation 193 of 2002
Concerning the Promotion of Cooperatives

Significance of the Conference

The general conference of the International Labour Organization,

- ❖ having been convened at Geneva by the governing body of the International Labour Office, and having met in its 90th Session on 3 June 2002;
- ❖ recognizing the importance of cooperatives in job creation, mobilizing resources, generating investment and their contribution to the economy;
- ❖ recognizing that cooperatives in their various forms promote the fullest participation in the economic and social development of all people;
- ❖ recognizing that globalization has created new and different pressures, problems, challenges and opportunities for cooperatives, and that stronger form of human solidarity at national and international levels are required to facilitate a more equitable distribution of the benefits of globalization;
- ❖ noting the ILO Declaration on Fundamental Principles and Rights at Work, adopted by the International Labour Conference at its 86th Session (1998);
- ❖ noting the rights and principles embodied in International Labour Conventions and Recommendations, in particular the Forced Labor Convention, 1930; the Freedom of Association and Protection of the Right to Organize Convention, 1948; the Right to Organize and Collective Bargaining Convention, 1949; the Equal Remuneration Convention, 1951; the Social Security (Minimum Standards) Convention, 1952; the Abolition of Forced Labor Convention, 1957; the Discrimination (Employment and Occupation) Convention, 1958; the Employment Policy Convention, 1964; the Minimum Age Convention, 1973; the Rural Workers' Organizations

Convention and Recommendation, 1975; the Human Resources Development Convention and Recommendation, 1975; the Employment Policy (Supplementary Provisions) Recommendation, 1984; the Job Creation in Small- and Medium-Sized Enterprises Recommendation, 1998; and the Worst Forms of Child Labor Convention, 1999;

- recalling the principle embodied in the Declaration of Philadelphia that "labour is not a commodity;
- recalling that the realization of decent work for workers everywhere is a primary objective of the International Labor Organization;
- having decided upon the adoption of certain proposals with regard to the promotion of cooperatives, which is the fourth item on the agenda of the session; and
- having determined that these proposals shall take the form of a Recommendation; adopts this *twentieth day of June* of the year two thousand and two the following Recommendation, which may be cited as the Promotion of Cooperatives Recommendation, 2002.

Scope, Definition and Objectives

1. It is recognized that cooperatives operate in all sectors of the economy. This Recommendation applies to all types and forms of cooperatives.
2. For the purposes of this Recommendation, the term "cooperative" means an autonomous association of persons united voluntarily to meet their common economic, social and cultural needs and aspirations through a jointly owned and democratically controlled enterprise.
3. The promotion and strengthening of the identity of cooperatives should be encouraged on the basis of:
   (a) Cooperative values of self-help, self-responsibility, democracy, equality, equity and solidarity; as well as ethical values of honesty, openness, social responsibility and caring for others; and
   (b) Cooperative principles as developed by the international cooperative movement. These principles are: voluntary and open membership; democratic member control; member economic participation; autonomy and independence; education, training and information; cooperation among cooperatives; and concern for community.
4. Measures should be adopted to promote the potential of cooperatives in all countries, irrespective of their level of development, in order to assist them and their membership to:
   (a) create and develop income-generating activities and sustainable decent employment;

(b) develop human resource capacities and knowledge of the values, advantages and benefits of the cooperative movement through education and training;

(c) develop their business potential, including entrepreneurial and managerial capacities;

(d) strengthen their competitiveness as well as gain access to markets and to institutional finance;

(e) increase savings and investment;

(f) improve social and economic well-being, taking into account the need to eliminate all forms of discrimination;

(g) contribute to sustainable human development; and

(h) establish and expand a viable and dynamic distinctive sector of the economy, which includes cooperatives, that responds to the social and economic needs of the community.

5. The adoption of special measures should be encouraged to enable cooperatives, as enterprises and organizations inspired by solidarity, to respond to their members' needs and the needs of society, including those of disadvantaged groups in order to achieve their social inclusion.

Policy Framework and Role of Governments

6. A balanced society necessitates the existence of strong public and private sectors, as well as a strong cooperative, mutual and the other social and non-governmental sector. It is in this context that governments should provide a supportive policy and legal framework consistent with the nature and function of cooperatives and guided by the cooperative values and principles, which would:

(a) establish an institutional framework with the purpose of allowing for the registration of cooperatives in as rapid, simple, affordable and efficient a manner as possible;

(b) promote policies aimed at allowing the creation of appropriate reserves, part of which at least could be indivisible, and solidarity funds within cooperatives;

(c) provide for the adoption of measures for the oversight of cooperatives, on terms appropriate to their nature and functions, which respect their autonomy, and are in accordance with national law and practice, and which are no less favorable than those applicable to other forms of enterprise and social organization;

(d) facilitate the membership of cooperatives in cooperative structures responding to the needs of cooperative members; and

(e) encourage the development of cooperatives as autonomous and self-managed enterprises, particularly in areas where cooperatives have an important role to play or provide services that are not otherwise provided.

7. (a) The promotion of cooperatives guided by the values and principles should be considered as one of the pillars of national and international economic and social development.

(b) Cooperatives should be treated in accordance with national law and practice and on terms no less favorable than those accorded to other forms of enterprise and social organization. Governments should introduce support measures, where appropriate, for the activities of cooperatives that meet specific social and public policy outcomes, such as employment promotion or the development of activities benefiting disadvantaged groups or regions. Such measures could include, among others and in so far as possible, tax benefits, loans, grants, access to public works programmes, and special procurement provisions.

(c) Special consideration should be given to increasing women's participation in the cooperative movement at all levels, particularly at management and leadership levels.

8. (a) National policies should notably:

- promote the ILO fundamental labour standards and the ILO Declaration on Fundamental Principles and Rights at Work, for all workers in cooperatives without distinction whatsoever;
- ensure that cooperatives are not set up for, or used for, non-compliance with labour law or used to establish disguised employment relationships, and combat pseudo cooperatives violating workers' rights, by ensuring that labor legislation is applied in all enterprises;
- promote gender equality in cooperatives and in their work;
- promote measures to ensure that best labour practices are followed in cooperatives, including access to relevant information;
- develop the technical and vocational skills, entrepreneurial and managerial abilities, knowledge of business potential, and general economic and social policy skills, of members, workers and managers, and improve their access to information and communication technologies;
- promote education and training in cooperative principles and practices, at all appropriate levels of the national education and training systems, and in the wider society;

- promote the adoption of measures that provide for safety and health in the workplace;
- provide for training and other forms of assistance to improve the level of productivity and competitiveness of cooperatives and the quality of goods and services they produce;
- facilitate access of cooperatives to credit;
- facilitate access of cooperatives to markets;
- promote the dissemination of information on cooperatives; and
- seek to improve national statistics on cooperatives with a view to the formulation and implementation of development policies.

(b) Such policies should:

- decentralize to the regional and local levels, where appropriate, the formulation and implementation of policies and regulations regarding cooperatives;
- define legal obligations of cooperatives in areas such as registration, financial and social audits, and the obtaining of licences; and
- promote best practice on corporate governance in cooperatives.

9. Governments should promote the important role of cooperatives in transforming what are often marginal survival activities (sometimes referred to as the "informal economy") into legally protected work, fully integrated into mainstream economic life.

Implementation of Public Policies for the Promotion of Cooperatives

10. (a) Member States should adopt specific legislation and regulations on cooperatives, which are guided by the cooperative values and principles, and revise such legislation and regulations when appropriate.

(b) Governments should consult cooperative organizations, as well as the employers' and workers' organizations concerned, in the formulation and revision of legislation, policies and regulations applicable to cooperatives.

11. (a) Governments should facilitate access of cooperatives to support services in order to strengthen them, their business viability and their capacity to create employment and income.

(b) These services should include, wherever possible:

- human resource development programmes;
- research and management consultancy services;
- access to finance and investment;
- accountancy and audit services;
- management information services;
- information and public relations services;
- consultancy services on technology and innovation;
- legal and taxation services;
- support services for marketing; and
- other support services where appropriate.

(c) Governments should facilitate the establishment of these support services. Cooperatives and their organizations should be encouraged to participate in the organization and management of these services and, wherever feasible and appropriate, to finance them.

(d) Governments should recognize the role of cooperatives and their organizations by developing appropriate instruments aimed at creating and strengthening cooperatives at national and local levels.

12. Governments should, where appropriate, adopt measures to facilitate the access of cooperatives to investment finance and credit. Such measures should notably:

(a) allow loans and other financial facilities to be offered;

(b) simplify administrative procedures, remedy any inadequate level of cooperative assets, and reduce the cost of loan transactions;

(c) facilitate an autonomous system of finance for cooperatives, including savings and credit, banking and insurance cooperatives; and

(d) include special provisions for disadvantaged groups.

13. For the promotion of the cooperative movement, governments should encourage conditions favouring the development of technical, commercial and financial linkages among all forms of cooperatives so as to facilitate an exchange of experience and the sharing of risks and benefits.

Role of Employers' Workers' and Cooperative Organizations, and their Relationships

14. Employers' and workers' organizations, recognizing the significance of cooperatives for the attainment of sustainable development goals, should seek, together with cooperative organizations, ways and means of cooperative promotion.

15. Employers' organizations should consider, where appropriate, the extension of membership to cooperatives wishing to join them and provide appropriate support services on the same terms and conditions applying to other members.

16. Workers' organizations should be encouraged to:

(a) advise and assist workers in cooperatives to join workers' organizations;

(b) assist their members to establish cooperatives, including with the aim of facilitating access to basic goods and services;

(c) participate in committees and working groups at the local, national and international levels that consider economic and social issues having an impact on cooperatives;

(d) assist and participate in the setting up of new cooperatives with a view to the creation or maintenance of employment, including in cases of proposed closures of enterprises;

(e) assist and participate in programmes for cooperatives aimed at improving their productivity;

(f) promote equality of opportunity in cooperatives;

(g) promote the exercise of the rights of worker-members of cooperatives; and

(h) undertake any other activities for the promotion of cooperatives, including education and training.

17. Cooperatives and organizations representing them should be encouraged to:

(a) establish an active relationship with employers' and workers' organizations and concerned governmental and non-governmental agencies with a view to creating a favourable climate for the development of cooperatives;

(b) manage their own support services and contribute to their financing;

(c) provide commercial and financial services to affiliated cooperatives;

(d) invest in, and further, human resource development of their members, workers and managers;

(e) further the development of and affiliation with national and international cooperative organizations;

(f) represent the national cooperative movement at the international level; and

(g) undertake any other activities for the promotion of cooperatives.

International Cooperation

18. International cooperation should be facilitated through:
    (a) exchanging information on policies and programmes that have proved to be effective in employment creation and income generation for members of cooperatives;
    (b) encouraging and promoting relationships between national and international bodies and institutions involved in the development of cooperatives in order to permit:
        (i) the exchange of personnel and ideas, of educational and training materials, methodologies and reference materials;
        (ii) the compilation and utilization of research material and other data on cooperatives and their development;
        (iii) the establishment of alliances and international partnerships between cooperatives;
        (iv) the promotion and protection of cooperative values and principles; and
        (v) the establishment of commercial relations between cooperatives;
    (c) access of cooperatives to national and international data, such as market information, legislation, training methods and techniques, technology and product standards; and
    (d) developing, where it is warranted and possible, and in consultation with cooperatives, employers' and workers' organizations concerned, common regional and international guidelines and legislation to support cooperatives.

Final Provision

19. The present Recommendation revises and replaces the Co-operatives (Developing Countries) Recommendation, 1966.

Summary

❖ The general conference of the International Labour Organization, having been convened at Geneva by the governing body of the International Labour Office, and having met in its 90th Session on 3 June 2002.

❖ It is recognized that cooperatives operate in all sectors of the economy.

❖ The promotion and strengthening of the identity of cooperatives should be encouraged on the basis of cooperative values and principles.

❖ Measures should be adopted to promote the potential of cooperatives in all countries, irrespective of their level of development, in order to assist them and their membership.

❖ A balanced society necessitates the existence of strong public and private sectors, as well as a strong cooperative, mutual and the other social and non-governmental sector. It is in this context that Governments should provide a supportive policy and legal framework consistent with the nature and function of cooperatives and guided by the cooperative values and principles.

❖ Member States should adopt specific legislation and regulations on cooperatives, which are guided by the cooperative values and principles, and revise such legislation and regulations when appropriate.

❖ Employers' and workers' organizations, recognizing the significance of cooperatives for the attainment of sustainable development goals, should seek, together with cooperative organizations, ways and means of cooperative promotion.

❖ International cooperation should be facilitated through exchanging information on policies and programmes that have proved to be effective in employment creation and income generation for members of cooperatives.

Self-Learning Activity

1. What should the national policy on cooperatives?
2. What sort of support services should the Government facilitate access of cooperatives?

12 Cooperative Policies and Cooperative Law in African Countries

In this unit the legislation and policies of cooperatives in African countries—the cooperative development policies, weakness and problems of such policies, cooperative legislation models/patterns and new trends in cooperative law in African countries — are discussed.

Cooperative Development Policies

Sound cooperative development is directly influenced by the cooperative development policy of the government and of other cooperative promotion institutions. It is one of the most important factors determining the creation of a favourable climate for cooperative development since it lays down the framework within which cooperative development activities take place. It gives cooperative promotion a particular direction which can be favourable or unfavourable for cooperative development. In the following, this aspect of cooperative development policy in African countries is analysed with regard to its present situation, the problems associated with it and measures for improvement in the cooperative development policies.

Situation of Cooperative Development Policy

One of the most important factors responsible for sound cooperative development is the existence of a consistent, realistic and well-planned, long-term cooperative development policy of the government. A good example of such policy statement is the Sessional Paper No. 8 of 1970 of Kenya. The Gaborone Conference emphasized the need for such a policy in each country and as a result steps have been undertaken in many African countries to formulate policy statements, have them approved in Parliament and to integrate such policies in the national development plans. Progress has been very diverse in various countries, as may be seen from the following examples:

In Botswana, the government policy on cooperatives has been clear although there was a felt need to include a specific policy statement on cooperative development in the country's national development plan. As a result, a policy statement on cooperative development was drafted and submitted to the government in the late 1986 for its approval and notification.

In Kenya, cooperatives have been accorded an important role in the implementation of the government's development policy as laid down in the Sessional Paper No. 10 of 1965 on "African Socialism and its Application to Planning in Kenya". Further, the specific policy on cooperative development has been laid down in the Sessional Paper No. 8 of 1970 and No. 14 of 1975 on Cooperative Development Policy. However, the swift changes within the cooperative movement in the last few years have made this Sessional Paper obsolete and created a need for its reviewal.

In Lesotho, the government's commitment to the promotion of viable socio-economic people's organizations, which include cooperatives, has been emphasized at various occasions. However, there is still a dire need for a clear national policy statement on cooperative development and legislation, which is lacking so far and which could contribute to the development of a viable and autonomous cooperative movement if implemented effectively.

The cooperative development policy of Mauritius follows the national objectives of agricultural diversification, industrialization and employment creation. The government has identified a number of problem areas which have to be tackled in the future such as the improvement of audit and supervision, the diversification of cooperatives into industrial areas, education and training of members and employees, the participation of women and youth in cooperatives, the promotion of cooperative research and cooperative trade and the financial autonomy of the cooperative movement.

In the 1980's the cooperative development policy of Tanzania could be derived from a variety of declarations and guidelines concerning cooperatives, although no single, comprehensive policy statement on cooperative development existed. Among the sources which throw light on the government policy on cooperatives were the African Declaration of 1967, which still forms the basis of the socio-economic development in Tanzania and is geared towards promoting socialism and self-reliance through cooperatives. The party directive on production-oriented cooperatives of 1985 formed a further base for cooperative development in the country. The directive summarizes the various policies, decisions and directives of the party and the government since the Arusha Declaration and strives for the promotion of production-oriented cooperatives.

Zimbabwe has laid great emphasis on having a cooperative development policy for the country. A cooperative policy paper was approved by the government in 1983. A new cooperative development policy paper has been issued together with the enactment of the new cooperative law in 1990. The establishment of a national cooperative training institution and of a cooperative bank has been envisaged in the policy paper as well. Cooperative development plans are an integral part of the national development plan and the ministry's policy on cooperative development is integrated into the national policies of social and economic development. The attitude of the State in Zimbabwe towards cooperative development is hence positive. The State has been the driving force behind the development and expansion of the cooperative movement after independence.

In Guinea, a new cooperative development strategy has been introduced since 1984 which does not differ very much from the policies pursued before 1984. Administrative structures have been decentralized and a cooperative promotion institution of the State has been established, namely the Service National d'Assistance Technique aux Cooperatives (SNATC).

In Tunisia, at the beginning of the decade 1960-70 the political party which took over the government proposed a programme for the cooperativisation of the country. In short, it was an utopian and ill-conceived project which ten years later ended in disaster.

In Madagascar, the economic development programme conceived and launched in 1964 by the government of the First Republic proclaimed that a cooperative is at the same time one of the means and one of the fundamental objectives of development. The basic law of 1964 laid down in more detail in section 31 that cooperative organizations and in particular the buying and selling stations have to participate in the execution of this plan. This was an unrealistic ambition which could not be implemented in view of the prevailing situation.

In Burundi, the party Union Pour le Progres National (UPRONA) as well as the government planned a general policy in favour of using cooperatives for achieving development goals. The Central Committee of the party devoted a good deal of its work at its second session in July 1985 to the programme of cooperativisation. The IV Economic and Social Development Plan for the period 1983-1987 devoted several pages to cooperatives.

In Ethiopia, the history of the cooperative movement dovetails the policy of cooperative development during three regimes, viz., Imperial, Derg and present FDRE government. During Imperial period and Derg regime cooperatives were organized as a government policy, say a target approach was followed. During the present FDRE period some policy reforms have been made and cooperatives are organized for the development. Now slowly the cooperative movement with new Cooperative Proclamation No. 147/ 1998 is flourishing in the country.

To sum up, it can be stated that irrespective of which power laid down the national policy on cooperative development, this policy was always basically motivated by political problems and goals and was not devised to create favourable climate for cooperatives. Political parties and governments wanted to take over the existing cooperative structure especially in the rural areas, in order to have a better control of the population and to use them for carrying out tasks planned from above. These policies were utopian, ambitious and neither in consonance with the existing realities and needs nor with the means at their disposal. The people concerned were not given the chance to participate in the elaboration of these national programmes.

Weakness and Problems

The role of governments in cooperative development and the relationship between the State and cooperatives are two important factors in the African context. It has been seen that a great majority of African governments have recognized cooperatives as instruments for socio-economic development. They used top-down approach of initiating and promoting cooperatives hence continuing with a readily available model which existed from colonial times. The relationship between State and cooperatives over the decades have changed and vary from country to country in Africa. However, in spite of the differences, the intervention of the State in the cooperative movement has generally increased over the years.

Official attitudes towards cooperatives can be manifold. The State might be hostile to cooperatives as was the case in countries like Ghana in 1960 and Tanzania in 1975 where cooperatives were dismantled overnight and restructured. Secondly, the State might be neutral or indifferent to cooperatives and show no interest in them except for providing legal framework. This is now the case in Senegal and Cameroon under their new development policies. Thirdly, the State might have a top-down approach to cooperatives whereby it participates in the organization, management, supervision and control of the cooperatives using them to siphon off their surplus earnings but also taking charge of their losses and, if necessary, keeping them alive artificially. Finally, the State might have a benevolent approach to cooperative development whereby it creates a favourable climate for the development of cooperatives, provides them assistance and incentives without infringing in the affairs of the cooperatives.

The experiences in the African countries have shown that the most common patterns of the relationship between the State and cooperatives seem to be either of massive State paternalism and control or a hostile approach to cooperatives. Cooperatives have lost their self-help character and members see themselves as suppliers to a para-statal organization. This is the result of violation of cooperative values and principles. Since membership was made compulsory, surpluses were extracted through marketing boards and government officers intervened in the day-to-day affairs of cooperatives.

In most countries there seems to be confusion as to what direction cooperative development should take and how to go about achieving this goal. One notices great contradiction in the plans and activities of the State with regard to cooperative development.

A further problem concerning cooperative development policy seems to be the lack of continuity in many countries. Frequent and sudden changes in policy have wide-ranging negative effects on cooperative development as was the case in Tanzania and Ghana. This includes the frequent changes of Ministries responsible for cooperatives and changes of leading officials of the civil service from one post to another. Many cooperative development policies in African countries have turned out to be unrealistic. As a result there are large discrepancies between the officially declared policy and its implementation.

Measures for Improvement

One of the basic ingredients for the creation of a conducive climate for cooperative development is to have an effective cooperative development policy and implement it successfully. However, before any development policy for cooperatives is formed, one has to be clear about the concept and objectives of cooperative development. This would mean that the State has to take a clear decision whether it wants to follow the concept of State-sponsored cooperation whereby the cooperative should finally become self-reliant institutions or whether it wants to follow the concept of State-controlled cooperatives, where the cooperatives are used as instruments to fulfill its development goals by implementing development programmes of the State. This discrepancy between proclaimed policy and policy implementation needs to be removed and a well-planned strategy of either State-sponsored or autonomous cooperation needs to be implemented.

A proper concept can only be conceived by the State with the participation of the cooperative movement and the NGOs concerned. The results of such a participatory process should then be coined an official policy for the development of cooperatives and other SHOs. The formulation of such a policy is frequently a process of political bargaining, of coordination and of harmonization of conflicting interests and often ends up in a compromise. However, it is important to find a consensus and lay down the policy in a policy statement. Such a statement has to be:

1. Clear, i.e., avoid the ambiguity of combining State-sponsorship of SHOs with State intervention and State-control;

2. Consistent, i.e., follow a logical pattern in which all components of the programme of State-sponsorship fit together;
3. Realistic, i.e., be based on solid research and knowledge of facts, taking full account of present possibilities and constraints and future probable development, especially with regard to the speed of socio-economic change, the scope of self-help activities, the target population and available resources for self-help promotion; and
4. Officially pronounced, i.e., be published in form of white paper or a statement of objects and reasons of the cooperative law.

Any constructive policy statement on the development of cooperatives should highlight the government's role and intention to promote cooperatives and how it intends doing so, a clear description of the role which cooperatives and other SHOs are to play in the economic system of the country. Cooperative development policy has to be continuous and long-term and should be laid down in a policy paper. However, the implementation should be subject to periodical reviews so as to be able to accommodate new trends which may occur as a result of the development of the country.

The most important step, however, is to have seriously committed government which has sincere intentions of promoting cooperatives without controlling them. The de-officialisation cannot be achieved simply by making an official statement to this effect. It is necessary to clearly limit the function of the cooperative department officers. Government officers should withdraw totally from interfering in the management affairs of cooperatives at all levels. Further, cooperative development policies need to be integrated at all levels of development planning. This implies that cooperatives must be given a voice in planning national development programmes, including measures for the promotion of cooperative development in sectoral programmes. Cooperatives should be represented in the policy-making and programme reviewing organs of the government.

At the regional and international level there are a number of policy statements and recommendations. Perhaps the most important of these is the ILO Recommendation No. 127 which has assumed a position of being the basis for discussion on cooperative policies in developing countries today. The recommendation outlines in a concise form the basic ingredients of a national cooperative policy, the methods to be adopted and the measures to be taken to implement these policies.

Besides the initiatives of the ILO, the resolution taken at the series of Ministerial Conferences of East, Central and Southern African countries organized by the ICA (in Gaborone 1984, Lusaka 1987, and Nairobi 1990) also mark a progress in formulating cooperative policies in Africa. The conferences are trend setters and encouraging factors in the process of creating a favourable climate and conditions for cooperative development.

Cooperative Legislation

Most of the African countries have experienced decades of colonial rule. One of the results of this period of foreign domination is the existence of parallel systems of original local norms and values and value systems imported from and imposed by the former colonial powers. Such dualism of value system and structures exists in the field of law as well as other fields of life. In most of the African countries there are widely spread informal organizations based on local custom and rules of unwritten customary law working side-by-side with officially recognized, registered cooperative and pre-cooperative societies operating under modern, i.e., imported cooperative legislation. The colonial origin of modern cooperative law and the fact that many of the provisions of this modern cooperative legislation — although following internationally recognized cooperative principles — are alien to the majority of the people in developing countries and sometimes run counter the prevailing traditional systems of norms and values, are among the root causes for the problems encountered by promoters of cooperative development in Africa up till today.

The cooperative legislation in the 22 countries covered by a report can be subdivided by their origin into three categories:

1. Countries following the classical British-Indian Pattern of Cooperation: Botswana, Egypt, the Ghana, Lesotho, Mauritius, Nigeria, Tanzania and Zimbabwe.
2. Countries following the French Model of State-controlled Cooperatives: Algeria, Burkina Faso, Cameroon, Chad, Cote d'Ivoire, Guinea, Madagascar, Mali, Niger, Senegal, Togo and Tunisia; and
3. Burundi as a former Belgian dependency.

Out of these countries, six tried to develop their own cooperative development policy and legislation following socialist models for a shorter or longer period of time, replacing one imported model by another, namely Algeria, Guinea, Madagascar, Mali, Tanzania and Tunisia. But except for Algeria and Tunisia, they returned to their original system with some modification. Ten of these have developed special legal provisions for pre-cooperative forms of organizations. Burkina Faso (Village Groups 1983), Cameroon (Common Interst Groups 1992), Cote d'Ivoire (Groupements a vocation cooperative 1966), Guinea (Groupements Villageois ou de quartier 1985), Madagascar (fokonolona), Mali (tons villageois), Niger (groupements mutualistes villageois 1978), Senegal (associations d'interet rural 1960-83),

Tanzania (Provisionally registered cooperatives 1968 and villages and ujamaa villages 1975-1982), Zimbabwe (provisionally registered pre-cooperatives 1990).

The two models still strongly influence the legislation governing cooperative societies in most of the African countries. Apart from radical changes, replacing colonial models with socialist structures, the innovative force of law-making in the field of cooperative legislation has been rather limited.

Classical British-Indian Pattern of Cooperation

Cooperative legislation in the African countries having experienced British colonial rule was almost uniform at the time when these countries reached independence. All these countries used cooperative legislation based on the classical British-Indian pattern of cooperation. In a nutshell, the ideas underlying this model are as follows:

- ❖ The objective of government is to encourage the development of self-reliant economically viable cooperatives;
- ❖ For an initial period, the government sponsors this development by offering guidelines, advice and supervision, carried out by a specialized government agency;
- ❖ The policy of government is to hand over its promotional functions to cooperative support structures as soon as possible, limiting its role to skeleton functions like registration, cancellation of registration and normative control.

During 1930's the Model Cooperative Societies Ordinance was applied without major changes by the British dependencies which had not already introduced this type of cooperative law. In recent years, efforts have been undertaken in some countries to correct the shortcomings of this legislation. The central assumptions on which the entire concept is based, are not respected in the laws and in their application, namely that government influence on cooperatives is strictly temporary, that it only serves to make cooperatives self-reliant as soon as possible and that government shall phase out as soon as the cooperatives are strong enough to look after their own affairs.

The French Model

During colonial times the French colonial government introduced a type of semi-public provident society, the SIP in what was then called Afrique occidental francais (AOF) (French West Africa), established by administrative circulars in 1902 and 1909 with bylaws to be approved by the governer and under the control of the district officer. The Africans saw SIPs/ socialist africaine de prevoyance – SAPs as extensions of the colonial government.

After the Second World War, SIPs/SAPs continued to operate, but parallel to them the liberal French cooperative legislation of 1947 was declared applicable in the overseas territories. In 1955, the direct application of the French cooperative law in the French dependencies was repealed and a decree governing the legal status of cooperatives in French overseas territories came into force. During the years 1977-83 a new legislation for village groups and cooperative societies was developed in a process of participative law-making. This was revised again in 1990. Still some countries opted for models of cooperative legislation following socialist patterns.

New Trends in Cooperative Law of the African Countries

When analyzing the recent development of cooperative law in the African countries, several new trends emerge in policy statements and revisions of cooperative legislation, namely the recognition of cooperatives as private SHOs of their members, a pluralism of forms of SHOs, a rethinking of the role of government in cooperative development, improvement of the external conditions for cooperative development in the economic sphere, and participative law-making.

Recognition of cooperatives as private SHOs of their members: For decades cooperatives in Africa were treated by policy-makers, development planners and foreign donors as if they were development tools which governments could use to implement their programmes and to exercise control mainly over the production of agricultural cash crops for export markets. It has become inevitable to allow citizens to form genuine SHOs financed and controlled by their members and operating in their members' interest. This has, for instance, been declared at the First African Ministerial Cooperative Conference in Gaborone, Botswana in 1984, where it was stated that governments should be prepared to release those income-generating activities presently being run by parastatal bodies to be undertaken by cooperatives so as to help them in attaining self-reliance and that governments were willing to help cooperatives attain increased strength and capability.

Pluralism of forms: During colonial regimes and in many African countries up till very recently, State controlled registered cooperative societies were the only officially recognized form of organizations. In due course people wanted to have their self-help organizations based on the cooperative principles and values. Apart from the legal forms of simple SHOs in the Feench speaking countries, various kinds of associations, groups, societies and clubs are formed as alternatives or preliminary stages of registered cooperative societies and these alternatives developed as a means to bypass rigid cooperative structures will lose some of their attractions.

Rethinking of the role of government in cooperative development: Structural adjustment programmes are forcing governments to reduce their involvement in economic affairs, to deregulate and liberalize the markets and to give more room and responsibility to private initiative. This means the role of government in cooperative development should be reconsidered with a trend to limit government's control over the cooperatives. Government's role in promoting cooperatives will concentrate on creating favourable conditions for private business organizations including cooperatives and offering education, training and consultancy services to those who seek these services.

Improving the external conditions for cooperative development in the economic sphere: Instead of promoting cooperatives directly by grants, soft loans, subsidies and tax exemptions which tend to make them dependent on donors and serve as justification for government control, cooperatives have to be allowed access to income-generating activities so as to enable them to build up their own capital base and to become truly independent. The proceedings of the First African Ministerial Cooperative Conference in Gaborone contain the recommendations on these lines for improving the external conditions for cooperative development.

Participative law-making: In some of the African countries, a new method of participative law-making has been applied which gives cooperatives and their elected representatives a chance to express their views already at an early stage of the process of law making and which emphasizes the free flow of information at all stages of the process of law making relevant reports and drafts available to all interested parties and by having them discussed in workshops, seminars and conferences at all levels.

Summary

- The cooperative development policies are of different in nature based on the models adopted in African countries. French model, British-Indian model, and other models are followed.
- Some states were under colonial regime and some were not; there is no uniform cooperative policy in states of Africa.
- The African countries need to revise the cooperative development policies and laws for cooperatives according to the changes.

Self-Learning Activity

1. Critically discuss on Cooperative Development Policies in African countries?
2. Cooperative Legislation should be revised for the development of cooperatives in Africa – discuss?

Part - II

Development of Cooperative Law in Ethiopia during the Periods of Imperial Government and DERG Regime

13 Farm Workers Cooperative Decree No. 44 of 1960 Made by Imperial Government

Traditional Cooperatives in Ethiopia

Ethiopia is known as a country with diversified nationalities, ethnic groups, languages; each has its own unique culture and custom of living in entertaining different social activities. Working in group (ploughing, harvesting, trashing, house construction), habits of eating together (in holidays, festivals), and living together is the common phenomena of Ethiopians. In Ethiopia there are three well known traditional cooperatives or self-help groups. They are discussed below.

Edir

Edir is one of the traditional forms of cooperatives still operating almost in all parts of Ethiopia, urban and rural. It is similar with burial cooperatives or organization that mainly stands for performing burial ceremonies and to condolence. The main objective for the establishment of this form of traditional cooperative (Edir) is to help a family who is the member of Edir in case of getting sorrow (A family lost one of its members, because of dying) and happiness (marriage and other occasions) which require personal, material and financial support from all of the Edir members based on the rules and regulations stated in the bylaw of the Edir. If a person is going to get this assistance he has to fulfil the membership criteria set by the traditional society. Edir gets its legal personality from ministry of justice or regional justice bureau by paying registration fee. The member's participation is very high in Edir because its foundation is based on the willingness of each and every member.

Ekub

Ekub is other form of traditional cooperative or traditional self-help group in Ethiopia. Ekub is a traditional financial cooperative formed voluntarily. In this members make regular contributions to a revolving loan fund. The formation of Ekub is based on classes of people who have identical (similar) earning or income. Unlike saving and credit cooperatives, it does not bear interest on the money saved (collected). The person who has got the money on his turn basis solves his immediate economic and social problem. To minimize risk in an Ekub personal guarantee should be given by payee to the traditional society when he/she is taking the money from the Ekub members. Many people use this form of traditional cooperative as a means of financial solution to their economic problems. Ekub is to certain extend similar to the modern saving and credit cooperatives. Therefore, there is a chance that this traditional form of cooperative could be changed in to modern cooperative societies with some modifications on their operation and making them to have legal bases. The amount of money which is now serving for immediate problem solving could be transformed in to sustainable and continues problem solving system of modern cooperative by convincing and promoting the Ekub members.

Debo/Wenfal/Lefenty

Debo is a system of farmer's cooperation during the time of farming, weeding, harvesting, trashing, and house construction etc. Debo/Wenfale/ Lefenty do not have a system of administration like the other form of associations, it is based on equivalent labour or material contribution (mainly Ox) by each farmer. It is a mechanism by which all farmers helping each other on turn basis. Since each types of work are being done in time, the productivity per farmers can be increased. Generally, these three traditional forms of association which are having the values and customs of our society should be brought to modern form of cooperatives so that they can contribute to the economic and social development of the people of Ethiopia.

Modern form of cooperatives started in Ethiopia during the ruling era of Emperor Haile Selassie I. In 1960 the first legislative called "Farm Workers Cooperatives Decree" was declared as Decree No. 44/1960. The objectives needed to enact this decree were:

- ❖ To accelerate the development of the agricultural economy of the country.
- ❖ The organization of cooperative enterprise was believed to be as it can contribute measurably to this end.
- ❖ And it was also found necessary that the proper framework be created for the establishment of such cooperative enterprises.

The Ministry of National Community Development was charged with the responsibility of ensuring systematic cooperative promotion and development. Various efforts were made to ensuring systematic cooperative promotion and development. Various efforts were made to establish farm workers' and service cooperatives for the settlement for the landless or evicted tenants to engage in collective farming on government land. The provisions of Farm Workers Cooperative Decree No. 44/1960 are discussed hereunder.

Necessity for the Issuance of the Decree

Whereas, it is desirable that steps be taken further to accelerate the development of the agricultural economy of Our Empire; and

Whereas, the organization of cooperative enterprises can contribute measurably to this end; and

Whereas, it is necessary that the proper framework be created for the establishment of such cooperative enterprises;

Now, therefore, in accordance with the provisions of Article 92 of Our Revised Consultation, and on the advice of Our Council of Ministers, We hereby decree as follows:

Article 1: Short Title

This decree may be cited as the "Farm Workers' Cooperative Decree, 1960".

Section I: Creation, Purposes and Objectives of Cooperatives

Article 2: Authorization of Creation of Cooperatives

There are hereby authorized to create Farm Workers Cooperative(s) thereafter the "Cooperative"(s), which shall be organized, administered, and regulated in accordance with the provisions hereof.

Article 3: Purposes and Objectives of Cooperatives

Cooperatives organized hereunder shall have as their principal purpose and object the promotion of the economic interests of Ethiopia and of their members through the efficient cultivation and development of land made available to them and the profitable sale of products produced on said land.

Without the generality of the foregoing, the cooperative shall:

(a) Arrange for the cooperative production, processing, transportation and marketing of agricultural products and commodities and the taking of other action calculated to achieve the most profitable production, processing, and marketing of agricultural products and livestock produced owned by the cooperative;

(b) Operate and administer livestock and agricultural and other machinery owned by the cooperative for the benefits of its members;

(c) Promote good farming and agricultural practices;

(d) Promote cooperation among members of the cooperative;

(e) Promote cooperation among cooperatives generally by the pooling of common resources and the taking of other action appropriate to this end.

Section II: Manner of Organization of Cooperatives

Article 4: Designation of Land Available for Transfer

(a) From time to time, the Ministry of National Community Development (hereafter the Ministry) shall designate areas of land which have been placed at its disposal as available for transfer as Rist land to Cooperatives. The Minister shall, taking into account the size and quality of each area of land, fix the number of shares which shall be issued by the Cooperative to which transferred.

(b) In determining the location and size of an area of land pursuant to paragraph (a) of this Article 4 and the number of shares to be issued by the Cooperative to which transferred, the Ministry shall take into account and give due weight to the economic interests of the Empire and the need for assuring a balanced agricultural development throughout the Empire.

Article 5: Application for Membership

Persons wishing to apply for membership in a cooperative shall appear in person at the Ministry or at a branch office thereof and shall complete and file with the office where registering an application form which shall be supplied to them free of charge.

Article 6: Qualification as a Member

A person applying to the Ministry for membership pursuant to Article 5 hereof shall be registered by the Ministry if he meets the following conditions:

(a) is a national of Ethiopia

(b) is over eighteen (18) and under sixty (60) years of age;

(c) declares that he is willing to join a cooperative and to accept all of the duties of a member thereof; and

(d) is found by the Ministry physically fit to discharge all of the duties of a member thereof.

Article 7: Formation of Cooperative Group

(a) When a sufficient number of applicants have been registered by the Ministry, the Ministry shall designate a tract of land to be placed at the disposal of members which shall comprise said Cooperative.

(b) Simultaneously therewith, the Ministry shall designate from among the applicants registered with it a group to constitute the nucleus for the creation of the Cooperative. Said group shall represent at least one-half (½) of the number of members which shall comprise said Cooperative. To the maximum extent possible, the wishes of the applicant with respect to the area of Ethiopia in which or the Cooperative with which he desires to be associated with relatives or other designated individuals in the same Cooperative, shall be taken into account by the Ministry.

Article 8: Right of Applicant to Elect Not to Become a Member of a Cooperative

Each applicant registered with the Agency pursuant to Article 5 hereof shall, when named to a group of applicants to create a Cooperative be given an opportunity to reject said nomination and shall remain eligible to be named subsequently to another group provided however that any applicant who rejects three (3) such nominations shall be stricken from the register maintained by the Ministry and shall thereafter be ineligible to become a member of a Co-operative.

Article 9: Organizational Meeting

Under its formation each group shall hold an organizational meeting and elect the administrative bodies of the Cooperative. A representative of the Ministry shall be present at the meeting so held to ensure that all necessary formalities are fulfilled and to render such assistance and advice as may be requested.

Article 10: Registration as a Cooperative

(a) Upon the election of the administrative bodies of the Cooperative and the adoption of a resolution authorising and directing the same, an application shall be made to the Ministry for registration as Farm Workers' Cooperative. Said application shall contain such information as the Ministry may require.

(b) The fact of registration shall be entered by the Ministry in a Register of Farm Workers' Cooperatives to be maintained by it.

(c) Registration with the Ministry shall confer upon the Cooperative full status as a juridical person under the laws of the Empire with all of the powers and rights attaching thereto, which shall include subject to the restrictions and conditions set forth herein. The power to:

(i) Contract and borrow money in its own name

(ii) Sue and be sued; and

(iii) Acquire, hold and alienate movable and immovable property.

Article 11: Transfer of Rist Land to the Cooperative

(a) Within three (3) months of the date of registration of the Cooperative with Ministry, the Ministry shall cause the area of land designated for transfer to the Cooperative to be recorded in the appropriate land register as Rist land held by the Cooperative, and shall take or cause to be taken all other action necessary to confirm said transfer and to vest ownership of said Rist land in the Cooperative.

(b) Land so transferred shall be grant by the Ministry to the Cooperative and shall be transferred to the Cooperative without cost or charge to the latter.

Article 12: Issuance of Membership Certificates

When any person becomes a member of the Cooperative, the Cooperative shall cause to be issued and delivered to him a certificate representing his membership in the Cooperative which shall be registered in his name in the register maintained by the Cooperative pursuant to Article 20 thereof.

Section III: Acquisition of Membership in the Cooperative

Article 13: Original Members of the Cooperative

Upon the registration of the Cooperative pursuant to Article 10 hereof, the persons comprising the group formed pursuant to Article 7 hereof shall be registered as members on a membership register to be maintained by the Cooperative, which register shall show, with respect to original members and all persons who subsequently become members of the Cooperative:

(a) The name of the member;

(b) The date and manner of acquisition of membership; and

(c) Such other pertinent data as the Cooperative may deem appropriate.

Article 14: Admission of New Members by Application after Cooperative Formed

After registration of the Cooperative pursuant to Article 10 hereof, a new member be admitted to the Cooperative by making application to the Managing Committee there for and being accepted as a member by the said Managing Committee, subject to confirmation at the next General Meeting of the members of the Cooperative; provided, however;

(a) That any such applicant shall meet the conditions set forth in Article 6 hereof;

(b) That any applicant whose application is rejected by the Managing Committee of the Cooperative shall have a right of appeal to the members of the Cooperative at the next General Meeting thereof; and

(c) That so long as the membership of the Cooperative is less than the maximum number of members fixed by the Ministry pursuant to Article 4 thereof, any applicant whose application is rejected by the members of the Cooperative shall have a right of appeal to the Ministry, which may either confirm the rejection or direct that the applicant be admitted as a member of the Cooperative.

Article 15: Acquisition of Membership by inheritance or as the Legal Representative of a Member

(a) Persons meeting the condition set forth in paragraph (a) of Article 6 hereof may become a member of a Cooperative by inheritance from a deceased member. If the deceased member has nominated in his will one or more persons to whom, on his death, his membership in the Cooperative shall pass, said person or persons shall, if he or they fulfil the conditions set forth in paragraph (a) of Article 6 hereof, become a member of the cooperative. If said person or persons fulfil all of the conditions set forth in Article 6 hereof, he or they shall become a working member of the Cooperative. If the deceased member has made no will, the person or persons taking as intestate heirs shall succeed to the membership of the deceased member, subject to the same conditions set forth in the first two sentences of this paragraph (a).

(b) The Legal representative of a member who is declared to be unsound mind shall represent said member in the operations of the Cooperative.

(c) The person determined by civil law to be the legal representative of a member who is declared to be of unsound mind or of a minor who is the heir of a member shall be the legal representative of said member or heir for the purposes of this Decree.

Article 16: Acquisition of Membership by Purchase

Membership in the Cooperative shall be alienable, and my be sold to any person who fulfils all of the conditions set forth in Article 6 hereof 'provided however, that any member, whether a working or a non-working member of the cooperative, who desires to sell his membership therein, shall first offer the same for sale to employees of the Cooperative who are not already members thereof, and shall not sell said share to any other person if such an employee of the cooperative desires to purchase said membership; and provided, further that unless the consent of the Cooperative shall have been first obtained and if the transferee shall himself become a working member of the Cooperative shall be effective for so long as any debt is owing by the Cooperative to the Ministry, and any member purporting to make such sale shall be considered as withdrawing from the Cooperative pursuant to Article 21 hereof.

Article 17: Limitations of Membership

(a) No member may acquire, except by inheritance, more than one membership in the cooperative.

(b) Except in the case of persons who become members of the Cooperative in common by inheritance, there shall be no partial or fractional memberships.

(c) Only persons who have become members of the Cooperative by inheritance or who are the legal representatives of a member declared to be of unsound mind may be non-working members thereof.

Section IV: Rights, Duties, Privileges and Responsibilities of Members

Article 18: General Rights of Members

(a) Membership in the cooperative shall entitle the members:

(i) To a proportionate share in the net profit of the Cooperatives;

(ii) To elect, and if a working member, to be elected to and serve on, the administrative bodies of the Cooperative;

(iii) To attend the General Meeting of the members and to vote on all questions within the competence of said General Meeting; each member in the cooperative shall have the right to one vote; persons owning a membership in common shall be entitled to only one vote among them;

(iv) If a working member:

1. To be allotted a parcel of land pursuant to article 30 hereof on which he may build his house and produce such products and commodities as he may choose for his and his family's needs or for marketing in such manner as he may choose;
2. To receive a monthly sum which shall be allotted to him by the cooperative as a working member's allowance, which allowance shall be fixed by the Managing Committee on the basis of the type of work performed by said working member for the Cooperatives;
3. To such other special privileges and rights as the Cooperative may decide to extend to working members.

(b) No member of a Cooperative shall be personally liable for the debts of the Cooperative.

Article 19: General Duties of Members

Every member of the Cooperative shall have the following duties:

(a) To work for the attainment of the purposes and objects of the Cooperative according to his capacity;

(b) To implement loyally all decisions of the administrative bodies of the Cooperative;

(c) To promote the spirit of cooperation among the Cooperative's members; and

(d) If a working member, to work at least two hundred (200) days annually for the Cooperative.

Article 20: Maintenance of Membership Register

Each Cooperative shall maintain a Membership Register which shall show, with respect to each member thereof:

(a) The name of the member;

(b) The number of memberships held;

(c) The date and manner of acquisition of membership;

(d) Such other pertinent data as the Cooperative shall deem appropriate.

Section V: Loss of membership in the Cooperative

Article 21: Termination of Status as a Working Member

A working member of the Cooperative shall lose his status as such upon the occurrence of one of the following events:

(a) Death;

(b) Expulsion from the Cooperative;

(c) Voluntary withdrawal as a working member;

(d) A declaration by the competent authorities that he is of unsound mind; or

(e) Alienation of his membership in the Cooperative.

Article 22: Termination of Status as a Working Member by Death

(a) The membership of a deceased member shall pass in the manner specified in Article 15 hereof.

(b) Any person who becomes a member of a Cooperative by inheritance shall have the following election:

(i) If he meets all of the conditions set forth in Article 6 hereof

1. To become a working member of the Cooperative and to be allotted the parcel of land held by the person from whom he inherited the membership; or

2. To receive the payment specified in Article 27 hereof.

(ii) If he does not meet all the conditions set forth in Article 6 hereof:

1. To become a non-working member; or

2. To receive the payment specified in Article 27 hereof.

Article 23: Termination of Status as a Working Member by Expulsion

(a) The Managing Committee, or the members of the Cooperative at a General meeting, may expel any working member who:

(i) Is convicted of an offence involving dishonesty;

(ii) Is found to have acted against the best interests of the Cooperative; or

(iii) Without excuse, fails to work the minimum number of days specified in paragraph (d) of Article 19 hereof.

(b) Any working member expelled by the Managing Committee shall have the right of appeal to the members of the Cooperative at the next General Meeting thereof.

(c) Any working member so expelled shall have the right to receive the payment specified in Article 27 hereof, subject to the conditions provided in said Article 27.

Article 24: Termination of Status as a Working Member by Withdrawal

Any working member who withdraws from the cooperative shall , lose all of the rights specified in Article 18 hereof, but shall have the right to receive the payment specified in Article 27 hereof; provided, however, that no payment shall be made pursuant to Article 27 hereof if said working member is in debt to the cooperative in an amount in excess of the amount which he would receive pursuant to said Article 27, nor shall any such payment be made if at the time of withdrawal the cooperative is in debt to the Ministry.

Article 25: Termination of Status as a Working Member by a Declaration that the Member is Unsound Mind

The legal representative of any working member, who is declared to be of unsound mind, shall have the following election:

(a) If he meets all of the conditions set forth in Article 6 hereof, to become a working member of the Cooperative and to be allotted the parcel of land held by the person whose legal representative he is.

(b) To become a non-working member: or

(c) To receive the payment specified in Article 27 hereof.

Article 26: Termination of Status as a Working Member by Alienation of Membership

(a) The alienation of membership in the cooperative shall be subject to the provisions of Article 16 hereof.

(b) Any working member who alienates his membership in the cooperative shall, effective on the date upon which the name of the person to whom alienated entered in the Membership register, lose all of the rights specified in the Article 18 hereof.

(c) No sale of a membership in the cooperative made in violation of the provisions of Article 16 hereof shall be effective to vest a membership in, or confer any of the rights specified in Article 18 hereof upon, the transferee and any member purporting to make any such sale shall be considered as withdrawing from the Cooperative pursuant to Article 23 hereof.

Article 27: Payment to be made upon Termination of Status as a Working Member

(a) Any person who becomes entitled thereto pursuant to the provisions of Articles 22, 23, 24, 25 or 26 thereof shall receive the following amounts, after deduction of any debt owing to the Cooperative by the member who are on whose behalf payment thereof it claimed:

(i) Any amount due as of the date on which status as a working member was terminated representing the member's share in the net profits of the Cooperative;

(ii) Any deposit or sum held by the Cooperative on said member's behalf; and

(iii) The value of the member's share in the Cooperative as fixed by the Managing Committee and approved by the Ministry.

(b) Upon the receipt of the payments specified in paragraph (a) of this Article 27, all rights of the working member or his heirs or representatives, as the case may be, with respect to the Cooperative, its lands, buildings, livestock and funds shall cease and terminate.

Section VI: Rights and Duties of the Cooperatives

Article 28: Rights of the Cooperative to Own Property

The Cooperative shall have the right to own and hold the Rist land transferred to it by the Ministry pursuant to Article 11 hereof, together with all buildings, livestock, machinery, equipment and funds as may be necessary for the attainment of its purposes and objects.

Article 29: Limitation upon the Right of the Cooperative to Alienate Property

(a) Land transferred as Rist land to the Cooperative pursuant to Article 11 hereof and buildings owned by the Cooperative may not be sold or otherwise alienated by the Cooperative without the priority consent of the Ministry.

(b) For so long as any debt is owing by the Cooperative to Ministry, machinery and equipment owned by the Cooperative may not be sold or otherwise alienated by the Cooperative without the prior consent of the Ministry.

Section VII: Cultivation of Land

Article 30: Allotment of Land to Working Members

(a) The Cooperative shall allot to each working member a parcel of land not greater than one (1) hectare in area which he possess and use in the manner specified in paragraph (a)(iv)(1) of Article 18 hereof.

(b) Parcel of land allotted to working members pursuant to paragraph (a) of the Article 30 shall remain a part of the Rist land transferred to the Cooperative by the Ministry pursuant to Article 11 hereof.

(c) Upon the transfer of membership in the Cooperative by a working member, the person acquiring said membership shall subject to his fulfilling and discharging all of the conditions and duties of a working member and subject to all of the provisions hereof, acquire the right to possess and use the parcel of land possessed and used by his transferor.

(d) Anything herein to the contrary notwithstanding, a family, which for this purpose shall be deemed to consist of father, mother and all unmarried children, shall be allotted no more than one (1) hectare of land, whether it holds one or more memberships in the Cooperative.

(e) Persons holding a membership in the Cooperative in common shall be entitled to not more than one (1) hectare of land to be held by them in common.

Article 31: Cultivation of Cooperative Land

All land placed at the disposal of the Cooperative by the Ministry pursuant to Article 11 hereof, which is not allotted to working members pursuant to Article 30 hereof, shall be cultivated by the working members of the Cooperative in the manner decided by the administrative bodies thereof.

Section VIII: Governing Bodies of the Cooperative

Article 32: Supreme Authority in the Membership

(a) The Supreme Authority in the Cooperative is, subject to the limitations herein specified, vested in the members thereof, who shall exercise said authority through decisions taken at General Meetings of the membership. A General Meeting shall be held at least once each year to elect the Managing Committee and the Supervisory Board of the Cooperative, to consider the financial report and audited accounts of the Cooperative, and to take decisions with respect to the general affairs of the Cooperative.

(b) A special General Meeting may be convened at any time by the Managing Committee of the Cooperative, and said meeting shall be convened upon the request of the Agency or of ten per cent (10%) of the members of the Cooperative.

(c) The procedures governing the conduct of the General Meeting shall be prescribed in bylaws adopted at the first General Meeting.

Article 33: Managing Committee

(a) The Managing Committee shall be the executive body of the Cooperative and shall take all action and decisions, subject to the decisions of the members of the Cooperative, necessary to carrying out the day-to-day operations thereof.

(b) Members of the Managing Committee shall serve for one (1) year and may be re-elected. The composition, manner of election, procedures, powers and duties of the Managing Committee shall be prescribed in bylaws adopted by the members of the Cooperative at a General Meeting.

Article 34: Supervisory Board

(a) The Supervisory Board shall have general responsibility for the overseeing of the business and operations of the Cooperative. Said Board shall present to each annual General Meeting of the membership of the Cooperative a report setting forth the results of its activities during the past year and making recommendations and suggestions with respect to the future operations of the Cooperative.

(b) The composition, manner of election, procedure, powers and duties of the Supervisory Board shall be prescribed in bylaws adopted by the members of the Cooperative at a General Meeting; provided, however, that at least one-third (1/3) of the members of said Board shall be appointed by the Ministry.

Article 35: General Manager

(a) The General Manager of the Cooperative, who shall be appointed as such by the Ministry and paid by the Cooperative, shall be responsible for the conduct and the carrying out of the day-to-day operations of the Cooperative under the direction of the Managing Committee.

(b) The General Manager shall be directly responsible to the Managing Committee to the Ministry and shall render periodic reports to said Committee and to the Ministry.

(c) The General Manager, in accordance with policies established by the Managing Committee and approved by the Ministry, is empowered to employ and discharge all personnel necessary to its proper and efficient functioning, to dispose of their services and to fix their salaries, wages and allowances.

Section IX: Operations and Financing of the Cooperative

Article 36: Preparation of Initial Plan of Operations

Promptly upon registration of the Cooperative pursuant to Article 10 hereof, the Managing Committee of the Cooperative shall consult with the Ministry and, in conjunction therewith, shall prepare plans for the programme to be carried out by the Cooperative during the first year of its operation.

Article 37: Financing of Cooperative Operations by the Ministry

(a) The Ministry shall, as soon as the Cooperative has been registered pursuant to Article 10 hereof, and pursuant to authorization thereof as required by the law, arrange to advance to said Cooperative the funds required to settle the members thereof on the land placed at the disposal of the Cooperative pursuant to Article 11 hereof, to finance the construction of dwelling and other necessary buildings thereon, to make the minimum monthly payments to the members thereof, to purchase the necessary equipment, seed and livestock to commence its activities, and generally, to finance the operations of the Cooperative in accordance with the plans worked out between the Managing Committee of the Cooperative and the Ministry pursuant to Article 36 hereof.

(b) In thę event that, following the first year of operations of the Cooperative, further financial assistance shall be required by the Cooperative, the Ministry shall consult with the Managing Committee of the Cooperative in order to arrive at a mutually satisfactory plan of financing for subsequent operations.

(c) Funds advanced to the Cooperative pursuant to this Article 37 shall be loaned by the Ministry at such terms and upon such conditions as shall be agreed upon between the Cooperative and the Ministry which shall not, however, be less favourable than the terms and conditions available at other lending institutions operating within Ethiopia.

(d) Funds advanced to the Cooperative pursuant to this Article 37 shall be secured by a pledge of the equipment and machinery purchased by the Cooperative and a mortgage of the Rist land and buildings held by it;

provided, however, that the Ministry may agree at any time to subordinate its lien on said property to that of third person for good cause.

(e) All funds loaned by the Ministry to Cooperatives under this Article 37, shall be repaid to the Ministry of Finance in accordance with the repayment schedule agreed upon between the Ministry and the Cooperative and shall become receipts of the General treasury.

(f) The Ministry shall see to the application of all funds loaned by it to Cooperatives and shall assure that said funds are used in an efficient manner and for the purpose for which loaned.

Article 38: Technical Assistance to be Provided to Cooperatives

The Ministry shall, at its own expense, provide technical advice and assistance to the Cooperative in the fields of agronomy, animal husbandry, marketing and related fields.

Section X: Funds and Property of Cooperative

Article 39: Borrowing by the Cooperative

Until all debts owing by the Cooperative to the Ministry shall have been repaid, no Cooperative may borrow funds or otherwise contract indebtedness except from the Ministry.

Article 40: Lending by the Cooperative

No Cooperative may make any loan to any person not a member thereof.

Article 41: Disposal of Profits

After the payment of or the making of provision for all expenses and obligations for the current year, nay net profits remaining to the Cooperative shall be disposed of in the following fashion:

(a) Ten per cent (10%) thereof shall be paid in to a General Reserve Fund;

(b) A percentage thereof fixed by the General Meeting, which may not exceed fifty per cent (50%), shall be distributed to the members of the Cooperative as their share of net profits;

(c) A percentage thereof fixed by the General Meeting with the approval of the Ministry shall be paid in to a fund for the purchase of equipment and other capital goods;

(d) Any balance remaining thereafter may be disposed of by payment in to a fund for the care of old, ill or minors in the Cooperative or in improving the educational, health or other facilities of the Cooperative.

Section XI: Dissolution

Article 42: Dissolution upon Initiative of Shareholders

The membership of the Cooperative may at any time, by a decision taken at a General Meeting and approved by two-thirds (2/3) of the members, request that the Ministry undertake the dissolution of said Cooperatives. If the Ministry agrees to the dissolution of the Cooperative, it shall proceed in the manner specified in Article 44 hereof. If the Ministry shall not approve said dissolution, the Cooperative shall continue to carry out its operations as therefore.

Article 43: Dissolution upon Initiative of Ministry

For so long as any debt is owed by the Cooperative to the Ministry, the Ministry may proceed to the dissolution of the Cooperative in the manner specified in Article 44 hereof.

Article 44: Appointment of Liquidator

In any case in which the Ministry proceeds to the dissolution of the Cooperative pursuant to either Article 42 or 43 hereof, it shall appoint a liquidator whose duty shall be to wind up the affairs of the Cooperative in an expedition and efficient fashion, and who shall have all powers necessary thereto, including, without limiting the generality of the following, the power:

1. To take immediate possession of all of the books, records and documents belonging the Cooperative;
2. To investigate all claims against the Cooperative and to decide on priority of payment among them;
3. To give instructions regarding the collection and distribution of assets;
4. To arrange for the distribution of assets when a plan of liquidation has been drawn up and approved by the Ministry.

Section XII: General and Transitory Provisions

Article 45: Veto Powers during Period of Indebtedness

For so long as any debt is owed by the Cooperative to the Ministry, the Ministry:

(a) Shall retain, and may exercise at any time, a power of veto over decisions taken by the Managing Committee or the shareholders of the Cooperative acting at a General Meeting, in addition to those powers which are specifically reserved to the Ministry herein; and

(b) Shall appoint the General Manager of the Cooperative and such other personnel as may be deemed necessary to the proper and effective functioning thereof.

Article 46: Completion of Repayment of Debt to the Ministry

Promptly upon completion of repayment of the debt owed by the Cooperative to the Ministry, all of the rights of the Ministry with respect to the Cooperative provided herein shall terminate and be of no further validity; provided, however, that the provisions of Article 29(a) hereof which require the prior consent of the Ministry to the sale or alienation by the Cooperative of land transferred to the Cooperative and the provisions of Article 42 hereof with respect to the right of the Ministry to disapprove the proposed dissolution of the Cooperative, shall remain in full force and effect.

Article 47: General Legislation Applicable

Unless a provision hereof shall be inconsistent therewith, the Cooperative, its shareholders, operations and activities shall be subject to and shall comply with all applicable legislation in force in the Empire of Ethiopia.

Article 48: Effective Date

This Decree shall come in to force on the date of its publication in the Negarit Gazeta. Done at Addis Ababa this 27th day of October, 1960.

Limitations of the Farm Workers Cooperative Decree

The following are some of the limitations of the Farm Workers Cooperative Decree which retarded the growth of cooperative movement in Ethiopia.

- No clear mention about the organization structure, its duties and responsibilities.
- Lacks the basic values and principles of cooperation.
- No recognition of the cultural, social and economic problems of societies.
- Not clear and definite to understand as a cooperative law.
- Provision was made only to form cooperatives among farm workers i.e., the scope of this decree was limited to only farm workers.

Summary

- In Ethiopia there are three well known traditional cooperatives or self-help groups such as Edir, Ekub and Debo/Wenfal/Lefenty.
- Modern form of cooperatives started in Ethiopia during the ruling era of Emperor Haile Selassie I. In 1960 the first legislative called "Farm Workers Cooperatives Decree" was declared as Decree No. 44/1960.
- The objectives needed to enact this decree were: To accelerate the development of the agricultural economy of the country; the organization of cooperative enterprise was believed to be as it can contribute

measurably to this end; and it was also found necessary that the proper framework be created for the establishment of such cooperative enterprises.

- The Ministry of National Community Development was charged with the responsibility of ensuring systematic cooperative promotion and development.
- The Decree was designed in to twelve major sections comprised of 48 articles.
- Under this decree provision was made to establish farm workers cooperatives which should be organized, administered and regulated by the provisions.
- Cooperatives organized under the decree shall have as their principal purpose and object the promotion of the economic interests of Ethiopia and of their members through the efficient cultivation and development of land made available to them and the profitable sale of products produced on said land.
- The Ministry of National Community Development shall designate areas of land which have been placed at its disposal as available for transfer as Rist land to Cooperatives.
- Persons wishing to apply for membership in a cooperative shall appear in person at the Ministry or at a branch office thereof and shall complete and file with the office where registering an application form which shall be supplied to them free of charge.
- Nationality, age, willingness and physical fitness were the requirements to become a member of the cooperative.
- Disposal of land was made according to the number of members registered with the cooperative.
- Under its formation each group shall hold an organizational meeting and elect the administrative bodies of the Cooperative.
- Upon the election of the administrative bodies of the Cooperative and the adoption of a resolution authorising and directing the same, an application shall be made to the Ministry for registration as Farm Workers' Cooperative.
- Land so transferred shall be granted by the Ministry to the Cooperative and shall be transferred to the Cooperative without cost or charge to the latter.
- When any person becomes a member of the Cooperative, the Cooperative shall cause to be issued and delivered to him a certificate representing

his membership in the Cooperative which shall be registered in his name in the register maintained by the Cooperative pursuant to Article 20 thereof.

- Provisions were made in the decree for Admission of New Members by Application after Cooperative Formed, Acquisition of Membership by inheritance or as the Legal Representative of a Member, and Acquisition of Membership by Purchase,
- Provision was made on Rights, Duties, Privileges and Responsibilities of Members in a cooperative.
- As per the provision, all cooperative should maintain a membership register.
- Provisions were made for Termination of status as a Working Member, Termination of status as a Working Member by Death, Termination of status as a Working Member by Expulsion, Termination of status as a Working Member by Withdrawal, Termination of status as a Working Member by a Declaration that the Member is unsound Mind, Termination of status as a Working Member by Alienation of Membership, and Payment to be made upon Termination of status as a Working Member
- Provisions were also made on the Rights of the Cooperative to Own Property and Limitation upon the Right of the Cooperative to alienate property.
- Provisions were made for the Allotment of Land to Working Members and Cultivation of Cooperative Land.
- As for organs of management, provisions were made for Supreme authority in the Membership, Managing Committee, Supervisory Board and General Manager.
- Provisions were also made for Operations and Financing of the Cooperative, Funds and Property of Cooperative, Dissolution, and General and Transitory aspects.

Self-Learning Activity

1. What are the qualifications of membership as prescribed by the decree?
2. What are the limitations on membership as per the decree?
3. What are the rights and privileges of a working member of a cooperative as per the decree?
4. List down the provisions relating to termination of status as a working member by a declaration that the member is of unsound mind?
5. What do you know about veto powers during the period of indebtedness as per the decree?

14 Proclamation No. 241 of 1966

Proclamation Made by Imperial Government to Provide for the Formation of Cooperative Societies

Prelude

In 1966, the Cooperatives Societies Proclamation no. 241 was issued. It was only after this decree that cooperatives began to emerge in Ethiopia. Efforts to mobilize people were intensified and rationalized. This was an encouraging start bearing in mind the fruitless initial efforts. The first cooperatives were mainly formed to provide inputs, to process, and to facilitate the marketing of crops and products. Primary cooperative societies formed unions, which in some cases exported directly to the world market.

The mid-1960s saw the establishment of savings and credit cooperative societies in Ethiopia, pioneered by the employees of Ethiopian Artiness in 1964. By 1973, the societies formed their own national apex body known as Ethiopian Thrift and Credit Cooperative Societies with 6,247 members and savings amounting to US $627,752. Spontaneous as they were, the societies flourished. You will have a detailed understanding of the provisions of the Cooperative Societies proclamation in the following paragraphs.

Necessity for the Enactment of the Proclamation

Whereas, Our people have understood the usefulness of cooperative activities and it is expedient to provide a proper basis for the formation of Cooperative Societies, which shall promote thrift, mutual help and self-help among persons sharing common needs and desires;

Now therefore, in accordance with Articles 34 and 88 of Our Revised Constitution, We approve the resolutions of Our Chamber of Deputies and Senate and

We hereby proclaim as follows:

Part 1– Preliminary

1. *Short Title*

This proclamation may be cited as the "Cooperative Societies Proclamation, 1966".

2. *Repeal*

The Farm Workers' Cooperative Decree, 1960 (Decree No. 44 of 1960) is hereby repealed.

3. *Definitions*

In this proclamation, unless the context otherwise requires:

1. "Amendment" shall mean an amendment of the rules and shall include a new rule and the rescission of a rule;
2. "Executive committee" shall mean the directing body of a society entrusted with the management of such society;
3. "Legal representative" shall mean a person so declared under the provisions of the Civil Code of 1960 by a competent court;
4. "Member" shall mean any physical or juridical person who is a member of a society and shall include a nominal member;
5. "Minister" and "Ministry" shall mean, respectively, the Minister and Ministry of National Community Development and Social Affairs.
6. "Officer" shall mean a president, vice-president, secretary, manager, member of an Executive Committee, treasurer, administrator or liquidator of a society and shall include any other person empowered under the regulations or the rules to give directions in regard to the conduct of business of a society;
7. "Prescribed" shall mean prescribed by regulations;
8. "Registrar" shall mean a person appointed under Article 5 hereof and shall include any person when exercising such powers of the Registrar as may be delegated to him;
9. "Regulations" shall mean regulations issued under this Proclamation by the Minster;
10. "Rules" shall mean the rules of a society and shall include all amendments thereto;
11. "Society" shall mean a Cooperative Society registered under this Proclamation;
12. "Society with limited liability" shall mean a society whose members are, in the event of its being wound up, liable for such society's obligations to the extent of any amount still owing on account of shares held by them and, in addition, to any multiple of the value of such shares as provided in the rules of such society;

13. "Society with unlimited liability" shall mean a society whose members are, in the event of its being wound up, personally, jointly, severally and fully liable for such society's obligations; and

14. "Special resolution" shall mean a resolution passed by a majority of two-thirds (2/3) or such higher quorum or majority as may be specified in the rules.

4. *Purposes and Objects of Societies*

Societies organised under this Proclamation shall have as their principal purposes and objects the promotion, in accordance with cooperative principles and the requirements of social justice, of better living, better business and better methods of production by such means as:

1. reducing the cost of credit and other expenses;
2. reducing the cost of goods and services for production and consumption;
3. minimizing and reducing the individual impact of risks and uncertainties;
4. spreading knowledge of practical technical improvements; or
5. may otherwise contribute to achieve the above mentioned purposes and object.

5. *Registrar*

1. A Registrar of Cooperative Societies and, if necessary for the effective administration the duties and responsibilities of the Registrar as set forth in this Proclamation or as may be prescribed, a Deputy Registrar of cooperative societies shall be appointed by us upon the recommendation of the Minister. The Minister may appoint an Assistant Registrar or Assistant Registrars of Cooperative Societies as necessary. All of these shall be persons of long experience in the public service and, where possible in the administration of societies.
2. The Deputy Registrar and any Assistant Registrars shall exercise such powers of the Registrar and discharge such of his duties and responsibilities as may be prescribed.

Part II – Formation and Registration of Societies

6. *Types of Societies*

Societies shall be of two (2) categories:

1. Primary societies, which shall be comprised of not less than ten (10) individual members; and

2. Secondary societies which, in addition to other members who may be either physical or juridical persons, shall be comprised of at least one (1) member which is another society and shall in all cases possess limited liability.

7. *Name of Society*

1. The word "cooperative" shall appear in the name of every society.

2. The word "limited" shall appear in the name of every society with limited liability.

3. The name of every society shall be conspicuously affixed on any place in which the business of the society is carried out and shall appear in all notices, advertisements, correspondence and other publications of the society and on all negotiable instruments purporting to be signed by or on behalf of the society.

8. *Formation of Society*

1. The formation of a society shall be initiated through a general meeting of promoters which shall take all decisions necessary for the formation and registration of the proposed society and its by-laws:

(a) adopt the proposed rules; and

(b) prepare the application for registration.

2. The rules shall conform to such requirements as may be prescribed and may follow such model rules as may be prepared by the Ministry.

9. *Application*

1. Application for registration of a society shall be submitted to the Registrar in the form specified by him and shall include the following:

(a) the name, objects and area of operations of the proposed society;

(b) whether the liability of the proposed society is limited or unlimited;

(c) the names of the applicants, who shall not be fewer than ten (10) where the application relates to the registration of a primary society, together with such particulars as are necessary for membership under Article 14 hereof;

(d) two (2) copies of the proposed rules; and

(e) such other particulars as may be prescribed.

2. The application shall be signed by each individual applicant and by the duly authorized representative of any juridical person which is an applicant.

3. The Registrar may require the applicants to furnish to him additional information relating to the economic background and potential of the proposed society.

10. *Registration*

1. Where the Registrar is satisfied that an application conforms with the requirements set forth in this Proclamation and in the regulations and that the purposed society will serve the purposes and objects set forth in Article 4 hereof, he shall register such society and its rules and shall issue to the applicants a registration certificate signed by him and showing the date of such registration.

2. A registration certificate issued pursuant to paragraph (1) of this Article 10 shall, unless the registration of the society has been cancelled, be conclusive evidence that the society therein mentioned is a society duly registered under this Proclamation.

11. *Society to Have Juridical Personality*

A society shall become and be a juridical person as of the date of registration thereof.

12. *Amendment of Rules*

1. A society may amend its rules on such conditions as are provided in this Proclamation and as may be prescribed or specified in the rules.

2. No such amendment shall be valid until it has been registered hereunder, for which purpose two (2) copies of any proposed amendment shall be forwarded to the Registrar who shall register the same when he determines that the effect thereof will be consistent with the purposes and objects set forth in Article 4 hereof and shall thereupon issue to the society a copy of such amendment dated and certified by him which shall be conclusive evidence of the fact that such amendment has been approve and has on such date been duly registered.

13. *Change of Liability, Transfer of Assets and Liabilities, Division or Amalgamation*

1. A society may by a special resolution containing all the particulars regarding the carrying into effect of such resolution and upon registration of such resolution pursuant to paragraph (3) of this Article 13:

(a) change the nature or extent of liability of its members;

(b) transfer all or part of its assets and liabilities to another society;

(c) divide into two (2) or more societies; or

(d) Amalgamate with one (1) or more societies to form a new society.

2. A society shall cause such resolution to be served on its creditors and on such of its members as did not attend the meeting at which the resolution was passed and shall inform them that they will be deemed to have agreed thereto unless they state their disagreement within forty-five (45) days from the date of such service.

3. The Registrar shall register such resolution when he determines that:

(a) all the members and creditors have either specifically or impliedly agreed thereto; or

(b) any dissenting members have withdrawn from the society and have been paid off or the payment of any such dissenting members or creditors has been guaranteed to the satisfaction of the Registrar.

4. Upon registration of such special resolution:

(a) any transfer to be undertaken pursuant to subparagraph (1) (b) of this Article 13 shall be effected automatically;

(b) the registration of the transferring society or of the former society or societies, as the case may be, shall, if appropriate, be cancelled and such society or societies shall thereupon cease to exist; and

(c) the Registrar shall, where appropriate, issue to the society a copy of such special resolution dated and certified by him, which shall be conclusive evidence of the fact that such special resolution was on such date duly passed in accordance with the law.

Part III – Members of Societies and their Rights and Obligations

14. *Persons who may Become Members*

No person other than:

1. a physical person as defined in the Civil Code of 1960;
2. another society; or
3. a ministry, chartered government agency or other public authority,

may become member of a society.

15. *Nominal Members*

1. A society may admit any physical or juridical person as a nominal member.

2. Except as otherwise provided herein or in the rules, a nominal member shall have the same rights, duties and liabilities as a member; provided, however, that a nominal member shall not be entitled to any share, in any form whatever, of the assets or profits of the society.

16. *Register of Members*

Every society shall keep a register to be called the "Register of Members" wherein shall be entered:

1. the name, address and occupation of each member;

2. the date on which any person became a member or ceased to be a member;

3. the share in the society held by such member; and

4. any other details that may be specified in the rules

17. *Member not to Exercise Rights till Due Payment Mode*

No member shall exercise the rights of a member unless he has made such payments to the society in respect of membership or has acquired such interests in the society as may be specified in the rules.

18. *Voting*

1. Every members shall, regardless of the number of shares owned or controlled by him, have one (1) vote at meetings of the society; provided, however, that:

   (a) a nominal member shall have no vote;

   (b) a juridical person shall have such number of votes as is specified in the rules of the society and shall appoint an equivalent number of representatives to exercise its voting rights;

2. Except as provided in sub-paragraph (1) (b) of this Article 18 and in Article 23 hereof, all members shall vote in person.

19. *Restriction on Holding Shares*

No member of a primary society shall hold more than one-fifth (1/5) of the total paid-up share capital of such society.

20. *Restrictions on Transfer of Shares or Interest*

1. No transfer by a member of his share of interest in a society shall be valid unless:

(a) the member has held such share or interest for at least one (1) year;

(b) the transfer is made to a member; and

(c) the transfer is approved by the Executive Committee.

2. Transfer of any share or interest in a primary society shall be subject to the restriction set forth in Article 19 hereof.

21. *Transfer of Interest on Death of Member*

1. On the death of a member, his share or interest shall be transferred to one of his heirs who has been specifically mentioned to inherit such share or interest in the will of the deceased, or, failing such mention, to the heir-law. Where such heir is a member or is admitted as a member.

2. Where such heir is not a member and does not wish to become or is not admitted as a member, he shall be paid the value of the share or interest of the deceased member.

3. Where in pursuance of the provisions of this Article 21 a member's share or interest exceeds the limits laid down in Article 19 hereof, such member shall be paid the value of the excess.

4. Any transfer or payment made under this Article 21 shall be valid and effectual against any demand made on the society by any third party.

22. *Liability of Past or Deceased Member*

The liability of a past member or of the estate of a deceased member for the debts or obligations of a society as of the date of his ceasing to be a member or of his death shall continue for two (2) years from such date unless

(a) an order for the dissolution of the society is issued within said period of two (2) years, in which case such liability shall continue until the winding-up proceedings are completed; or

(b) the first audit of the society's accounts after such date shows a credit balance in favour of the society, in which case such liability shall forth with terminate.

Part IV – Organs of Societies

23. *Supreme Authority in Society*

The supreme authority in a society shall rest in the general meeting of the members thereof; provided, however, that where the rules allow for the constitution of a smaller body consisting of delegates of members, such body shall exercise such delegated powers as may be specified in the rules.

24. *Ordinary General Meeting*

1. An ordinary general meeting of the members shall be held at least once annually and shall:

   (a) consider the annual report and the author's report;

   (b) decide on the allocation of the net profits;

   (c) examine and approve the programme of the activities of the society prepared by the Executive Committee for the coming year;

   (d) elect the members of the executive committee; and

   (e) decide any other matter that may be submitted to it in accordance with the rules.

2. Other ordinary general meetings of the members may be called by the Executive Committee as necessary.

25. *Special General Meeting*

1. The Executive Committee shall call a special general meeting within one (1) month from having been required in writing so to do by the Registrar or by such number or proportion of the members as may be specified in the rules.

2. Where the Executive Committee fails to call a special general meeting in accordance with paragraph (1) of this Article 25, such meeting shall be called by the Registrar and shall in such case be deemed to have been called by the Executive Committee.

26. *Executive Committee*

1. In every society, there shall be an Executive Committee comprising such number of members and elected in such manner as shall be specified in the rules.

2. The Executive Committee shall meet at such times and shall proceed in such manner as shall be specified in the rules.

3. The Executive Committee shall have such powers and duties as shall be specified in the rules and shall, in particular, be responsible for:

   (a) keeping records of its management and meetings;

   (b) keeping books and accounts in the manner to be prescribed;

(c) preparing annually a report on the society's operations and a programme for the coming year and submitting same to the general meeting;

(d) convening meetings in accordance with the rules;

(e) setting up a reserve fund and such other funds as are provided for in Article 34 hereof, in the regulations and in the rules; and

(f) carrying out all decisions of the general meeting.

27. *Supervision of Executive Committee*

1. Where the Registrar has reason to believe that an Executive Committee has persistently failed or is unable satisfactorily to perform its duties, or is acting in a manner in consistent with the objectives and purposes set forth in Article 4 hereof or otherwise appears by its actions to be endangering the interests of the society, he may order a hearing to be held to which the members of such Executive Committee or their representative shall be summoned, and such members or representative shall be required to testify and to present books and records to explain the situation which gave rise to such hearing.

2. Where the Registrar has reason to believe that the assets or general welfare of a society would suffer serious or irreparable damage as a result of any delay necessary to carry out the hearing required under paragraph (1) of this Article 27, he may without formal hearing as otherwise required under Article 49 hereof issue a temporary order restraining all or any of the members of the Executive Committee from further exercise of their powers as such members and providing for their replacement in accordance with paragraph (3) of this Article 27 pending a final determination in said hearing. Upon completion of said hearing such temporary order shall be confirmed, modified or vacated in accordance with the determination of the Registrar pursuant to said paragraph (3); provided, however, that in the event such temporary order is either confirmed or modified a new order shall be issued pursuant to said paragraph (3) and the period specified in such new order in accordance with paragraph (4) of this Article 27 shall run from the date of such temporary order.

3. Where the Registrar determines as a result of the hearing called pursuant to paragraph (1) of this Article 27 that such action is necessary to ensure the continued successful operation of a society in accordance with the purposes and objectives set forth in Article

4 hereof, he shall order the removal from office of all or any of the members of the Executive Committee and their replacement by other members of the society, in such number as he shall fix, and/ or one (1) or more administrators who need not be members of the society.

4. Where an administrator or administrators are appointed pursuant to paragraph (2) or (3) of this Article 27, they and any such member or members of the Executive Committee as remain thereon or have been placed thereon pursuant to either of said paragraphs shall be deemed to constitute an Executive Committee as though elected by the general meeting and shall exercise the powers of such Committee subject to the general supervision of the Registrar for such period not exceeding two (2) years as shall be specified in the order mentioned in said paragraph (3) and as may there after by further order in writing be extended by the Registrar; provided, however, that such period, including all extensions thereof, shall not exceed four (4) years.

5. On expiration of the period mentioned in paragraph (4) of this Article 27, the Executive Committee deemed constituted pursuant thereto shall call a general meeting to elect new Executive Committee in accordance with the rules.

28. *Securing Possession of Books and Records*

Whenever the members or past members of an Executive Committee or an employee of a society refuse or fail within a reasonable time to hand over to the proper person or persons the books and records of the society, the possession of such books and records shall be secured in accordance with the law.

Part V – Privileges of Societies

29. *Priority of Claims by Society*

Notwithstanding any provision to the contrary in whatever law contained, any debts owed to a society by a member or past member or the estate of a deceased member, in respect of such membership, shall take precedence over all other debts of such person, except debts owed to the Government.

30. *Charge and Set-off in Respect of Shares or Interest of Members*

A society shall have a charge upon the shares or interest in the capital and on the deposits of a member, past member or deceased member, and upon any dividend, bonus or profits payable to a member or past member or to the estate of a deceased member in respect of any debt or outstanding demand due to the society from such member or past member or estate and may set-off any sum credited or payable to a member or past member or estate of a deceased member in or towards payment of any such debt or outstanding demand.

31. *Shares of Interest Not Liable to Attachment or Sale*

Except as provided in Article 30 hereof, the shares or interest of a member in the capital of a society shall not be liable to attachment or sale under any judgment or order of a court in respect of any debt or liability incurred by such member, and neither his trustee in bankruptcy nor a receiver duly appointed shall be entitled to, or have any claim on, such share or interest.

32. *Government Aid and Exemption from Taxes*

1. Income of a society earned through operations conducted within the scope of this proclamation shall be exempt from income tax;

2. The appropriate administrative authorities shall have power in accordance with the law to;

   (a) give to any society any kind of financial assistance and, in particular, give loans, advances subsidies or *ad hoc* grants to a society and guarantee the payment of share capital of a society and dividends thereon, at such rates as may be prescribed; and

   (b) allot government land to any society in such manner as shall be prescribed.

Part VI – Properties and Funds of Societies

33. *Funds not to be Divided*

No part of the funds other than the net profits of a society shall be paid by way of bonus or dividend or otherwise distributed among its members; provided, however, that a member may be paid remuneration on such scale as may be specified in the rules for any services rendered by him to the society.

34. *Disposal of Net Profits*

1. A society shall, out of its net profits in any year:

   (a) transfer not less than twenty-five per cent (25%) of such profits to a reserve fund until it amounts to such percentage of the share capital as may be prescribed; and

   (b) create such other fund or funds as may be prescribed.

2. The reserve fund created pursuant to sub-paragraph (1) (a) of this Article 34 shall be indivisible and no member shall be entitled to claim any share in it.

3. The balance of the net profits over and above the amounts to be employed pursuant to paragraph (1) of this Article 34 may be utilized for all or any of the following purposes:

(a) payment of dividends to members on their paid up share capital at a rate not exceeding ten per cent (10%) of such share capital per annum;

(b) payment of bonuses to member, based on the amount or volume of business transacted by them with the society, to the extent and in the manner specified in the rules;

(c) constitution of or contribution to such special funds as may be specified in the rules;

(d) donation of amounts not exceeding ten per cent (10%) of such net profits for any charitable purpose or common good fund; and

(e) payment of bonuses to employees of the society to the extent and in the manner specified in the rules.

35. *Investment of Funds*

A society shall invest or deposit its funds only in such manner as shall be prescribed.

36. *Restrictions on Borrowings*

A society shall receive, deposit and loans only to such extent and on such conditions as may be prescribed or as may be specified in the rules.

37. *Restrictions on Loans*

A society shall not make a loan to any person other than a member; provided, however, that a society may make loans to another society with the approval of the Registrar or to a depositor on the security of his deposit.

Part VII – Audit, Inquiry and Inspection

38. *Audit*

1. The Registrar shall require the accounts of every society to be audited at least once annually by such person as he shall appoint, and, if justified and necessary, he may determine the charges to be paid by the society concerned to words the cost of such audit.

2. The audit conducted pursuant to paragraph (1) of this Article 38 shall include examination of overdue debts; if any, verification of cash balance and securities and valuation of the assets and liabilities of the society.

3. The auditor's report shall be served on the Executive Committee in the prescribed manner.

39. *Inquiry*

1. The Registrar may hold or cause to be held by such person as he shall appoint an inquiry into the constitution, working and financial condition of a society.

2. An inquiry of the nature referred to in paragraph (1) of this Article 39 shall be undertaken on application therefore by:

   (a) a secondary society of which the society concerned is a member;

   (b) a majority of the members of the Executive Committee; or

   (c) not less than one-third (1/3) of this total number of members.

40. *Inspection*

1. The Registrar may of his own motion inspect or cause to be inspected by such person as he shall appoint the books of a society;

2. An inspection of the nature referred to in paragraph (1) of this Article 40 shall be undertaken on application there for by a creditor of the society where such applicant;

   (a) satisfies the Registrar that the debt is exigible and that he has demanded payment but has not received satisfaction within a reasonable time; and

   (b) deposits with the Registrar such sum as security for the proposed inspection as the Registrar may require.

41. *Powers in Respect of Audit, Inquiry and Inspection*

Any person acting in pursuance of Article 38, 39, or 40 hereof shall have such powers and shall carry out such duties as are set forth in Article 52 hereof and as may be prescribed.

42. *Surcharge*

1. If in the course of an audit, inquiry, inspection or the winding up of a society, it is found that any person who is or was entrusted with in the organisation or management of such society or who is or has at any time been an officer or an employee of the society has made any payment contrary to this Proclamation, the regulations or the

rules or has caused any deficiency in the assets of the society by breach of trust or wilful negligence or has misappropriated or fraudulently retained any money or other property belonging to such society, the Registrar may, of his own motion or on the application of the Executive Committee, liquidator or any creditor, inquire himself or direct any person authorized by him, by an order in writing in this behalf, to inquire into the conduct of such person.

2. Where an inquiry is made under paragraph (1) of this Article 42 the Registrar may, after giving the person concerned an opportunity of being heard, make an order requiring him to repay or restore the money or property or any part thereof, with interest at such rate, or to pay contribution and costs or compensation to such extent, as the Registrar may consider just and equitable.

Part VIII – Arbitration

43. *Disputes to be Referred to Arbitration*

1. Where a dispute regarding the constitution, management or operations of a society arises between;

   (a) members, past members and persons claiming through members, past members or decreased members; or

   (b) a member, past member or person claiming through a member, past member or decreased member and the society, its Executive Committee or any officer, agent or employee of the society; or

   (c) the society or its Executive Committee and any past Executive Committee, any officer, agent or past employee or the nominee, heirs or legal representatives or any deceased officer, deceased agent or deceased employee of the society; or

   (d) the society and any other society, such dispute shall be referred to the Registrar for decision.

2. For the purposes of paragraph (1) of this article 43 the term "dispute" shall be deemed to include, in particular but without limitation, the following:

   (a) a claim by the society for any debt or demand due to it from a member or the nominee, heirs or legal representatives of a deceased member;

   (b) a claim by a surety against the principal debtor where the society has recovered from the surety any amount in respect of any debt or demand due to it from the principal debtor; and

(c) any dispute arising in connection with the election of any officer of the society.

44. *Settlement of Disputes*

1. On a dispute being referred to the Registrar pursuant to Article 43 hereof, he may;

   (a) decide the dispute himself; or

   (b) refer it for disposal to one or more arbitrator whom he shall appoint.

2. The Registrar may revoke any appointment made pursuant to sub-paragraph (1) (b) of this Article 44 and decide the dispute himself.

Part IX – Dissolution and Winding-up of Societies

45. *Dissolution*

1. A society shall be dissolved pursuant to paragraph (3) of this Article 45 where:

   (a) it passes a special resolution to this effect; or

   (b) it is a primary society and the number of its members falls below ten (10).

2. A society may be dissolved pursuant to paragraph (3) of this Article 45 where:

   (a) following audit, inquiry or inspection conducted, respectively, pursuant to Article 38, 39 or 40 hereof, the Registrar determines that the society should be dissolved; or

   (b) the society has not commenced working within one (1) year from the date of its registration or has ceased to work.

3. Where a society is to be dissolved, the Registrar shall issue a written order for such dissolution in the prescribed form; provided, however, that such order may be revoked at any time before the completion of the winding-up proceedings, where the Registrar determines that the situation so warrants.

4. An order of dissolution issued pursuant to paragraph (3) of this Article 45 by reason of the occurrence of one of the conditions mentioned in paragraph (1) of this Article 45 shall take effect from the date of such order.

5. An order of dissolution issued pursuant to paragraph (3) of this Article 45 by reason of the occurrence of one of the conditions mentioned in paragraph (2) of this Article 45 shall be subject to

appeal pursuant to Article 51(1) hereof, and where no such appeal is presented within two (2) months from the date of such order, the order shall take effect upon expiration of such period. Where an appeal is presented within such period, the order shall not take effect unless it is confirmed.

46. *Liquidator*

1. Upon issuing an order pursuant to Article 45 (3) hereof, the Registrar shall appoint a liquidator and, if necessary, fix his remuneration which shall be paid out of the funds of the liquidate society.
2. A liquidator shall, on appointment, take into his custody or under his control all the books records and documents of the society and all the property, effects and actionable claims to which the society is or appears to be entitled and shall take such steps as he may deem necessary or expedient to prevent loss or deterioration of or damage to such property, effects or claims.
3. Where an order for dissolution is set aside on appeal the books, documents, records, property, effects and actionable claims of the society shall revest in the society.

47. *Powers and Duties of Liquidator*

1. The liquidator shall, under the guidance and control of the Registrar, have such powers and carry out such duties as are necessary to complete the winding up proceedings, and, in particular, but without limitation, shall:
   (a) investigate all claims against the society and decide on priority of payment among them;
   (b) determine the contribution to be made by members or past members or by the estates or legal representatives of deceased members or by any officers or former officers to the assets of the society;
   (c) collect the assets of the society;
   (d) distribute such assets in accordance with a plan of liquidation approved by the Registrar;
   (e) carry on the business of the society in so far as may be necessary for the proper liquidation of the affairs of the society;
   (f) represent the society in legal proceedings;
   (g) determine whether any person is a member, past member or nominee of a deceased member; and

(h) call such meetings of the members as may be necessary for the proper conduct of the liquidation.

2. Upon completion of the winding-up proceedings the liquidator shall make a report to the Registrar and deposit the records of the society in such place the Registrar may direct.

48. C*ancellation of Registration*

When the winding-up proceedings are completed the certificate or registration shall be surrendered to the Registrar who shall cancel the registration of the society, and the society shall upon such cancellation be dissolved and cease to exist.

Part X – Decision, Appeal and Execution

49. *Principles of Decision*

Except as otherwise expressly provided in this Proclamation, every decision, order or award, whether resolving a dispute or otherwise of a judicial or arbitral nature, required to be made hereunder shall be made on the basis of a proper hearing conducted in accordance with the Civil Procedure Code.

50. *Cooperatives Tribunal*

1. There shall be established within the Ministry a Cooperatives Tribunal (hereinafter called the "Tribunal").
2. The Tribunal shall have its principal office at Addis Ababa but may hold sittings at such other places as it deems appropriate.
3. The Tribunal shall consist of three (3) members appointed by us upon the recommendation of the Minister. One (1) of the members shall be designated as Chairman of the Tribunal.
4. Members of the Tribunal shall be persons of high reputation and impartiality and with legal experience, preferably in the field of societies.
5. Members of the Tribunal shall be appointed for a term of three (3) years; provided, however, that the initial appointments to the Tribunal shall be for terms of one (1), two (2) and three (3) years, respectively, so that the term of not more than one (1) member then serving shall expire in each subsequent year. A retiring member shall be eligible for reappointment.
6. The Minster may recommend the withdrawal of an appointment of a member in case of negligence of duty or malfeasance in office.
7. Any vacancy in the membership of the Tribunal shall be filled in accordance with paragraph (3) of this Article 50.

8. The Tribunal shall conduct its hearings and fulfil its duties in accordance with the Civil Procedure Code.
9. The remuneration or fee to be paid to the members of the Tribunal shall be decided, from time to time, by the Minster.
10. The Minster shall assign such staff to the Tribunal as may be necessary for its proper functioning. Such staff shall be carried on the payroll of the Ministry.

51. *Appeal*

1. An appeal may be taken to the Tribunal from a decision made by the Registrar under Article 10, 12, 13, 27, 42, 45, or 47 of this Proclamation; provided, however, that no appeal may be taken to the Tribunal from a decision of a subordinate official made under Article 10, 12, 13, 27, 42, 45, or 47 hereof unless it is first reviewed by the Registrar.
2. A special section of the Supreme Imperial Court consisting of the Afa Negus or Vice Afa Negus and four (4) other judges shall have appellate and final jurisdiction in all matters of appeal and proceedings in error which may be taken from a decision, order or award of the Registrar made under Article 44 of this Proclamation and from decisions of the Tribunal made under paragraph (1) of this Article 51 in all matter of law, fact or equity, where the rules of law or the principle of equity appear from the files, exhibits or records of the Tribunal or Registrar to have been erroneously determined; provided, however, that no appeal may be taken to the Supreme Imperial Court from a decision, order or award made under Article 44 (1) (b) hereof unless it is first reviewed by the Registrar.
3. Whenever it is deemed necessary, the special section of the Supreme Imperial Court established under this Proclamation may hold its sittings in any place in the Empire where societies have been formed.

52. *Persons to Have Powers of Civil Court*

Every authority required to making a decision, order or award under this Proclamation shall have the same powers as a civil court with regard, in particular, but without limitation, to the summoning of witnesses, the production of evidence, the conduct of the proceedings and the making of injunctions.

53. *Execution*

Any decision, order or award made under this Proclamation shall, where appropriate, be executed as through made by a civil court, and the courts of the Empire shall have jurisdiction to order the enforcement of any such decision, order or award.

Part XI – Miscellaneous

54. *Use of Term "Cooperative"*

No person other than a society shall carry on business under any name or title of which the word "cooperative" is a part.

55. *Address of Society*

Every society shall have an address registered in the prescribed manner where service of process shall be made and to which all notices and communications shall be sent and shall inform the Registrar of any change in such address within thirty (30) days.

56. P*roclamation, Regulations and Rules to be Open to Inspection*

Every society shall keep a copy of this Proclamation and of the regulations and the rules open to inspection free of charge at all reasonable times at the registered address of the society.

57. *Service of Documents*

Any decision or other document required to be served under this Proclamation shall be served in accordance with the provisions of the Civil Procedure Code.

58. *Acts of Societies not to be Invalidated by Certain Defects*

No act of a society or of any Executive Committee or officer of a society shall be deemed to be invalid by reason only of the existence of any defect in the composition of such Executive Committee or in the appointment or election of such officer or on the ground that such officer was not properly qualified for such office unless such defect directly involves or affects the substance of such act.

59. *Commercial Code not Applicable*

The provisions of the Commercial Code of 1960 shall not apply to societies except in so far as such provisions are consistent with the purposes and provisions of this Proclamation, and in particular but without limitation, societies shall not be subject to any requirement of organization, registration or internal management otherwise applicable to trades or business organizations under the Commercial Code.

60. *Regulations*

The Minster may issue regulations for the better carrying into effect of the provisions hereof.

Limitations of Cooperative Proclamation No. 241/1966

The following were identified as the major limitations of the Proclamation No. 241/1966.

- Members of the society were only land-owners. Only land-owners and rich farmers were being admitted as members who could pay highest amount of share capital.
- Poor farmers could not become members of cooperative societies.
- The cooperatives were established only in the cash crop growing areas.
- The main reason for the establishment of the cooperative societies was to provide credit to the rich farmers and to produce and sale the cash crops to earn foreign currency.

Summary

- In 1966, the Cooperatives Societies Proclamation No. 241 was issued. It was only after this decree that cooperatives began to emerge in Ethiopia. Efforts to mobilize people were intensified and rationalized.
- This proclamation was contained in eleven parts comprised of 60 articles.
- As for formation and registration of societies, provisions were made on types of societies, name of society, formation of society, application, registration, society to have juridical personality, amendment of rules, and change of liability, transfer of assets and liabilities and division or amalgamation.
- As for members of societies and their rights and obligations, provisions were made on persons who may become members, admission of nominal members, register of members, member not to exercise rights till due payment made, voting, restriction on holding shares, restriction on transfer of shares or interest, transfer of interest on death of member, and liability of past or deceased member.
- As for organs of societies, provisions were made on supreme authority in society, ordinary general meeting, special general meeting, executive committee, supervision of executive committee and securing possession of books and records of the society.
- As for as privileges of societies are concerned, provisions were made on priority of claims by society, charges and set off in respect of shares or interest of members, shares or interest not liable to attachment or sale and government aid and exemption from taxes.
- As for properties and funds of societies, provisions were made on funds not to be divided, disposal of net profits, investment of funds, restrictions on borrowings and restrictions on loans.
- Provisions were made on audit, inquiry, inspection, powers in respect of audit, inquiry and supervision, and surcharge.

❖ As for arbitration, provisions were made on the disputes to be referred to arbitration and settlement of disputes.

❖ As for dissolution and winding-up of societies, provisions were made on dissolution, liquidator, powers and duties of liquidator, and cancellation of registration.

❖ As for decision appeal, and execution, provisions were made on principles of decision, cooperatives tribunal, appeal, persons to have powers of civil court and execution.

❖ Under miscellaneous, provisions were made on use of term cooperative, address of society, proclamation, regulations and rules to be open to inspection, service of documents, acts of societies and to be invalidated by certain defects, commercial code not applicable, and regulations.

Self-Learning Activity

1. What type of societies could be formed and registered under the Proclamation No. 241/1966?
2. What do you mean by regulation?
3. What do you know about admission of nominal members under the proclamation?
4. What do you know about the restriction on holding shares by a member in a cooperative?
5. What do you understand about the provision relating to priority of claims by society?
6. Write down the provision relating to inquiry?

15 Peasant Association Proclamation No. 71 of 1975 Issued by DERG Regime

Introduction

During its thirteen-year existence (1974 to 1987), the Derg worked to spread administrative reform down to the lowest echelons of regional administration. To this end, it took several important steps in 1975.

With its Land Reform Proclamation in March 1975, the Derg abolished the lowest level of rural administration, the *balabat*, and called for the formation of peasant associations that would be responsible for the implementation and enforcement of the land reform measures.

Later in the year, the Derg issued Proclamation No. 71, which gave peasant associations legal status and authorized them to create "conditions facilitating the complete destruction of the feudal order." It also empowered the associations' executive committees to draft internal regulations that would, in theory, devolve more power to local communities. These associations were to be guided initially by students in the development through Cooperation Campaign (commonly referred to as *zemecha*), who were expected to teach peasants about the revolution's goals. Students were also supposed to help local communities plan and implement development programmes in their areas.

Initially, it was not clear how much power, authority, or autonomy the regime intended to devolve to local institutions. Consequently, state agents often came into conflict with local organizations under the guidance of students who were often more radical and politically astute than government functionaries. By 1976, to bring local communities under tighter central control, the Derg introduced laws spelling out the rights and obligations of peasant associations and *kebeles*.

Salient Features of the Proclamation No. 71 of 1975

This proclamation provided for the organization and consolidation of peasant associations to organize and develop cooperatives in all places at all levels in order to lay down the foundation for socialist agriculture so that the peasant may benefit from joint labour.

In this proclamation, the peasant associations were given broader powers and duties, which aimed at better organization and consolidation of the peasantry.

Some of the Powers and Duties of Peasant Associations

- To enable peasants to secure and safeguard their political and economic and social rights.
- To enable the peasantry to administer itself.
- To establish cooperative societies.
- To enable the peasantry to work collectively and to speed up social development by improving the quality of the instruments of production and the level of productivity.
- To sue and be sued.
- To issue and implement its internal regulations in order to achieve its goals and aims.

Moreover, this proclamation for the first time incorporated provisions for the organization of two types cooperative societies such as Service Cooperatives and Agricultural Producers Cooperatives.

Service Cooperatives

Organization and Membership of Service Cooperatives

The requirements to form a service cooperative society stated in the proclamation were:

- Not less than three and not more than ten peasant associations may form a service cooperative society without affecting the legal personality of each association.
- As prescribed by the law, service cooperative societies may establish one service cooperative society at the *Woreda* level and were necessary, higher service cooperative societies.
- Woreda Peasant Associations shall supervise all service cooperative societies established under the jurisdiction of Woreda.
- However, the peasant associations shall not interfere with the day-to-day activities of service cooperative society i.e., the law limited the interference of PAs role.

Objectives, Powers and Duties of Service Cooperative Society

The Objectives, Powers and Duties of Service Cooperative Society included the following:

- To procure agricultural crops from the farmers.
- To provide agricultural extension service.
- To market the produce of members at fair price.
- To provide loans at fair rate of interest.
- To provide storage and savings services.
- To supply consumer goods to the members according to their needs.
- To provide education in socialist philosophy and cooperative work in order to enhance the political consciousness of the peasantry.
- To supply improved agricultural implements and provide tractor services.
- To collect contributions.
- To give flour mill service.
- To organize craftsmen in order to promote cottage industry.
- To provide political education with a view to establishing agricultural producers' cooperative societies by forming, promoting, and consolidating mutual aid teams like Debo.
- To sue and be sued.
- To draw up its internal regulations.

Agricultural Producers' Cooperative Society

In the proclamation, it was written that an Agricultural Producers' Cooperative Society is a society that is established voluntarily by peasant associations.

Objectives, Powers and Duties of Agricultural Producers' Cooperative Society

Agricultural Producers' Cooperative Society shall have the following objectives, powers and duties:

- To put the main instruments of production under the control of and when necessary to gradually transfer their ownership to the society.
- To divide members in to working groups to enable them to work collectively for the society especially by organizing members with special abilities in order to obtain mutual benefits.
- To give priority to the interests of poor and middle peasants and to ensure that the leadership of the association is drawn from such peasants.
- To raise production and to gradually improve the instruments of production.

- To pay the members according to the quality and quantity of their work.
- To assign a special fund for the welfare and security of the members.
- To struggle for continuous improvement, democratic rights and unity.
- To struggle for the gradual abolition of exploitation from the rural areas and to refrain from any kind of exploitation.
- To engage in continuous political movement in order to enhance the political consciousness of its members.
- To sue and be sued.

Summary

- Derg issued Proclamation No. 71, which gave peasant associations legal status and authorized them to create "conditions facilitating the complete destruction of the feudal order." It also empowered the associations' executive committees to draft internal regulations that would, in theory, devolve more power to local communities.
- These associations were to be guided initially by students in the Development through Cooperation Campaign (commonly referred to as *zemecha*), who were expected to teach peasants about the revolution's goals. Students were also supposed to help local communities plan and implement development programmes in their areas.
- The Proclamation No. 71 of 1975 provided for the organization and consolidation of peasant associations to organize and develop cooperatives in all places at all levels in order to lay down the foundation for socialist agriculture so that the peasant may benefit from joint labour.
- In this proclamation, the peasant associations were given broader powers and duties, which aimed at better organization and consolidation of the peasantry.
- Not less than three and not more than ten peasant associations may form a service cooperative society without affecting the legal personality of each association.
- As prescribed by the law, service cooperative societies may establish one service cooperative society at the Woreda level and were necessary, higher service cooperative societies.
- Woreda Peasant Associations shall supervise all service cooperative societies established under the jurisdiction of Woreda.
- In the proclamation, it was written that an Agricultural Producers' Cooperative Society is a society that is established voluntarily by peasant associations.

Self-Learning Activity

1. What are the requirements needed for the formation of service cooperatives?
2. State any three objectives of agricultural producers' cooperative society as stipulated by Peasant Associations Proclamation?

16 Proclamation No. 138 of 1978

Proclamation Made during DERG Regime to Provide for the Establishment of Cooperative Societies

Necessity for the Enactment of the Proclamation

Whereas, the stage of progress our revolution has reached necessitates that the growing demand of peasants, artisans and workers for the increase of production and just distribution of goods of production and consumption be satiated;

Whereas, to raise the living standards of peasants, artisans and workers and to develop the national economy it is necessary to combat the remnant feudalistic and capitalistic means of exploitation, such as usury, laissez faire pricing, and the like, by enabling peasants, artisans and workers to secure necessary services and retain the fruits of their labour;

Whereas, in order to assure the broad masses the fruits of their labour according to the quantity and quality of their work, it is necessary to encourage collective ownership of the means of production;

Whereas, the organization of the broad masses in cooperatives and the pooling together of their efforts and resources aid in protecting their economic, political and social rights and in obtaining goods and services essential for production and living purposes;

Whereas, central planning can have a wider spectrum and involve the participation of the broad masses if peasants, artisans and other workers are organized in cooperatives and define their common economic and social problems;

Whereas, in order to implement the objectives specified above, it is necessary that the broad masses establish appropriate cooperative societies;

Now, therefore in accordance with Article 5(6) of the Redefinition of Powers and Responsibilities of the Provisional Military Administration Council and the Council of Ministers Proclamation No. 110 of 1977, it is hereby proclaimed as follows:

Major Provisions of the Proclamation

1. *Short Title*

This Proclamation may be cited as the "Cooperative Societies Proclamation No. 138 of 1978."

2. *Definitions*

In this Proclamation unless the context otherwise requires:

1. "appropriate authority" shall mean the Ministry of Agriculture and Settlement concerning agricultural cooperative societies; Handicrafts and Small-Scale Industries Development Agency concerning artisans, producers and service cooperatives; the Ministry of Urban Development and Housing concerning housing cooperatives; and the National Bank of Ethiopia concerning thrift and credit cooperatives;
2. "cooperative" shall mean a cooperative society established and registered under this Proclamation;
3. "peasant association" shall mean a peasant association established or to be established under the Public Ownership or Rural Lands Proclamation No. 31/1975.

3. *Objectives of Cooperatives*

Cooperatives shall be organized for the following objectives:

1. To develop self-reliance and to promote the interest of their members;
2. To put the means of production under the control of cooperatives and to transform them gradually to collective property as may be necessary;
3. To increase production;
4. To expand industries;
5. To conduct political agitation;
6. To eliminate reactionary culture and customs;
7. To participate in the building up of a socialist economy;
8. To accumulate capital and to mobilize human resources to sustain economic development.

4. *Cooperatives to be Established*

The following types of cooperative may be established:

1. Producers' cooperative societies;
2. Service cooperative societies;
3. Thrift and credit cooperative societies; and
4. Housing cooperative societies.

5. *Agricultural Producers' Cooperatives*

1. Farmers in a peasant association may form agricultural producers' cooperatives.
2. Subject to this Proclamation, agricultural producers' cooperative societies shall have the powers and duties indicated in Article 8 of the Peasant Associations Organization and Consolidation Proclamation No. 71 of 1975.

6. *Agricultural Service Cooperatives*

Notwithstanding sub-article 1 of Article 6 of the Peasant associations Organization and Consolidation Proclamation No. 71 of 1975:

1. Two or more *Kebele* peasant associations may form an agricultural service cooperative;
2. Subject to this Proclamation, agricultural service cooperatives shall have the powers and duties of the Peasant Associations Organization and Consolidation Proclamation No. 71 of 1975.

7. *Artisans Producers' Cooperatives*

Artisans producers' cooperatives may be formed by individual artisans to work collectively and to gradually transfer the means of production to the ownership of the cooperative and to get benefits according to the services they render and the work they contribute.

8. *Artisans' Service Cooperatives*

Artisans' service cooperatives may be formed by individual artisans to cooperate in production and in the provision of means of production, marketing facilities and other necessary services to their members.

9. *Housing Cooperatives*

Housing cooperatives may be formed by individuals for the purpose of building dwelling houses for their members.

10. *Thrift and Credit Cooperatives*

Thrift and credit cooperatives may be formed by individuals working in one undertaking or office for making regular savings and to obtain credit for individual needs or productive purposes.

11. *Formation of Cooperatives*

1. The appropriate authority shall be responsible for the formation and promotion of cooperatives in its respective field of activity.
2. The formation of a cooperative shall be initiated through a meeting of prospective members who shall take all decisions as to the formation and registration of the proposed cooperative.

12. *Registration*

1. All cooperatives shall be registered in the following manner:
   (a) Agricultural service and producers cooperatives shall be registered by the Ministry of Agriculture and Settlement;
   (b) Artisans' service and producers' cooperatives shall be registered by the Handicrafts and Small Scale Industries Development Agency;
   (c) Housing cooperatives shall be registered by the Ministry of Urban Development and Housing;
   (d) Thrift and credit cooperatives shall be registered by the National Bank of Ethiopia.
2. Cooperatives registered in accordance with sub-article 1 of this Article shall have juridical personality.

13. *Articles of Association of Cooperatives*

1. Each cooperative shall have its own Articles of Association prepared in accordance with this Proclamation and regulations issued hereunder.
2. The Articles of Association shall, among other things, provide for the following:
   (a) The name of the cooperative;
   (b) The address of the cooperative and the area of its operations;
   (c) The objectives and activities of the cooperative;
   (d) The rights and duties of members;
   (e) The terms and requirements for admission of members and the conditions for the termination of membership;
   (f) Membership fees and other contribution;
   (g) The election, duties and responsibilities of the executive committees, supervisory committees and other committees;

(h) The procedure for convening and conduction the general meeting and other meetings of the association; the duties and responsibilities of such meetings;

(i) The procedures for amending the Articles of Association of the cooperative;

(j) The manner for appropriating surplus for reserve and other funds;

(k) The conditions under which the shares and other interests of a member can be transferred to his legal heirs;

(l) Other matters which are not contrary to the provisions of this Proclamation or regulations issued hereunder.

14. *Establishment of a Cooperative Board*

There is hereby established a Board to coordinate and supervise all activities of cooperative under this Proclamation.

15. *Members of the Board*

1. The Board shall have the following members

(a) The Minister of Agriculture and Settlement .... Chairman

(b) The Minister of Industry or his representative .... Member

(c) The Minister of Commerce and Tourism or his representative .... Member

(d) The Minister of Housing and Urban Development or his representative member"

(e) The Minister of Labour and Social Affairs or his representative member"

(f) The Minster of Education, or his representative member"

(g) The Planning Commissioner or his representative member"

(h) The Governor of the National Bank or his representative .... Member

2. When the matter being discussed by the Board concerns other government offices, such offices shall send representatives as members.

16. *Meetings of the Board*

1. The Board shall meet as often as its operations require.
2. The Board's meeting shall be convened at the request of the chairman or in accordance with its rules of procedure.

3. The presence of a majority of its members constitutes the quorum.
4. Decisions of the Board shall be made by majority vote; and in case of a tie the Chairman shall have a casting vote.
5. The Board shall determine its own rules of procedure.

17. *Powers and Duties of the Board*

The Board shall have the following powers and duties:

1. To study the progress of cooperatives and advise the government on policy measures to be taken with respect thereto;
2. To issue policies and guidelines for the establishment and development of cooperatives;
3. To issue directives for the implementation of this Proclamation and regulations issued hereunder;
4. To delegate its powers under this Proclamation to other organizations and offices as may be necessary.

18. *Secretariat*

1. The Board shall have a secretariat in the Ministry of Agriculture and Settlement.
2. The secretariat shall:
   (a) assist the Board by making various studies necessary for making decisions and issuing directives;
   (b) keep a record of all cooperatives.

19. *Powers of the Appropriate Authority*

1. Subject to Article 17 of this Proclamation, the appropriate authority shall have the power to implement this Proclamation, regulations issued hereunder and the policies and decisions of the Board.
2. Without limiting the generality of the foregoing, the appropriate authority shall:
   (a) prepare and submit to the Board for approval the necessary studies, plans, model Articles of Association and guidelines on cooperative organization and promotion;
   (b) supervise the execution of the powers and duties of cooperatives;
   (c) give orientation to the public on the benefits and purposes of forming cooperatives and on cooperative polices and objectives;

(d) train the necessary man-power for cooperative development;

(e) prepare and submit the necessary report on cooperative development.

20. *Government Assistance*

All public distribution and service rendering organizations and public authorities shall give priority to cooperatives over private persons and organizations in providing their services.

21. *Indivisibility of Common Service Funds*

Funds of cooperatives allocated for reserve, social welfare, education, health and for other common purposes in accordance with their Articles of Association shall not be distributed among members.

22. *Reorganization, Amalgamation and Dissolution of Cooperatives*

Cooperatives may reorganize, amalgamate with other similar cooperatives or be dissolved in accordance with regulations issued by the Board.

23. *Charge or Set-off in Respect of Shares or Interest of Members*

A cooperative shall have a charge upon the deposits or other interests of its member in respect of any debt or outstanding demand due to the cooperative from such member, and may set-off any sum on or towards payment of any such debt or outstanding demand.

24. *Shares or Interest not Liable to Attachment or Sale*

Except as provided in Article 23 hereof, the share or interest of a member in the capital of a cooperative shall not be liable to attachment or sale in respect of any debt or liability of such member.

25. *Limitation on Loans*

A cooperative may make loans only to its members or other cooperatives.

26. *Audit*

1. The accounts of any cooperative shall be audited at least once a year by the appropriate authority or by such other person designated by the latter at the expenses of the cooperative.
2. The audited report shall be submitted to the Board and to the general meeting of the cooperative for action in accordance with regulations issued hereunder.

27. *Inspection*

The appropriate authority may at any time inspect or cause the inspection of the books of any cooperative. The said authority shall submit the report to the executive committee or the general meeting of the cooperative, as the case may be, for proper action by the latter.

28. *Societies formed under Cooperative Societies Proclamation*

1. Societies formed under the Cooperative Societies Proclamation No. 241/1966 that qualify under this Proclamation shall be re-registered in accordance with this Proclamation.
2. Societies formed under Proclamation No. 241/1966 may be dissolved by the decision of the Board where their objectives and membership are inconsistent with this Proclamation. Such cooperatives shall be liquidated in conformity with the said Proclamation.

29. *Settlement of Disputes*

1. In rural areas:
   - (a) Disputes between producers' cooperatives and their members shall be settled by the Kebele Judicial Tribunal formed under the Peasant Associations Organization and Consolidation Proclamation No. 71/1975. Appeal against the decision of this tribunal may be taken to the Woreda Judicial Tribunal whose decision shall be final.
   - (b) Disputes between:
     - *(i)* service cooperatives and their members;
     - *(ii)* cooperatives;
     - *(iii)* cooperatives and peasant associations shall be settled in accordance with Articles 33 and 37 of the Peasant Associations Organization and Consolidation Proclamation No. 71/1975.
2. In urban areas:
   - (a) Dispute between housing cooperatives and their members shall be settled by the Kebele Judicial Tribunal, formed under the Urban Dwellers Associations Consolidating and Municipalities Proclamation No. 104/1976; appeal against the decision of the Kebele Judicial Tribunal may be taken to the Judicial Tribunal of Higher Urban Dwellers' Association whose decision shall be final.
   - (b) Disputes between housing cooperatives and Kebele Urban Dwellers' Association shall be settled by the Judicial Tribunal of Higher Urban Dwellers' Association or in the absence

thereof, by the Special Judicial Tribunal, appeal against such decision may be taken to the Judicial Tribunal of Central Urban Dwellers' Association whose decision shall be final.

3. Disputes between artisans' cooperatives and their members and thrift and credit cooperatives and their members shall be settled by an Arbitration Committee appointed by the general meeting of their respective cooperatives. Appeals against the decision of the Committee may be taken to Judicial Tribunals whose decision shall be final.

30. *Use of Term "Cooperative"*

No person, association or organization, other than cooperatives registered under this Proclamation, may carry on activities under any name or title of which the word "cooperative" is a part.

31. *Repeal and Conflict with Other Laws*

1. Subject to Article 28 of this Proclamation the Cooperative Societies Proclamation No. 241/1966 is hereby repealed.
2. No law, regulation, practice or procedure, written or customary shall, in so far as it is inconsistent with this Proclamation have force or effect in respect of situations provided for by this Proclamation.

32. *Penalty*

Any person who violates or obstructs the implementation or contravenes the provisions of this Proclamation or regulations issued hereunder shall be punishable in accordance with the Penal Code.

33. *Power to Issue Regulations*

The Board may issue regulations for the better carrying out of the provisions of this Proclamation.

Summary

- By taking in to account the problems in the implementation of Peasant Associations Proclamation, the Derg Regime enacted an elaborate proclamation called Cooperative Societies Proclamation No. 71/1978 in order to create and consolidate agrarian institutions in the rural areas.
- Under this proclamation, provisions were made to establish only producers' cooperative societies; service cooperative societies; thrift and credit cooperative societies and housing cooperative societies.
- The appropriate authority shall be responsible for the formation and promotion of cooperatives in its respective field of activity.

Comparison of Cooperative Laws

Points of Distinction	Farm Workers' Cooperative Decree No. 44/1960	Cooperative Societies Proclamation No. 241/1966	Cooperative Societies Proclamation No. 138/1978
Number of sections	Twelve sections	Eleven parts	No sections or parts
Number of articles	48 articles	60 articles	34 articles
Definition of terms	Not mentioned	Mentioned	Mentioned
Organization of cooperatives	Ministry of National Community Development	Registrar appointed by the Ministry of National Community Development and Social Affairs	Ministry of Agriculture and Settlement, Handicrafts and Small Industries Development Agency, Ministry of Urban Development and Housing, National Bank of Ethiopia
Types of Cooperatives formed	Only Farm Workers' Cooperatives Societies	Primary and Secondary types of all categories of societies	Producers' cooperative societies, Service cooperative societies, Thrift and credit cooperatives, Housing cooperatives
Registration	By the Ministry	By the Registrar	By agencies/ministries in charge for different types of cooperatives
Privileges of society	No provision	Provision was made	No provision
Audit and supervision	No provision	Provision was made	Provision was made
Arbitration	No provision	Provision was made	No provision
Cooperative Tribunal	No provision	Provision was made	Provision was made
Settlement of Disputes	No provision	Provision was made	Provision was made

- Agricultural service and producers' cooperatives shall be registered by the Ministry of Agriculture and Settlement.
- Artisans' service and producers' cooperatives shall be registered by the Handicrafts and Small Scale Industries Development Agency.
- Housing cooperatives shall be registered by the Ministry of Urban Development and Housing.
- Thrift and credit cooperatives shall be registered by the National Bank of Ethiopia.
- Each cooperative shall have its own Articles of Association prepared in accordance with this Proclamation and regulations.
- There is hereby established a Board to coordinate and supervise all activities of cooperative under this Proclamation.
- All public distribution and service rendering organizations and public authorities shall give priority to cooperatives over private persons and organizations in providing their services.
- Funds of cooperatives allocated for reserve, social welfare, education, health and for other common purposes in accordance with their Articles of association shall not be distributed among members.
- Cooperatives may reorganize, amalgamate with other similar cooperatives or be dissolved in accordance with regulations issued by the Board.
- The accounts of any cooperative shall be audited at least once a year by the appropriate authority or by such other person designated by the latter at the expenses of the cooperative.
- Provision was made on settlement of disputes according to the types of cooperative societies.

Self-Learning Activity

1. What do you know about appropriate authority as per proclamation 1978?
2. What types of cooperatives could be established under the proclamation 1978?
3. What do you know about the constitution of the members of the Board as per the proclamation 1978?

Part - III
Development of Cooperative Law in Ethiopia During Transitional Government (At Present)

17 Agricultural Cooperatives Societies Proclamation No. 85 of 1994

Background

After the downfall of the Derg regime, there was a gap in between 1991-1995 in cooperative movement of Ethiopia. This gap was created due to the fact that the government attention was mainly drawn towards stabilizing, bringing peace and creating administration organs. Later on due to cooperative experts' dedication and devotion and the government's commitment towards cooperative development, it became necessary to enact new cooperative proclamation which suits to the current economic system.

Agricultural Cooperative Societies Proclamation No. 85 of 1994 was enacted to give more thrust on all round development of the economy of Ethiopia.

Whereas, it has become necessary to make conditions convenient so that an Ethiopian peasant living in rural areas in scattered manner by being organized on free will may be able to solve jointly the economic and social problems facing him;

Whereas, it has become essential to make the societies play their roles properly in a free market system by getting rid of the governmental intervention in the internal affairs of the Agricultural Cooperative societies;

Whereas, it has become imperative to issue legislation by which agricultural cooperative societies be organized and administered in order to achieve the foregoing mentioned objectives;

Now, therefore, in accordance with Article 9 (d) of the Transitional Period Charter, it is hereby proclaimed as follows:

Part One: General

1. *Short Title*

This Proclamation may be cited as "Agricultural Cooperative Societies Proclamation No. 85/1994".

2. *Definitions*

Unless the context otherwise requires in this Proclamation:

1. "Society" means a primary or a higher level agricultural cooperative society registered under this proclamation;
2. "Member" means any physical person or a society, having juridical personality which is registered after fulfilling its membership obligation;
3. "General Meeting" means a meeting of members of the primary cooperative society;
4. "General assembly" means a meeting of a higher society in which individual persons representing member societies attended;
5. "Special Resolution" means a resolution passed by a majority of (2/3) or such higher quorum or majority as may be specified in the by-laws;
6. "Management Committee" means a body elected and empowered by the general meeting or assembly with the responsibility to manage the activities of the society;
7. "Ministry" means Ministry of Agriculture;
8. "Agricultural Bureau" means a national/regional self-government agricultural bureau;
9. "Appropriate Authority" means an agricultural bureau, in case the matter to be entertained by it relates to members of a society found in a certain nation/regional self-government a Ministry in the case the matter to be entertained by it relates to members of society found in more than one national/regional self-governments;

3. *Objectives of the Society*

The society to be established under this proclamation shall have the following objectives:

1. To improve the living condition of members by increasing production and productivity;
2. To promote self-reliance among members;
3. To solve problems collectively which a peasant cannot personally achieve;
4. To make members obtain modern technologies products which are capable to increase agricultural production and materials necessary for their livelihood easily and at fair price;

5. To satisfy the needs of a community and increase the income of a peasant by processing agricultural product to industrial products; and

6. To promote the cultures of the members by teaching and training.

4. *Guiding Principle of Societies*

The society shall be guided by principles:

1. Individuals who are supposed to be voluntarily members must have similar type of work and interest. Any kind of discrimination or influence based on religion, sex, nationality and political outlook shall not be made on those who want to be members.

2. The society shall carryout any of its activities on a democratic basis. One member shall have only one vote.

3. Surplus of the society shall be distributed to members according to their participation in the economic activities of the society.

4. The society shall stand non-aligned and free from any political influence.

Part Two: Formation and Registration of Societies

5. *Formation of a Primary Society*

1. A primary society to be established shall be on the free will of the peasants living within a given area.
2. The number of members in a primary society to be established shall not be less than ten.

6. *Formation of Higher Level Society*

Two or more primary societies may be establish a higher level society.

7. *Types of Societies*

1. A society may engage in either one type of activity or in activities with multipurpose and may have a character of either service rendering or producing.

2. The field of area to be engaged in by any society shall be determined by the by-laws of the society.

8. *Name of a Society*

1. Any society shall have a name.

2. The word "Cooperative Society" shall appear in the name of every primary society.

3. The word "Union" or "Federation" shall appear in the name of higher level society.

9. *Registration of Society*

1. Any society shall be registered by the appropriate authority.
2. Any society when established shall submit an application for registration together with the following particulars to the appropriate authority:
   (a) the by-laws of the society
   (b) names, address, and signature of the members
   (c) names, address, and signature of the members of the management committee of the society
   (d) names, address, and signature of the leaders of member primary societies.
3. The appropriate authority shall register a society and issue a certificate of registration within 15 days when he satisfies that application for registration submitted to him has fulfilled the requirement for registration.

10. *Juridical Personality and Responsibility*

1. Any society registered in pursuance of Article 9 of this proclamation shall have juridical personality from the date of its registration.
2. Any society shall not be liable for any claim worthing more than its total asset.

11. *By-laws of Society*

1. Every society shall have, its own by-law.
2. The contents of the bylaw shall include the following particulars:
   (a) name of the society
   (b) address of the society
   (c) objectives of the society
   (d) requirements necessary for membership of society and conditions for dismissal from membership
   (e) the rights and duties of the members of the society
   (f) the responsibilities and working mechanism of management bodies
   (g) allocation and distribution of surplus; and
   (h) other cases not contrary to this proclamation.

3. The by-laws of society may be amended by the general meeting or assembly;

4. The amendment of the by-laws of society shall be effective only where it is submitted and registered.

12. *Amalgamation and Division of Societies*

1. The general meeting of a society through a special resolution may:

   (a) by dividing itself in to two or more societies, or

   (b) by amalgamating itself with one or more societies form a new society.

2. Amalgamation and division of the society shall be effective through a special resolution:

   (a) if the members and creditors of the society fully agree of its amalgamation or division; or

   (b) if the special resolution is registered by the appropriate authority in that the members and creditors have been paid off or the payment is guaranteed to the satisfaction of the appropriate authority.

3. The previous records of societies shall be cancelled from the register as soon as the newly formed society by amalgamation is registered or the newly formed societies by division are registered.

4. The rights and duties of societies which have lost their identities by amalgamation shall be transferred to the newly formed society.

5. The rights and duties of a society has lost its identity by division shall be transferred to the newly formed societies as specified in sub-article 2 of this Article.

Part Three: The Rights and Duties of a Society

13. *Requirements Necessary for Membership of Primary Society*

1. Any individual may become a member of primary society if:

   (a) his age is more than fourteen;

   (b) his regular work is agricultural;

   (c) his residence is within the working area of the society;

   (d) he is capable to pay the share capital, registration fee demanded by the society;

   (e) he is found willing to implement its obligation.

2. Any woman shall have the right to be a member of society if she fulfils the requirements set forth in sub-article 1 of this article.

14. *Rights and Duties of Members*

1. Any member of a society shall have the following rights:

(a) to obtain services and benefits according to his participation in the society;

(b) to participate in the meeting of the society and to vote;

(c) to elect or be elected; however a member who has not attained the age of 18 shall not have the right to be elected;

(d) to withdraw from the society according to his request after due respect of his benefits.

2. Any member of a society shall have the following duties:

(a) to pay respect to the by-laws, directives and decisions of the society;

(b) to work those activities which ought to be worked collectively in accordance with the by-laws and directives of the society;

(c) to pay share capital and registration fee;

(d) to protect the common property of the society.

15. *Dismissal from Membership*

1. Any member of a society may leave from the society on his own initiative.

2. Any member of a society may leave from the society when it is decided by the general meeting or assembly to dismiss him from the society because of committing repeated faults.

3. The benefits of any dismissed member shall be respected in accordance with the by-laws of the society.

4. Without prejudice to the provisions of Article 13 hereof, any dismissed member may reapply for membership, however a member dismissed in accordance with the sub-article 2 of this Article may become a member of the society only if he obtains the approval of the general meeting or assembly.

16. *Payment of Shares*

1. The capital which enables the society to expand its work activities shall be obtained from paid up shares of each member in accordance of the decision of the general meeting or assembly.

2. The society may sell additional shares if it is found necessary to promote the financial capacity of the society subject to the decision of the general meeting or assembly.

3. No member shall hold more than one-fifth of the total paid up share capital of such society.

4. The society may pay interest on the share issued in accordance with the bylaws of the society; however the rate of interest shall not exceed the bank interest rate.

17. *Register of Members*

Every society shall keep a register wherein shall be entered.

1. The name, address, age and sex of each member;
2. The date on which he become a member or ceased to be a member;
3. The amount of shares held by each member;
4. The name of the heir of the member; and
5. Any other details that may be specified in the by-laws.

18. *Voting*

1. Any member shall, regardless of the number of shares owned by him have only one vote at meeting of the society.
2. Any member shall not cast a vote through a representative.

19. *Restriction on Transfer of Share or Benefit*

1. No transfer, by a member, of his share or benefit shall be valid unless:

   (a) the member has held such share or benefit for at least one year before he transfers;

   (b) a transfer is made to another member; and

   (c) the transfer is approved by the management committee.

2. On the death of a member, his share or benefit shall be transferred to one of his heirs who has been specifically mentioned in the register of society inherit such share or benefit in the will of the deceased, or failing such mention to the heir at law where such heir is a member or is admitted as member.

3. Where such heir is not a member and does not become or is not admitted as a member, he should be paid the value of the share or benefit of the deceased member.

4. If the shares or benefit to be transferred to a member under this article are found to be beyond the limitation as prescribed in sub-article 3 Article 16 here the member shall be paid the difference in cash.
5. The transfer or payment concluded in pursuance of sub-article 2 or 3 of this Article shall not be reveres due to the claims paused by third parties on society.

Part Four: Management Bodies

20. *Supreme Organ of the Society*

1. The supreme organ of any society shall be the general meeting or the representative of general assembly.
2. The general meeting or the representatives of general assembly shall meet twice in a year. But if the management committee, on one-third of the members of general meeting or general assembly, requires a meeting to be called, emergency meeting may be held by giving 30 days prior notice.

21. *Powers and Duties of the General Meeting or General Assembly*

The general meeting or assembly of a society shall:

1. Pass decisions after evaluating the general work activities of the societies;
2. Issue and amend the by-laws and internal regulations of the society;
3. Elect and dismiss the members of the management committee, controlling committee and when necessary the members of other committees;
4. Determine the amount of shares of the society;
5. Decide how the annual net surplus of the society is distributed;
6. Give decision on the audit report;
7. Hear work reports and give proper decision;
8. Decide that a society either be amalgamated with another society or be divided in pursuance of this proclamation;
9. approve the annual work plan and budget;
10. decide any issue submitted by the management committee and other committees.

22. *Special General Meeting or General Assembly*

1. The management committee shall call a special general meeting or general assembly within one month from having required in writing to do so by the limited number or members as may be specified in the bylaws.

2. Where the management committee fails to call a special general meeting or general assembly in accordance with sub article 1 of this Article such meeting shall be called by the appropriate authority and shall in such case be deemed to have been called by the management committee.

23. *Management Committee*

1. There shall be a management committee having a limited number of members as prescribed in the bylaws of every society.

2. The term of office of the management committee shall be two years, however they may be either elected or dismissed at any time by the general meeting or assembly.

24. *Powers and Duties of the Management Committee*

The powers and duties of the management committee shall be determined in pursuance of the by-law and in particular shall include the following:

1. Holds the minutes of a meeting in writing.

2. Holds the documents and books of accounts of the society.

3. Prepares report on the work activities of the society, the next annual work programme and budget and submits to the general meeting or general assembly.

4. Calls general meeting or general assembly in accordance with the bylaw of the society.

5. Executes all decisions given by the general meeting or general assembly.

25. *Controlling Committee*

1. Every society shall have a controlling committee to which the number of members shall be specified in the by-laws of the society.

2. The term of office of the controlling committee shall be two years, however they may be either re-elected or dismissed at any time by the general meeting or assembly.

26. *Powers and Duties of the Controlling Committee*

The controlling committee:

1. Follows up that the management committee is carrying out its responsibilities properly.

2. Follows up that the funds and properties of the societies are properly utilized.

3. Controls that the various activities of the society are carried out pursuant to the by-laws of the society.
4. Performs other duties given by the general meeting or assembly.

27. *Other Sub-Committees*

Other sub-committees may be established as necessary pursuant to the by-laws of the society.

Part Five: Special Privileges of Society

28. *Priority of Claims by Society*

Notwithstanding any provision to the contrary in whatever law contained, any debt owed to the society by a member in respect of such membership, shall take precedence over all other debts of such person, except debt owed to the Government.

29. *Set-off in Respect of Share or Benefit of Members*

The shares or benefits of any member may be set-off for debts due to the society from such a member.

30. *Shares or Benefit not Liable to Attachment or Sale*

Except as provided in Article 29 hereof, the shares benefit of a member in the capital of a society shall be liable to attachment or sale.

31. *Government Assistance*

The central government and the national/regional governments shall render the necessary assistance for promotion and consolidation of the societies.

Part Six: Properties and Funds of Societies

32. *Funds of Society not to be Divided*

No part of the funds other than the net surplus determined to be allocated to members of the society shall be paid as a bonus, dividend or in any other form, however remuneration may be paid to any member for the services rendered to the society as prescribed in the by-law.

33. *Allocation of Net Surplus*

1. The society may allocate the net surplus obtained for the payment of the following things in accordance with the terms and conditions set forth in the bylaw and plan issued from time to time by the society.
   (a) for reserve;

(b) for the expansion of the work;

(c) for social services.

2. After deducting the amount prescribed in sub-article one of this article the remaining net surplus shall be divided to the members. Without prejudice to the sub-article 4 of Article 16 hereof, division is applicable on the basis of the shares of the members in the capital of the society:

   (a) the amount of goods sold to or purchased from the society by the members;

   (b) labour participation by the members in case of production activity.

34. *Restrictions of Borrowings*

A society shall receive deposits or loans from its members or other organizations to such extent and on such conditions as may be specified in the by-laws of society.

35. *Restrictions on Loans*

A society shall not extend loans other than to its members or a society established under this proclamation.

36. *Audit*

1. The account of every society shall be audited at least once annually.

2. The audit report shall be submitted to the general meeting or assembly.

Part Seven:

37. *Dissolution of a Society*

Any society shall be dissolved on the following grounds where:

1. Tt is dissolved by special resolution of the members; or
2. It is primary society and the number of its member falls below ten;
3. It is declared bankrupt by a court decision.

38. *Liquidation to be Concluded during Bankruptcy*

The provisions of book 5 of the commercial code with the necessary modifications made thereupon shall be applicable as regards the liquidation of the society that declared bankrupt.

39. *Liquidator*

1. The general meeting or assembly of a society shall assign a liquidator when a society is decided upon to be dissolved in pursuance of sub article 1 or 2 of Article 37 hereof.

2. The appropriate authority shall assign a liquidator upon the application of the management committee or members if a liquidator is not able to be assigned in accordance with sub-article 1 of this Article.
3. The liquidator shall receive records, documents and properties of the society as soon as he is assigned. He shall also take the necessary measures so that damage may not insure on the rights and properties of the society.

40. *Powers and Duties of Liquidator*

1. The liquidator shall have all the necessary powers to complete the winding-up proceedings. He shall in particular perform the following in order to carry out his duties properly:
   (a) investigate all claims against the society and decide on priority of payment among them;
   (b) collect the assets of the society;
   (c) distributes its assets in accordance with the plan of liquidation approved by the general meeting or assembly of the society;
   (d) carry on the work activities of the society in so far as may be necessary for the proper liquidation of the affairs of the society;
   (e) represents the society in legal proceedings;
   (f) calls meetings of the members as may be necessary for the proper conduct of the liquidation.
2. Upon complementation of the winding-up proceedings the liquidator shall make a report to the appropriate authority. He shall deposit the records of the society in such place as the appropriate authority may direct.

41. *Cancellation of a Society from the Register*

When the winding-up proceedings are completed the certificate of registration shall be surrendered to the appropriate authority who shall cancel the registration of the society, and the society shall upon such cancellation be dissolved and cease to exist.

Part Eight: Miscellaneous Provisions

42. *Address of Society*

Any society shall have a known and registered address where service of process shall be made and to which all notice and communication shall be sent and shall inform the appropriate authority of any change in such address within thirty days.

43. *By-laws to be Open to Inspection*

Every society shall keep by-laws open to inspection free of charge at all reasonable times at the registered address of the society.

44. *Employment of Workers*

1. Any society may employ a worker for an activity which requires special professional skill as necessary.

2. Any society may employ a worker on a temporary basis when it encounters workload and scarcity of manpower.

45. *Inapplicable Laws*

1. The provisions set forth in the proclamation to provide the establishment of cooperative societies, Proclamation No. 138/1978 as regards agricultural producers cooperative societies and agricultural service cooperative societies are repealed by this Proclamation.

2. No law, regulation or directive in so far it is in consistent with this Proclamation have force or effect in respect of matters provided for by this Proclamation.

46. *Transitional Provisions*

1. Agricultural producers, cooperative societies and agricultural service cooperative societies which have been established in accordance with cooperative societies Proclamation No. 138/1978 and still which are operating shall be reorganized under this Proclamation.

2. The societies Hall continue their operations holding their previous juridical personalities until they are reorganized and registered by the appropriate authority.

3. The appropriate authority shall facilitate all the conditions necessary for the reorganization of the society.

47. *Power to Issue Directives*

The Ministry may issue directives for the better and proper implementation of this Proclamation.

48. *Effective Date*

This Proclamation shall enter into force on the date of its publication in the Negarit Gazeta. Done at Addis Ababa, this 1st day of February 1994.

Summary

- Agricultural Cooperative Societies Proclamation No. 85/1994 was enacted to give more thrust on all-round development of the economy of Ethiopia.
- The society to be established under this proclamation shall have the objective to improve the living condition of members by increasing production and productivity.
- A primary society to be established shall be on the free will of the peasants living within a given area and the number of members in a primary society to be established shall not be less than ten.
- Two or more primary societies may establish a higher level society.
- A society may engage in either one type of activity or in activities with multipurpose and a society may have a character of either service rendering or producing.
- Under this proclamation, provision was made to establish only agricultural cooperative societies.
- In this proclamation, provisions were made on formation and registration of societies, rights and duties of members, management bodies, special privileges of societies, properties and funds of societies, and miscellaneous aspects.

Self-Learning Activity

1. What do you understand the provisions relating to employment of workers under 1994 proclamation?
2. What are the powers and duties of management committee as per 1994 proclamation?
3. What do you mean by management committee?
4. What are the powers and duties of controlling committee?

18 Cooperative Societies Proclamation No. 147 of 1998

Background

Whereas, it has become necessary to establish cooperative societies which are formed by individuals on voluntary basis and who have similar needs for creating savings and mutual assistance among themselves by pooling their resources, knowledge and property;

Whereas, it has become necessary to enable cooperative societies to actively participate in the free market economic system;

Whereas, it has become imperative to issue a comprehensive legislation by which cooperative societies are organized and managed in order to achieve the above-mentioned objectives;

Now, Therefore, in accordance with Article 55 (1) of the Constitution of the Federal Democratic Republic of Ethiopia, it is hereby proclaimed as follows:

Part One: General

1. *Short Title*

This Proclamation may be cited as the "Cooperative Societies Proclamation No. 147/1998."

2. *Definitions*

In this Proclamation unless the context otherwise requires:

1. "Society" means a cooperative society established and registered in accordance with this Proclamation and it shall in particular include the following:

    (a) Agricultural Cooperative Societies;

    (b) Housing Cooperative Societies;

(c) Industrial and Artisans Producers' Cooperative Societies;

(d) Consumers Cooperative Societies;

(e) Savings and credit Cooperative Societies;

(f) Fishery Cooperative Societies;

(g) Mining Cooperative Societies.

2. *"Cooperative Society"* means a society established by individuals on voluntary basis to collectively solve their economic and social problems and to democratically manage same;

3. *"Member"* mean any physical person, or society established under this proclamation, which is registered after fulfilling his membership obligations.

4. *"General Assembly"* mean a meeting of members of the Primary Cooperative society or representatives of societies above primary level.

5. *"Special resolution"* means a resolution passed by a two third majority of the members to be binding on all members;

6. *"Management Committee"* means a body elected and empowered by the General Assembly with the responsibility to manage the activities of the society;

7. *"Appropriate Authority"* means an organ established at federal level, or a bureau or an organ established for the same purpose at Regional or city Administration level, to organize and register cooperative societies and to give training, conduct research and provide other technical assistances to cooperative societies.

8. *"Person"* means a natural or juridical person.

3. ***Where the provisions of the Proclamation are set out in the masculine gender they apply equally to the feminine gender.***

4. *Objectives of the Society*

The society to be established under this proclamation shall have one or more of the following objectives:

1. To solve problems collectively which members cannot individually achieve;
2. To achieve a better result by coordinating their knowledge, wealth and labour;
3. To promote self-reliance among members;

4. To collectively protect, withstand and solve economic problems;
5. To improve the living standards of members by reducing production and service costs by providing input or service at a minimum cost or by finding a better price to their products or services;
6. To expand the mechanism by which technical knowledge could be put in to practice;
7. To develop and promote savings and credit services;
8. To minimize and reduce the individual impact of risks and uncertainties;
9. To develop the social and economic culture of the members through education and training.

5. *Guiding Principles of Co-operative Societies*

1. Co-operative societies are voluntary organizations open to all persons able to use their services and willing to accept the responsibilities of membership without gender, social, racial, political or religious discrimination.
2. Co-operative societies are democratic organizations controlled by their members who actively participate in setting their policies and making decisions. Every member has equal voting rights and accordingly one member shall have one vote.
3. Members shall receive dividends from profit according to their shares and contribution after deducting and setting aside an amount necessary for reserve and social services.
4. Co-operative societies are autonomous self-help organizations controlled by their members. If they enter into agreement with other organizations, including governments or raise capital from external sources, shall do so on terms that ensure democratic control by their members and maintain their autonomy.
5. Co-operative societies provide education and training to their members, elected representatives, managers and employees so as to enable them to contribute effectively to the development of their societies. They inform the general public, particularly youth about the nature and benefit of societies.
6. Co-operative societies serve their members most effectively and strengthen the societies movement by working together through local, national, regional and international structures.

7. Co-operative societies work for the sustainable development of their communities through policies approved by their members.

Part Two: Formation and Registration of Co-operative Societies

6. Formation of Co-operative Societies

1. Co-operative societies may, according to their nature, be established at different levels from primary up to the federal level.
2. A primary society shall be established by persons who live or work within a given area.
3. The number of members in a primary society to be established shall not be less than ten.
4. Notwithstanding sub-article (2) of this Article, the appropriate authority may specify in the directive, the minimum number of members that could make a society economically feasible.
5. A society may sell some of its shares to persons outside its area when the society faces shortage of capital.

7. *Types of Societies*

1. A society may engage in either production or service rendering activities or in both.
2. The field of activities to be engaged in by any society shall be determined by the by-laws of the society.

8. *Name of a Society*

1. Any society shall have its own name.
2. The words "Cooperative Society and Limited Liability" shall appear in the name of every society.
3. A name or distinguishing mark registered by one society shall not be used by any other society.
4. The name of every society shall be written boldly and be put at every place where the society's activities are performed. It should also be written or sealed on every notices letters, other specifications and documents which are signed on behalf of the society.

9. *Registration of a Co-operative Society*

1. Any society shall be registered by the appropriate authority.
2. Any society, when established, shall submit an application for registration together with the following particulars to the appropriate authority:

(a) minutes of the founders meeting;

(b) the by-laws of the society in three copies;

(c) names, address and signature of the members;

(d) name, address and signature of the members of the management committee of the society;

(e) a detailed description which proves that the registered members of the society have met the requirements for membership in accordance with the provisions of this Proclamation and the by-laws of the society;

(f) name, address and signature of members of the societies above primary level;

(g) plan of the society;

(h) documents showing that the amount of capital of the society and the capital has been collected and deposited in a bank account, if there is no bank in the area, that it has been deposited in a place where the appropriate authority has designated;

(i) the description of the land on which the society operates;

(j) other particulars that may be specified in the regulations or directives issued for the implementation of this Proclamation.

3. The appropriate authority shall register a society and issue a certificate of registration within 15 days when it is satisfied that the application for registration submitted to it has fulfilled the requirements for registration.

4. When the appropriate authority rejects the application for the registration of a society, it shall give a written explanation to the representatives of the society within 15 days. The representatives may appeal to the high court which has jurisdiction on the decision of the appropriate authority.

5. The certificate of registration issued to a society pursuant to Sub-Article (3) of this Article is an evidence to prove that a society is registered in accordance with this Proclamation.

10. *Juridical Personality and Responsibility*

1. Any society registered in pursuance of Article 9 of this Proclamation shall have juridical personality as of the date of its registration.

2. Any society shall not be liable beyond its total asset. It has limited liability.

11. *By-laws of Society*

1. Every society shall have its own by-laws.
2. The contents of the by-laws shall include the following particulars:
   - (a) name and address of the society;
   - (b) objectives and activities of the society;
   - (c) working place (area) of the society;
   - (d) requirements necessary for membership of the society;
   - (e) the rights and duties of the members of the society;
   - (f) the powers, responsibilities, and duties of management bodies;
   - (g) conditions for withdrawal and dismissal from membership;
   - (h) conditions for re-election, appointment, term of office and suspension or dismissal of the members of the management committee or other management bodies;
   - (i) conditions for calling of meeting and voting of the society;
   - (j) allocation and distribution of profit;
   - (k) auditing;
   - (l) employment of workers;
   - (m) other particulars not contrary to this Proclamation.
3. By-laws of a society may be amended by the special resolution of the general assembly. However, the amendment of the by-laws of the society shall be effective on the date of its submission to and registration by the appropriate authority.
4. Where the society decides on the amendment of its by-laws three copies of the amendment and the special resolution of the society made in accordance with this Proclamation shall be submitted to the appropriate authority within 30 days from the date of the decision.
5. The appropriate authority shall register the amendment and give evidence or its registration to the society where it is satisfied that the amendment of the by-laws was made in accordance with this Proclamation and regulations issued for the implementation of this Proclamation.

12. *Amalgamation and Division of Societies*

1. Without prejudice to Article 6(3) and (4) of this Proclamation, the general assembly of a society through a special resolution may form a new society:

(a) by dividing itself into two or more societies; or

(b) by amalgamating itself with one or more societies.

2. The special resolution on the amalgamation or division of the society shall be effective on the date of its registration by the appropriate authority upon verifying that:

(a) the members and creditors of the society fully agree to the amalgamation or division; or

(b) the members and creditors that do not agree have been paid off or their payment is guaranteed.

3. The previous registration of societies shall be cancelled from the register as soon as the newly formed society by amalgamation or by division are registered.

4. The rights and duties of societies which have lost their identities by amalgamation shall be transferred to the newly formed society.

5. The rights and duties of a society which has lost its identity by division shall be transferred to the newly formed societies as specified in sub-article (2) of this Article.

Part Three: The Rights and Duties of Members of a Society

Tips for you

Type or kinds of member in cooperatives

Active member means the member who takes active part in the management and business affairs of the cooperative.

Associate member means a member who holds jointly a share of a cooperative with others, but whose name does not stand first in the share certificate.

In-active member means a member who simply holds shares of the cooperative, but does not take part in the business affairs and management of the cooperative.

Member cooperative means a primary or secondary cooperative which is in need of and is able to use the core services of a secondary cooperative, and which is admitted as a member of that secondary cooperative, in accordance with the provisions of law and the bylaws of that secondary cooperative.

Nominal member means a person admitted to membership after registration in accordance with the bylaws.

Prospective member means a person who needs the core services being rendered by a cooperative and is eligible to be a member of that cooperative, but is not yet admitted as its member.

Sympathizer member means a person who sympathies with the aims and objects of the cooperative and admitted as a member by the cooperative.

13. *Requirements Necessary for Membership of a Society*

Any individual may become a member of a society where:

1. he has attained the age of 14 if it is a primary society;
2. he is able to pay the share capital and registration fee required by the society;
3. he is willing to implement its obligation and observe the objectives and by-laws of the society;
4. he fulfills the other requirements which may be specified in the regulations and directives issued for the implementation of this Proclamation;
5. it is registered with the appropriate authority if it is a society above the primary society.

Case 1:

Principle of Open Membership

Restriction of membership to members of Roman Catholics under by-law is against the cooperative principle of open membership

A registered cooperative society under the law sought to exclude persons other than Roman Catholics from its membership. The Government came to the conclusion that to permit the said cooperative society to follow the rule of exclusion as provided in the bylaws is violation of the basic and fundamental cooperative principle of 'open membership'. The society raised objection to the above action of Government, hence, filed a case before High Court of Bombay (India). The said High Court, in this context, observed that restriction in bylaws of cooperative society imposing conditions or prescription of qualifications restricting membership to a particular religion or group is violative of the principle of open membership for the following reason:

One of the basic and fundamental principles underlying the cooperative movement is the principles of open membership. It necessarily meant that the cooperative society without sufficient reason or cause cannot refuse admission to membership to any person duly qualified otherwise under the law, rules and bylaws. As per law, any individual who is competent to contract under law is qualified to seek membership in a cooperative society. The membership in a cooperative society, therefore, is available to all without any discrimination i.e., social, political or religion, etc. whatsoever.

14. *Rights and Duties of Members*

1. Any member of a society shall have the following rights:
   (a) to obtain services and benefits according to his participation in the society;
   (b) to participate in the meetings of the society and to vote;
   (c) to elect and be elected;
   (d) to withdraw from the society on his request with payment of benefits.
2. Any member of a society shall have the following duties:
   (a) to respect the by-laws, directives and decisions of the society;
   (b) to perform those activities which ought to be performed in accordance with the by-laws and directives of the society ;
   (c) to pay for share of capital and registration fee;
   (d) to protect the common property of the society.

15. *Dismissal from Membership*

1. Any member of a society may leave the society on his own initiative.
2. Any member of a society may leave the society when it is decided by the General Assembly to dismiss him from the society because of committing repeated faults.

Case 2: Procedure to be followed for Expulsion of Members

As per law and rules, the resolution for expulsion of member has to be passed by a majority of not less than 3/4 of the members present and entitled to vote at the General Assembly held for the purpose of expelling members for acts which are detrimental to the interest or proper working of the cooperative society. The law required that before a resolution for expelling a member is passed, the member concerned must be given an opportunity of representing his case to the General Assembly. Second, the resolution so passed will become effective only when it is approved by the appropriate authority.

The matter came up before Bombay High Court (India) for decision while disposing this application. The High Court observed that the notice of expulsion must call upon the member concerned to show cause notice or reason top the General Assembly against such proposed expulsion. This procedure required is neither mechanical nor an empty formality. The material on the basis of which the show cause notice is to be issued and reply given by the member has to be considered by General Assembly before arriving at a decision of expulsion. Such decision has to arrive by a majority of 3/4 of the members entitled to vote and was present. Finally, the appropriate authority is empowered to hold an enquiry before according approval on the said resolution passed by the General Assembly. The issuance of show cause notice for expulsion of a member in a cyclostyled form and non-consideration of the same by General Assembly amounted to failure to follow the procedure required under law. Further, the failure to maintain the register for recording of the voting by members for expulsion confirmed the irregularities carried out, Hon'ble High Court observed. The court also held that stay of election proceedings in the above mentioned circumstances is just and proper.

3. The rights of any dismissed member shall be respected in accordance with the by-laws of the society.
4. Without prejudice to the provisions of Article 13 hereof, any dismissed person may reapply for membership. However a member dismissed in accordance with sub-article (2) of this Article may become a member of the society only if he obtains the approval of the General Assembly.

16. *Payment of Shares*

1. The capital which enables the society to expand its work activities shall be obtained from paid up shares of each member in accordance of the decision of the General Assembly.
2. The society may sell additional shares if it is found necessary to promote the financial capacity of the society subject to the decision of the General Assembly.
3. No member shall hold more than 10 per cent of the total paid up share capital of such society.

17. *Register of Members*

Every society shall keep a register wherein shall be entered:

1. the name, address, occupation, age and sex of each member;
2. the date on which he became a member or ceased to be a member;
3. the amount of shares held and the registration fee paid, by each member;
4. the name and address of the heir of the member;
5. any other particulars that may be specified in the by-laws.

18. *Voting*

1. Every member shall, regardless of the number of shares he has, have only one vote at the meeting of the society.

2. Every member in a primary society shall personally be present at the meeting of the society to cast a vote.

3. Members of a society above primary level shall cast a vote through their representatives.

19. *Transfer of Share or Benefit*

1. No transfer by a member of his share or benefit in a society shall be valid unless:

   (a) the member has held such share or benefit for at least one year before he transfers;

   (b) the transfer is approved by the management committee.

2. On the death of a member of a primary society, his share or benefit shall be transferred to one of his heirs designated as such in the register of society or failing such designation to his legal heir at law, and where such heir is a member or is willing to be a member.

3. Where such heir is not a member and does not wish to become or is not admitted as a member, he shall be paid the value of the share or benefit of the deceased member.

4. If the shares or benefit to be transferred to a member under sub-article (2) of this Article are found to be beyond the limitation prescribed in sub-article (3) of Article 16 hereof, the member shall be paid the difference in cash.

5. The transfer or payment concluded in pursuance of sub-article (2) of this Article shall not be reversed due to the claims caused by third parties on the society.

Part Four: Management Bodies

20. *Supreme Organ of a Society*

The supreme organ of any society shall be the General Assembly.

21. *Powers and Duties of the General Assembly*

The General Assembly of a socicty shall:

1. pass decisions after evaluating the general activities of the societies;
2. approve and amend the by-laws and internal regulations of the society;
3. elect and dismiss the members of the management committee, control committee and when necessary the members of other sub-committees;

4. determine the amount of shares of the society;
5. decide on how the annual net profit of the society is distributed;
6. give decision on the audit report;
7. hear work reports and give proper decision;
8. decide that a society either be amalgamated with another society or be divided in pursuance of this proclamation;
9. approve the annual work plan and budget;
10. decide any issue submitted by the management committee and other committees.

22. *Calling of General Assembly*

1. The General Assembly shall meet at least once in a year.
2. If the Management Committee or one-third of the members of the General Assembly require a meeting to be called, an emergency meeting may be held by giving 15 days prior notice.
3. Where the management committee fails to call an emergency General Assembly in accordance with sub-article (2) of this Article such meeting shall be called by the appropriate authority and shall in such case be deemed to have been called by the Management committee.

23. *Management Committee*

1. Every society shall have a Management Committee which is accountable to the General Assembly and whose members and manner of election to be determined in the by-laws of the society.
2. The term of office of the Management Committee shall be three years.
3. Members of the Management Committee shall not be elected for more than two consecutive terms. They may be dismissed at any time by the General Assembly.
4. When members of the Management Committee leave their office for whatever reasons, they have the obligation to submit for inspection the activities they performed during their term of office.

24. *Powers and Duties of the Management Committee*

The powers and duties of the Management Committee shall be determined in pursuance of the by-laws and in particular shall include the following:

1. maintain the minutes of a meeting in writing;
2. maintain the documents and books of accounts of the society;
3. prepare the annual work programme and budget of the society; implements the same upon approval;
4. call the General Assembly in accordance with the by-laws of the society;
5. execute such other decisions given by the General Assembly;
6. submit reports to the General Assembly on the activities of the society.

25. *Control Committee*

1. Every society shall have a control committee which is accountable to the General Assembly and the number of which shall be specified by the by-laws of the society.
2. The term of office of members of the committee shall be three years. No member of the control committee shall be elected for more than two consecutive terms. They may, while in term of office, be dismissed by the General Assembly.

26. *Powers and Duties of the Control Committee*

The Control Committee:

1. follows up that the Management Committee is carrying out its responsibilities properly;
2. follows up that the funds and property of the society is properly utilized;
3. controls that the various activities of the society are carried out pursuant to the by-laws and internal regulations of the society;
4. performs other duties given by the general assembly.

27. *Other Sub-Committees*

Other sub-committees may be established pursuant to the by-laws of the society.

Part Five: Special Privileges of Society

28. *Priority of Claims by Society*

Notwithstanding any provision to the contrary in any law, debts owed to the society by a member shall take precedence over all other debts, except the debt owed to the Government.

29. *Set-off in respect of Share or Benefit of Members*

The shares or benefits of any member may be set-off for debts due to the society from such a member.

30. *Share or Benefit not Liable to Attachment or Sale*

Except as provided in Article 29 hereof, the share or benefit of a member in the society shall not be liable to attachment or sale.

31. *Government Assistance*

1. Without prejudice to incentives permitted under investment laws and other laws, Societies which are organized and registered under this Proclamation shall be entitled to the following:
   (a) to be exempted from income tax; provided however, members shall pay income tax on their dividends;
   (b) to acquire land as determined by a Region or a City accountable to the Federal Government;
   (c) to receive other assistance from the Federal Government or Regional Government or City Administration accountable to the Federal Government.
2. An institute responsible for promoting cooperative movement, rendering man-power training and conducting studies and research shall be established.

Part Six: Asset and Funds of Societies

32. *Indivisibility of Asset and Fund of Society not Divisible*

Except as otherwise prescribed under Articles 33(2) and 44 of this Proclamation, the asset and fund of a society shall not be divided for the members or any other party.

33. *Allocation of Net Profit*

1. The society shall deduct 30 per cent of the net profit obtained and allocated for the following purposes in accordance with the terms and conditions set forth in the by-laws and plan issued from time to time by the society:
   (a) for reserve;
   (b) for the expansion of work;
   (c) for social services.
2. After the amount prescribed in sub-article (1) is deducted the remaining net profit shall be divided among the members; the division shall be made on the basis of the shares the members have in the society and on the amount of goods offered for the sale to the society or goods purchased from the society by members of the society.

34. *Restrictions on Borrowings*

1. A society shall receive loans from its members or other organizations to such extent and on such conditions as may be specified in the by-laws of the society.

2. Interest on loans received from its members shall not exceed the current interest rate of a bank.

35. *Restrictions on Loans*

A society shall not extend loans other than to its members or a society established under this Proclamation.

Part Seven: Audit and Inspection

36. *Audit*

1. The appropriate authority shall audit or causes to be audited by a person assigned by it, the accounts of any society at least once in a year.

2. The audit conducted pursuant to sub-article (1) of this Article shall include the examination and verification of overdue debts, if any, and cash balance, securities and assets, and liabilities.

3. The audit report shall be submitted to the General Assembly.

37. *Inspection*

1. The appropriate authority may make or cause to be made by such person to be assigned by it an inspection to the organization, work execution, documents and financial condition of a society.

2. Without prejudice to sub-article (1) of this Article, inspection may be made when:

   (a) a majority of the members of the executive committee request;

   (b) not less than one-third of the total number of members of the society request.

38. *Keeping Audit and Inspection Results*

Audit and Inspection results conducted pursuant to Articles 36 and 37 of this Proclamation shall be kept in the office of the authority and the society, open and easily accessible to everyone.

39. *Actions to be taken for Losses of Property or Fund of the Society*

1. The auditor or inspector shall make a report to the Management Committee or the General Assembly or the appropriate authority, as the case may be, where the person who is or was entrusted with

the management of the society or who is or has been an officer or an employee of the society, and who, in the course of an audit or inspection has been found to have committed the following acts:

(a) had made any payment contrary to this Proclamation, the regulations or the by-laws;

(b) had caused any damages to the assets of the society by breach of trust or willfully or negligently;

(c) has misappropriated the properties of the society.

2. The appropriate authority who received the report pursuant to sub-article (1) of this Article shall give the person concerned an opportunity to present his defense within fifteen days.

3. After fulfillment of the above mentioned conditions, the appropriate authority shall ask the person who has been found responsible for misappropriation of the fund or property of the society to return or pay the same with interest including compensation and damages. Where the person concerned is not willing to do so, the authority shall take the appropriate legal measure.

Part Eight: Dissolution and Winding-up of Societies

40. *Dissolution of a Society*

A Society shall be dissolved on the following grounds:

1. Where a special resolution for its dissolution is given by the members; or

2. Without prejudice to Article 6 (4) hereof, where the number of members of a primary society falls below ten.

3. Without prejudice to sub-articles (1) and (2) of this Article, a society the dissolution of which is decided shall notify the same to the appropriate authority within seven days from the decision for its dissolution.

41. *Liquidator*

1. Where the dissolution of a society has been decided upon pursuant to Article 40 of this Proclamation, the appropriate authority may, assign a liquidator. It may, if necessary, determine that his remuneration be paid out of the accounts of the society.

2. The liquidator shall receive records, documents and properties of the society as soon as he is assigned. He shall also take the necessary measures to protect the properties and rights, records and documents of the society from damages.

42. *Powers and Duties of the Liquidator*

1. The liquidator shall have all the necessary powers to complete the winding up proceedings. He shall in particular perform the following in order to carry out his duties properly:
   (a) investigate all claims against the society and decide on priority of payment among them;
   (b) collect the assets of the society;
   (c) distribute the assets in accordance with the plan of liquidation approved by the general meeting of the society;
   (d) carry on the work activities of the society in so far as may be necessary for the proper liquidation of the affairs of the society;
   (e) represent the society in legal proceedings;
   (f) call meetings of the members as may be necessary for the proper conduct of the liquidation.
2. The liquidator shall issue notice in a newspaper, before the distribution of the property of the society takes place in accordance with sub-article (1) (c) of this Article, that the society is to be dissolved. It shall proceed with the distribution where no claim is presented within two months from the date of such notice. No claimant shall have a right after the expiration of such limitation.
3. Upon completion of the winding up proceedings the liquidator shall prepare and submit a report to the appropriate authority, he shall deposit the records and documents of the society in such places as the appropriate authority may direct.

43. *Calling on Creditors*

1. Creditors shall be paid on the basis of a balance sheet prepared by the liquidator upon the commencement of his assignment.
2. Creditors shall be informed of the dissolution of the society and required to file their claims with supporting documents.
3. Creditors appearing in the society's records or who are otherwise known shall be notified directly by registered letter. Notice to other creditors shall be given by notice, published in two successive monthly issues of a newspaper, and also in the form laid down in the by-laws of the society.

44. *Protection of Creditors*

1. Until the creditors of the society have been paid or amounts required for payment be deposited, the liquidators may not distribute any part of assets among the members.

2. Where known creditors have failed to present their supporting documents, the amounts owing to them shall be deposited according to the decision of the court.
3. Sums shall be set aside to meet the claims in respect of undertakings of the society which are not completed or which are under liquidation unless the creditors are guaranteed or distribution of assets is postponed until such undertakings are completed.
4. After the payment of claims have been completed or verified that sufficient deposit for payment has been made, the liquidators may distribute the assets of the society among the members based on the amount due to them.

45. *Cancellation of a Society from the Register*

When the winding-up proceedings are completed the certificate of registration shall be returned to the appropriate authority who shall cancel the registration of the society, and the society shall, upon the date of such cancellation, cease to exist.

Part Nine: Settlement of Disputes

46. *Conciliation*

The disputes provided under Article 48 of this proclamation shall be heard by a third party appointed by the disputing parties before they are referred to the arbitrators.

47. *Arbitration*

1. When the disputes, provided under Article 49 regarding cooperative societies are not settled by conciliation they shall be referred to arbitration.
2. The arbitration shall consist of three persons of high reputation and impartiality.
3. The arbitrators shall conduct their hearing and fulfill any of their duties in accordance with the Civil Procedure Code.

48. *Appointment of the Arbitrators*

1. Each party to the dispute shall appoint one arbitrator. The third arbitrator, who shall be the chairperson, shall be appointed by both parties.
2. The appropriate authority shall appoint the chairperson arbitrator when the parties fail to reach an agreement.

49. *Disputes to be Referred to Arbitration*

The arbitrators shall have the power to hear disputes not settled by conciliation regarding the organization, management, or operations of a society which arises between:

1. members or former members and members or representatives of former members or persons claiming in the name of deceased members; or
2. members, former members or members or representatives of former members or heirs of deceased members and any officer, representative of the management committee or employee of the society; or
3. the society or the management committee and any former management committee, any officer, agent or employee, or any former officer, agent or employee or the nominee heirs or representatives or representatives of deceased former members or employees; or
4. the society and any other society.

50. *Civil Court Powers of Arbitrators*

The Arbitrators shall have the same power, with regard to the cases provided under Article 49 of this Proclamation, as a civil court for the summoning of witnesses, production of evidence, the issuing of orders or the taking of any legal measures.

51. *Execution*

Any decision, order or award made under this Proclamation shall be taken as though made by a civil court, and, where appropriate, the courts shall have jurisdiction to order the enforcement of any such decision, order or award.

52. *Power of Courts*

Appeals on the decisions given by the Arbitrators under Article 47 of this Proclamation may, as the case may be, be instituted in Federal High Court, or the Regional State High court or the Federal High Court of a city accountable to the Federal Government where the society is situated.

Part Ten: Miscellaneous Provisions

53. *Address of a Society*

Any society shall have an address registered pursuant to Article 9 of this Proclamation. All services of process, notices and other communications shall be sent in such address. The society shall inform the appropriate authority of any change in such address within thirty days.

54. *Supplying Information*

Every society shall have the obligation to transmit information to the appropriate authority about the activities it performs.

55. *Establishment of a Federal Organ*

A Federal Organ responsible for organizing and registering Apex organizations and for rendering training, conducting research and other technical support to societies may be established by law.

56. *Depositing of this Proclamation, Regulations and the By-laws*

Every society shall deposit at its address copies of this Proclamation, the Regulations and the By-laws, to be accessible free of charge.

57. *Repealed and Inapplicable Laws*

1. The Cooperative Societies Proclamation No. 138/1978 and the Agricultural Cooperatives Societies Proclamation No. 85/1995 are hereby repealed.
2. No law, regulation or directive in so far as it is inconsistent with this Proclamation have force or effect in respect of matters provided for by this Proclamation.

58. *Transitory Provisions*

1. The cooperative societies which have been established and operating in accordance with Proclamation No. 138/1978 shall be reorganized under this Proclamation.
2. The cooperative societies which have been established and operating in accordance with Proclamation No. 85/1995 shall be deemed to have been established under this Proclamation and shall continue to carry out their functions in accordance with this Proclamation.
3. The societies indicated in sub-article (1) of this Article shall continue their operations holding their previous juridical personalities until they are reorganized and registered by the appropriate authority.
4. The appropriate authority shall facilitate the conditions necessary for the reorganization of the societies in accordance with sub-article (1) of this Article.

59. *Issuance of Implementing Legislation*

The Council of Ministers of the Federal Government or the appropriate organ of a Region or City accountable to the Federal Government may issue legislation for the proper implementation of this Proclamation.

60. *Effective Date*

This Proclamation shall come into force on the 29th day of December 1998, done at Addis Ababa, this 29th day of December, 1998.

Summary

- The Cooperative Societies Proclamation No. 147/1998 was issued by the transitional government by taking in to account the latest developments and prospects of cooperative movement.
- Co-operative societies may, according to their nature, be established at different levels from primary up to the federal level.
- A primary society shall be established by persons who live or work within a given area.
- The number of members in a primary society to be established shall not be less than ten.
- Any society shall be registered by the appropriate authority.
- Any society, when established, shall submit an application for registration together with all the particulars to the appropriate authority.
- Amalgamation and division of societies can be done under this proclamation by passing special resolution in the general assembly.
- Members do have all rights and expected to perform duties as prescribed in the proclamation.
- Withdrawal/dismissal of membership is possible under this proclamation.
- As for management bodies, provisions were made on powers and duties of General Assembly, Board of Management, and Controlling Committee.
- Societies registered under this proclamation will be conferred upon with certain special privileges and government assistance.
- Provisions were made on assets and funds of societies, audit and inspection, dissolution of cooperative societies, settlement of disputes and on miscellaneous aspects.

Self-Learning Activity

1. What type of cooperative societies could be formed under the Proclamation of 1998?
2. What are the contents of by-laws as prescribed in the Proclamation of 1998?
3. What do you mean by prospective member?
4. What are the requirements necessary for membership of a cooperative society as per the Proclamation of 1998?
5. Discuss the provisions relating to dismissal from membership as per the Proclamation of 1998?
6. Discuss the provisions on government assistance to cooperatives as per the Proclamation of 1998?

19 Proclamation No. 274 of 2002 to Establish Cooperatives' Commission

Background

Whereas, it has become necessary to enable the rural and urban working people to solve the economic and social problems they face by themselves depending on local resources and become self-reliant by being organized in cooperatives societies different in type and standard.

Whereas, it has become imperative to establish an autonomous organ responsible for registering and supporting cooperative societies organized at federal level, conducting research, rendering training and other technical support to achieve the above mentioned objective.

Now, therefore, in accordance with Article 55(1) of the Constitution of the Federal Democratic Republic of Ethiopia and Article 55 of the Cooperatives Societies Proclamation No. 147/1998, it is hereby proclaimed as follows:

Provisions of establishment of Cooperative Commission

1. *Short Title*

This Proclamation may be cited as the "Cooperatives' Commission Establishment Proclamation No. 274/2002.

2. *Establishment*

The Cooperatives' Commission (hereinafter referred to as "the Commission"), is hereby established as an autonomous Federal Government Organ.

The Commission shall be accountable to the Ministry of Rural Development.

3. *Head Office*

The Head Office of the Commission shall be in Addis Ababa.

4. *Objective of the Commission*

The objective of the Commission is to enable rural and urban working people to solve the economic and social problem they face by themselves and become self-reliant by being organized in cooperatives different in type and standard depending on the local resources.

5. *Powers and Duties of the Commission*

The Commission shall have the powers and duties to:

1. Formulate policies and prepare draft laws suitable for the activities and development of cooperative societies, and submit the same to the government and follow-up their implementation.
2. Encourage that the organization of cooperative societies be in accordance with Cooperatives' Proclamation No. 147/98 and in line with the international principles of cooperatives' organization.
3. Direct and supervise cooperatives' training institute to be set up at federal level.
4. Undertake research and study to promote traditional and local self-help associations to modern cooperative societies, it shall make known and disseminate the results of the study, and follows up the implementation thereof.
5. Make that the values, principles, organization, and benefits of the cooperatives be further known by the society and educational establishments.
6. Organize, register, and issue licenses of the legal personality to, the cooperative societies to be organized at federal level, and the cooperatives societies to be established by:
   - Two or more primary societies found in different regions, and unable to be organized at regional level due to their peculiar nature.
   - Regional cooperative societies found in two or more regions.
   - The union cooperative societies organized pursuant to (a) and (b) of this sub-article, or by the union of different cooperative societies organized pursuant to (b) of this sub-article.
7. Audit and inspect the accounts of cooperative societies to be set up at federal level and assign a liquidator, cancel them from its record when dissolved; and it shall provide uniform standards of accounting and audit for cooperative societies throughout the country.

8. Promote the product of the cooperative societies so that they may find market, and facilitate conditions in order to bring consumers and producers to direct communication in the home market.
9. Provide professional and technical support to process agricultural products of the cooperative societies to industrial products so that they will have better added-value, and to develop artisans' products.
10. Provide professional assistance to create the organization of cooperatives based on the culture and experiences of pastoralists and which enables them to improve their living conditions.
11. Facilitate, in cooperation with regions as may be necessary, means to provide support for societies by studying and preparing projects suitable for the development of cooperative societies.
12. Facilitate conditions to enable the cooperative societies in different regions to exchange their products and information about the market, and to share experiences with one another.
13. Provide technical and professional assistance for the bureaus and cooperative societies to be set up in the regions.
14. Establish relationship with concerned local and international organizations in order to expedite the progress and the activities of the cooperative societies.
15. Formulate and distribute model by-laws of societies which may vary according to the type and level of societies.
16. Submit reports on its performances to the concerned government organ.
17. Own property, enter into contracts, sue and be sued in its own name.
18. Carry out other duties helpful for the implementation of its objectives.

6. *Organization of the Commission*

The Commission shall have:

1. A Commissioner and a Deputy Commissioner to be appointed by the government; and
2. The necessary staff.

7. *Powers and Duties of the Commissioner*

1. The Commissioner is the Chief Executive of the Commission and, shall direct and administer the activities of the Commission.

2. Without prejudice to sub-article (1) of the Article, the Commissioner shall:
   (a) Discharge the powers and duties stated in Article 5 herein.
   (b) Employ and administer the staff of the Commission pursuant to the Federal Civil Service Laws.
   (c) Draw up work programmes and budget; and implement the same upon approval.
   (d) Effect expenditures in accordance with approved work programmes and budget of the commission.
   (e) Represent the Commission in all its dealings with third parties.
   (f) Present reports on the activities of the Commission.
3. The Commissioner may delegate part of his powers and duties to other officials and employees of the Commission to the extent necessary for the efficiency of the Commission.

8. *The Deputy Commissioner*
   4. He shall act on behalf of the Commissioner in his absence.
   5. He shall carry out other activities to be entrusted to him by the Commissioner.

9. *Budget*

The income of the Commission shall be drawn from the following sources:

(a) The budget allocated by the Federal Government.

(b) Aid received from domestic and foreign donors and other resources.

10. *Books of Accounts*
    1. The Commission shall keep complete and accurate books of accounts.
    2. The books of accounts and financial documents of the commission shall be audited annually by the Auditor General or by auditors assigned by him.

11. *Inapplicable Laws*

Any law inconsistent with this Proclamation shall not be applicable to matters provided for herein.

12. *Transfer of Rights and Obligations*

All rights and obligations relating to the matters provided for by this Proclamation and given to other organs are hereby transferred to the Commission.

13. *Effective Date*

This Proclamation shall enter into force as of the 14th day of May, 2002, done at Addis Ababa, this 14th day of May, 2002.

Summary

- In accordance with Article 55 (1) of the Constitution of the Federal Democratic Republic of Ethiopia and Article 55 of the Cooperatives Societies Proclamation No. 147/1998, a proclamation was issued in the year 2002 to establish Cooperative Commission at the national level.
- The objective of the Commission is to enable rural and urban working people to solve the economic and social problem they face by themselves and become self-reliant by being organized in cooperatives different in type and standard depending on the local resources.
- The commission has powers and duties to be performed in the fields of cooperative education, extension, training and research in order to disseminate the values and philosophies of cooperatives in the country.

Self-Learning Activity

1. What are the powers and duties of the commissioner?
2. State any four powers and duties of cooperative commission?

20 Cooperative Societies (Amendment) Proclamation No. 402 of 2004

Background

Whereas, it is necessary to amend cooperative societies proclamation No. 147/1998; now, therefore, in accordance with Article 55(1) of the Constitution of the Federal Democratic Republic of Ethiopia, it is hereby proclaimed as follows:

Provisions

1. *Short Title*

This Proclamation may be cited as "Cooperative Societies (Amendment) Proclamation No. 402/2004."

2. *Amendments*

Cooperative Societies Proclamation No. 147/1998 shall be amended as follows:

1. *The following new sub-articles (6), (7), (8) and (9) are added after sub-articles 5 of Article 9:*

   6. Any cooperative society which has been legally registered pursuant to sub-article 3 of this Article shall engage in any business as of the date of registration without the necessity of securing additional trade license.

   7. Where the appropriate authority ensures that requirements indicated under sub-article 2(a)-(g) are met, it shall grant temporary certificate which may serve not more than a year and shall cause the rest requirements to be observed within a specified period of time.

   8. Where any society is found operating out of the objectives for which it is established, it may be suspended by the appropriate authority from carrying out activities permitted by this law.

9. Where the general assembly of a society suspended pursuant to sub- article 8 of this Article submits its request to reverse the decision for suspension and where the appropriate authority found the request appropriate, it may reverse the decision for suspension. Where the appropriate authority did not reverse the suspension it shall give a written explanation to the General Assembly. The General Assembly may appeal to the higher court which has jurisdiction on the decision made by the appropriate Authority."

2. *Articles 16(1)-(3) is hereby deleted and replaced by the following new "Article16: Payment of shares*

   1. Any cooperative society shall, after securing the decision of the General Assembly, sell shares that shall have equal number and par value with the view to enable the society to obtain capital necessary.

   2. Any cooperative society shall collect, upon its formation from the members at least 1/5 of the amount of the share that the General Assembly has decided to be sold. And it shall sell the rest of the shares within four years as of the time of its establishment.

   3. Where the need for additional capital is arose, upon completion of the sale of shares in accordance with the decision of the General Assembly, the General Assembly may decide once again for the sell of additional shares in accordance with sub-article 1 of this Article.

   4. The share that the society sells may be sold either in cash or in kind. Shares paid in kind shall be determined by the by-law of the society.

   5. Any member may not hold more than 10 per cent of shares out of those that the General Assembly decides to be sold.

   6. A society, which faces shortage of capital, may sell certain shares to a person who is not a member of the society without contradicting the principle of the society.

   7. Particulars as regards to manner of sale of shares to a person who is not member to the society shall be determined by the by-law of the society."

3. *The following new sub-articles (3) (4) are added after sub-article (2) of Article 31.*

   3. The council of ministers may make any society free from any court fees that is payable in connection with dispute entertained by courts.

4. Any right emanated from a contract concluded by the society involving its properties shall be barred by statute of limitation after 20 years".

4. *Article 33(1) and (2) are deleted and replaced by the following new Article 33*

   1. Any cooperative society shall deduct 30 per cent of the net profit and allocate for the reserve fund. The amount allocated for the reserve fund shall not exceed 30 per cent of the capital of the society and it shall be deposited in the saving account of the society.

   2. The distribution of the remaining net profit shall be determined by the General Assembly.

   3. Any member who has received net profit as per sub-article 2 of this Article can buy an additional share."

5. *Sub 2 of Article 34 is deleted.*

6. *The following new sub-article (3) and (4) are added after sub-articles (2) of Article 40.*

   3. Where the court decides for its dissolution.

   4. Where the auditing reveals that it is bankrupt and when the appropriate authority ensures that causes the dissolution and the General Assembly decides.

7. *Article 40(3) shall become Article 40(5).*

8. *Article 46 is deleted and replaced by the following new Article.*

   "46 Settling disputes through conciliation

   1. Disputes indicated under Article 49 may be settled through reconciliation of parties elected by disputants before they are submitted to arbitration.

   2. Each party shall elect reconciliation; the chairperson of the reconciliation shall be elected in accordance with the agreement of the two parties.

   3. Where the two parties failed to reach at agreement to elect the chairperson of the reconciliation, the chairperson shall be elected by the appropriate authority".

9. *Article 58(2) is deleted and replaced by the following new Article 58(2)*

   "2. Agricultural cooperative societies, which were established pursuant to Proclamation No. 85/1994 and which are still operating shall be registered once again in accordance with this Proclamation".

10. *The following new Article added as Article 59*

"59. Obligation to cooperate

Any concerned organ shall have the obligation to cooperate on matters provided in this Proclamation."

11. *Article 59 shall become Article 60*

12. *Article 61 Effective Date*

The Proclamation shall come into force on 11th date of May. 2004. Done at Addis Ababa, 11th day of May, 2004.

Summary

- Cooperative Societies Amendment proclamation was issued in the year 2004 by taking in to account the changes took place in the field of cooperative movement.
- Amendments were made on registration of cooperative societies, payment of shares, allocation of net profit, dissolution of cooperative societies and settlement of disputes.

Self-Learning Activity

1. State the new articles added under the part government assistance?
2. What are the amendments made on disposal of net surplus?
3. What are the amendments made on settlement of disputes?

21 Council of Ministers Regulation No. 106 of 2004 for Implementation of Cooperative Societies Proclamation

Part One: General

This Regulation is issued by the Council of Ministers pursuant to Article 5 of the definition of powers and Duties of the executive organs of the Federal Democratic Republic of Ethiopia Proclamation No. 4/1995 and Article 59 of Cooperative Societies Proclamation No. 147/1998.

1. *Short Title*

This Regulation may be cited as "Councils of Ministers Regulation No. 106/2004 to Provide for the implementation of Cooperative Societies Proclamation No. 147/1998.

2. *Definition*

In this Regulation, unless the context requires otherwise.

1. "Proclamation" means Cooperative Societies Proclamation No. 147/1998.
2. "Regular meeting" means a general assembly convened pursuant to sub article 1 of Article 22 of Proclamation No. 147/1998.
3. "Cooperative society" means an entity that has got a definition referred to (indicated) under Article 2(2) of the Proclamation mission established pursuant to Article 2(1) or Proclamation 274/2002 and includes Cooperative Promotion Bureaus and Offices established in each region.
4. "Union" means a union composed of more than one primary cooperative societies that have similar objectives.
5. "Federation" means a group consists of unions and cooperative societies with similar objectives.

6. "League" means cooperative society league of Ethiopia establish by cooperative societies at the national level.

Part Two: Establishment of Cooperative Societies

3. *Establishment of Primary Cooperative Societies*

   1. Primary cooperative society shall be established by voluntary individuals who live or work in the same area or engaged in the same profession. Number of members establishing the society shall not be less than ten. The appropriate authority shall, taking into account the economic efficiency, determine the least number of establishing members through directives issued by itself.
   2. The operational area of primary cooperative society established pursuant to sub-article 1 of this article may be confined to one-region or cover more than one regions.
   3. Different kinds of primary cooperative societies may be established in the operational area indicated in sub-article 2 of this Article.

4. *Establishment of a Union*

   1. Subject to the provision of this Regulation and that of other relevant laws on cooperative society, primary cooperative societies having similar objective may establish a union.
   2. Subject to the provision of this Regulation and that of other laws an individual who carries out similar activities to that of a union and who is willing to observe the principles of the society may become a member of the union.

5. *Establishment of Cooperative Federation*

   1. Subject to the provision of this Regulation and that of other relevant laws, unions having similar objectives at Federal level may establish a Federation.
   2. Subject to the provision of this Regulation and that of other relevant law, cooperative societies and an individual that carries out similar activities with that of the Federation may become a member of the Federation.

6. *Establishment of Cooperative League*

   1. Subject to the provision of this Regulation and that of other relevant laws, primary cooperative societies, unions, and federations may establish a League that represents all cooperative societies in Ethiopia.

2. The number of the League established pursuant to sub-article 1 of this article may not exceed one.

7. *Operational Area*

1. The operational area of a Union or a Federation established pursuant to Article 4 or 5 of this Regulation shall be determined by the by-laws of the Union or the Federation.

2. The League shall have an operational area throughout the territory of Ethiopia.

Part Three: Types and Functions of Cooperative Societies

8. *Functions of Cooperative Society*

A cooperative society may engage in production or service rendering activities or in both production and service rendering activities.

9. *Cooperative Society engaged in Production Activities*

Cooperative society engaged in production activities shall be one which takes part in production process or which converts raw materials or semi-finished products to finished products.

10. *Cooperative Societies engaged in Service Rendering Activities*

A cooperative society engaged in service rendering activities shall deliver various services to members or cause them to obtain the same.

11. *Cooperatives Societies engaged in Production and Service Rendering Activities*

A cooperative society engaged in production and service rendering shall carry out both activities indicated under Articles 9 and 10 of this regulation.

12. *Types of Cooperative Societies*

1. Cooperative societies of different type may be organized in any economic or social sector of the country.

2. Cooperative societies differ from each other based on their unique nature such as their working place, establishment, function and legal personality they have.

3. The unique nature of cooperative societies shall be determined by a directive issued by the appropriate authority.

Part Four: Registration of Cooperative Societies

13. *Registration*

1. The Federal Cooperative Commission shall register the league and the federations as well as unions at the national level.

2. Any society established pursuant to this regulation shall have legal personality as of the date of its registration.

14. *Particulars of By-law of a Cooperative Society*

Subject to the provision of Article 11 of the proclamation, by-law of a cooperative society shall contain the following particulars:

- Objectives, values and principles of cooperative societies.
- Administrative structure of the society.
- Budget year of the society.
- Manner of keeping the fund of the society and ways of its utilization.
- Procedures on loans.
- Procedure to be applied in the instance of withdrawal, dismissal or death of members.
- Rules of procedures for the meeting of the society and notifications to be given to members.
- Procedures for the appointment or employment of mangers and other officers of the society, their powers and duties and term of office.
- Administration of employee of the society.
- Matters requiring special or quorum resolutions (decision).
- Procedure to applied in cases where the by-law of the society is amended or in cases where the society is dissolved, divided or amalgamated with other societies.
- Other appropriate particulars.

15. *Share Certificate of Members of a Cooperative Society*

1. Any member shall be granted certificate for the amount of full shares he has paid for.
2. The share certificate shall be printed in confidence (secretly) and shall contain the following particulars;
   - Name, address and emblem of the society.
   - Date of registration and registration number of the society.
   - Identification number of share certificate.
   - Par value of each share.
   - Name and identification number of the member.

- ❖ The amount of shares he has paid for (bought) and the price of the share he has bought.
- ❖ Signature of a person entrusted with a power of leading the society.
- ❖ Seal of the society.
- ❖ Date, month and year of issuance of certificate.

3. The share of the society may not be transferred from one member to the other or from a member to a third party.

16. *Dismissal of members*

1. A member who failed to meet his obligation shall be deemed not to meet his obligation where he:
   (a) has failed to pay fully for the shares within a period specified.
   (b) has failed to meet his obligation emanated from the occupational sector granted by the society for more than two times.
   (c) has not participated for a year in any transaction or services rendered by the society.
   (d) has not participated in two consecutive regular meetings of the society without sufficient reason.

2. Any member who has committed a fault shall be dismissed from membership. The member shall be deemed to have committed a fault where he has:
   (a) committed a fault which is contrary to the objective of the society.
   (b) deliberately caused harm or caused to be harmed the properties of the society.
   (c) misappropriated the properties of the society that he has received for various reasons.
   (d) deliberately misappropriated the fund of the society or facilitated conditions for the same action to be committed.
   (e) bribed somebody or been bribed by somebody in the name of the society.
   (f) sold or caused to be sold under price or bought or caused to be bought over price the properties of the society with view to derive unlawful advantage.
   (g) reduced the amount or the quality of product or service that the society supplies.

17. *Charges*

Any cooperative society shall pay charges indicated in the schedule attached thereto to government upon receiving a share certificate or its substitute.

18. *Grant of Substitute Certificate*

1. A cooperate society that has lost its certificate may apply to appropriate authority for the grant of substitute certificate.
2. The appropriate authority shall grant the substitute certificate within 10 days as of the submission of the request.
3. The appropriate authority shall issue directives on the manner of granting substituted certificate.

19. *Conditions for the Prohibition of Registration*

Any cooperative society shall not get registered and be granted certificate where:

1. it has got similar name and emblem with the society that has already registered.
2. it lacks its own project proposal.
3. it doesn't observe registration requirements specified in this regulation and the proclamation.
4. its objective is found contrary to this regulation, the proclamation and directive issued by the appropriate authority.\

Part Five: Meetings of a Cooperative Society

20. *Regular Meeting of the General Assembly*

1. Any cooperative society shall convene its regular General Assembly at least once in a year.
2. There shall be a quorum where more than half members of the General Assembly are present.
3. Where there is no quorum of the General Assembly called, the second General Assembly shall be called within 15 days as of the date of the first General Assembly. Where there is no quorum for general assembly called for the second time, the meeting shall be convened by members present.
4. The decision passed by the General Assembly, which is convened in a situation where there is no quorum as is indicated in sub- article 3 of this Article, shall be deemed to have been made in the presence of all members.

21. *Emergency Meeting of the General Assembly*

1. Where there is no quorum in an emergency meeting called as per Article 22 of the Proclamation, the management committees shall call the second emergency meeting within 15 days as of the date of the first meeting. Where there is no quorum in emergency meeting called for the second time, the appropriate authority may call another meeting.
2. There shall be quorum where two thirds of members of the General Assembly are present.

22. *Call for the Meeting*

The management committee shall make a call, as per the provisions of the Proclamation to all members 15 days before the emergency meeting is convened through a Newspaper having nationwide circulation or using any means found convenient.

23. *Voting Procedure of a Cooperative Society*

1. Unless and otherwise provided in the by-law of the society, decision of regular or emergency meeting shall be passed by a majority vote.
2. In cases of a tie, the chairperson of the General Assembly shall have a casting vote.

Part Six: Assets and funds of the Cooperative Society

24. *Allocation of Net Profit*

1. 30 per cent of the net profit of the society shall be deducted and allocated for the reserve fund. The amount allocated for the reserve fund shall not exceed 30 per cent of the capital of the society.
2. The amount of fund deducted from the net profit and allocated for the reserve fund shall be deposited in a saving account opened in the name of the society. The utilization/application of this fund shall be determined by the directive issued by the appropriate authority.

25. *Indivisibility of Assets of the Society*

Where the asset of the society is:

(a) registered as a reserve fund account.

(b) obtained through donation or inheritance, shall remain indivisible and common asset of the society.

26. *Distribution of Assets of Dissolved Cooperative Society*

The assets of a dissolved cooperative society left after the creditors are paid as is indicated under Article 44, sub-article 4 of the Proclamation shall be distributed to a member who is active at the time when dissolution pronounced, to a member who is dismissed for the reason other than committing a fault, and to a substitute of a deceased member. Manner of distribution of the asset shall be determined by a directive issued by the appropriate authority.

27. *Repealed Laws*

Regulations or a directive inconsistent with this regulation shall be inapplicable.

28. *Power to Issue a Directive*

The appropriate authority shall issue a directive necessary for the implementation of this regulation.

29. *Effective Date*

This regulation shall come in to force on the date of its publication in the Negarit Gazeta. Done at Addis Ababa, this 28th day of June 2004.

Summary

- ❖ Council of Ministers Regulation No. 106/2004 was issued to provide for the implementation of Cooperative Societies Proclamation.
- ❖ The regulation gave clear cut direction for establishment of Union, Federation and League.

Self-Learning Activity

1. What do you mean by League?
2. What do you understand about grant of substitute certificate?
3. Discuss the conditions for prohibition of registration?
4. Discuss the provisions relating to allocation of net profit?

22 Model Bylaws of Select Cooperative Societies

BYLAWS OF FARMERS' COOPERATIVE UNION

Bylaws of _________ Farmers' Cooperative Union Limited Liability.

Article 1: Name and Address

1. Name of the society

   The name of the society shall be "_________ Farmers' Cooperative Union Limited Liability".

2. Address of the union

   The address of the union shall be:

   _________ Regional State

   _________ Zone

   _________ Administration

   _________ Woreda

   _________ Kebele

   _________ Telephone

   _________ PO Box

   The union shall notify the appropriate authority (as defined in the relevant law) of any change of address within 30 days of the change.

Article 2: Definitions

1. "Person" means a natural or juridical person.
2. "Member society" means a cooperative society registered under the Cooperative Proclamation No. 147/1998.

3. "Union" means a secondary cooperative whose members include member societies.

4. "Management Board" means a body elected and empowered by the General Assembly with the responsibility to manage the activities of the Union.

5. "Special resolution" means a resolution passed by a two-thirds majority vote of the representatives to the General Assembly from the member societies, which is binding on all member societies.

Article 3: Objectives and Activities of the Union

Article 3.1: Objectives

The objectives of the Union shall be as follows:

1. To solve problems collectively that member societies cannot individually solve.
2. To achieve a better result by coordinating the knowledge, wealth and labor of the member societies in solving their local, economic and social problems.
3. To improve the profitability and efficiency of member societies by reducing production and service costs, by providing inputs or services at minimum costs, and by finding better prices for member societies' products and services through increased bargaining power, economies of scale and market share.
4. To facilitate direct relationships between member societies and financial institutions.
5. To create expanded opportunities for member society access to modern technologies.
6. To increase the value of member society products through the application of technology.
7. To minimize the impact on member societies of risks and uncertainties.
8. To provide access to professional business and technical services for member societies.
9. To develop the social and economic culture of the member societies through education and training.
10. To promote self-reliance among member societies.

The objectives of the union may be changed from time to time by the general assembly.

Article 3.2: Activities

The activities of the union shall be to facilitate the following for member societies:

1. Providing wholesale purchasing or brokering of products.
2. Providing wholesale inputs necessary or beneficial to production operations, such as fertilizers, improved seeds, insecticides and herbicides, veterinary drugs and others.
3. Supplying milling, storage, equipment, transportation, value added processing and other services.
4. Providing auditing, accounting and financial planning.
5. Facilitating access to market information.
6. Providing wholesale consumer goods.
7. Developing saving and credit services.
8. Providing continuous education and training to members, management bodies, employed staff and the local community; and
9. Performing other activities that help to expand the union and fulfill its objectives.

Article 4: Area of Operation

The area of operation of the union shall be as follows:

The area of operation shall be expanded from time-to-time as determined by the General Assembly.

Article 5: Membership

Article 5.1: Membership Eligibility

Any registered cooperative that satisfies the following criteria shall be eligible for membership in the union:

1. Which is able to pay the registration fee and able to buy the minimum number of shares required by these bylaws.
2. Which is willing to implement and observe the union's bylaws, internal regulations, guiding principles and decisions.
3. Which has not been expelled from another cooperative union within the previous _______ years.
4. Which conducts its business within the boundaries of the union's operating area.
5. Which is not otherwise prevented by law from performing juridical acts.

Article 5.2: Membership Applications

1. Every applicant for membership shall fill out an application form.
2. The union shall accept applications for membership annually between the months of _______ and _______, inclusive.
3. Upon the receipt of the application form, the management board shall check the submitted application form against Article 5.1 and forwards its decision to accept or reject the application for membership within one month of the date that the application form is received.
4. Applicants not satisfied with the decision of the management board may appeal to the General Assembly at the next scheduled meeting. The decision of the General Assembly shall be final.
5. Upon acceptance to membership the new member shall pay a registration fee, as established by the General Assembly. The fee shall be non-refundable and shall accrue no benefits to the member.

Article 5.3: Member Register

The Union shall assign each member a unique number and keep the member register with the following details:

1. Name, address, and business of the member society;
2. Date registered as a member;
3. Date membership is terminated;
4. The amount of shares held and the registration fee paid by each member.

Article 5.4: Member Shares

1. The union may sell ______ shares having the face value of ______ Birr.
2. The number and face value of shares to be sold may be increased by the general assembly.
3. Each member society shall be required to buy at least one share.
4. Where the General Assembly requires member societies to purchase additional shares, other than in the ordinary course of business of the union, those member societies who cannot pay in full the value of additional share(s) at once shall pay within ______ months.
5. No member shall hold more than ______ per cent of the total paid up share capital of such union.

   [Note: The Proclamation 147/1998, 16 (3) provides that no member shall hold more than 10 per cent of the total paid-up share capital of the society. This may be based on the requirement that primary cooperatives have at least ten members (see Proclamation 6(3). However, this minimum number only applies to primary societies and not to unions. Where unions may have two or more members, the capitalization limitations of 16 (3) seem illogical, and should not apply to unions].

6. Each member society shall be given a share certificate or receipt for shares purchased.
7. Dividends shall be paid on share capital and patronage pursuant to Article 11.
8. No transfer by a member society of the member society's shares in the union shall be valid unless the member has held those shares for at least one year before the transfer, and the transfer is approved by the management board.
9. All transfers of shares must be registered with the management board, and no transfer shall be valid unless so registered.
10. A member society shall be required to give ______ days written notice of the intention to withdraw shares in whole or in part.
11. The shares and other benefits of any member society may be set off for debts due to the union from the member society.

Article 6: Member's Rights and Duties

Article 6.1: Rights

Each member society of the union shall have the following rights:

1. To attend, participate and vote at General Assembly meetings.
2. To have representatives elect or be elected to committees of the union.
3. To submit initiatives to the general assembly or to the committees of the union.
4. To use the union's services according to the policies and procedures approved by the union;
5. To receive periodically or upon request, and at least once a year, a statement of transactions with the union.
6. To withdraw from membership voluntarily with payment of benefits in accordance with the policies and procedures of the union.

Article 6.2: Voting Rights

[Note: The Proclamation 147/1998, 18 (1), (3) provide that every member shall have only one vote. The common practice in Ethiopian Unions, at the time of drafting these model Bylaws, is for the primaries to elect representatives based on membership at the primary level. This procedure is represented by option one below. However, this voting procedure based on primary membership appears to violate the above Proclamation provisions based on union membership because it gives larger primaries more votes than smaller primaries at the union level. Nonetheless, because this is the common practice, an option is provided below.]

Each member society shall have the following voting rights:

[Select one of the following options:]

Option 1

1. The member societies will name _____ representatives to the union's general assembly for each _____ members rounded to the nearest _____.
2. The following officers of the member societies shall also represent the primary society at the union's general assembly [fill in four or less]:

   (a) __________

   (b) __________

   (c) __________

   (d) __________
3. Each of the representatives and officers named above shall have one vote at meetings of the union's general assembly.

Option 2

1. Each member society shall designate _____ representatives to vote at meetings of the union general assembly. Such representatives shall include the following officers of the member society [fill in four or less]:

   (a) __________

   (b) __________

   (c) __________

   (d) __________
2. Each of the representatives, including the officers named above, shall have one vote at meetings of the union's general assembly.

Option 3

1. Each member society shall designate _____ representatives to vote at meetings of the union's general assembly. Such representatives may include the officers of the member society.
2. Each of the representatives shall have one vote at meetings of the union's general assembly.

Article 6.3: Duties

Each member society of the union shall be obliged to:

1. Comply with applicable laws, the bylaws, general assembly resolutions, and the policies and procedures of the union.
2. Buy shares and pay the fees decided by the general assembly.
3. Notify the union in writing of the intention to amalgamate or divide pursuant to the Proclamation.
4. Make use of the services of the union as stated in the objectives of the union.
5. Attend meetings and take part in decision-making.
6. Appropriately protect and safeguard the common property of the union.
7. Participate in projects undertaken by the union both physically and financially.
8. Participate in educational activities of the union.
9. Contribute to solving any problems affecting the union.
10. Sign and abide by a marketing agreement with the union.
11. Promote the union to non-member societies.
12. Abide by all contracts between the member society and the union.

Article 6.4: Shares not Liable to Attachment or Sale

The shares or benefits of a member society in this union shall not be liable to attachment or sale, except as provided in Article 5.4(11) of these bylaws.

Article 6.4: Right of Hearing and Appeal

1. The management board shall hear and determine matters relating to any alleged violation of bylaws or internal regulations of the union by a member society. The member society has the right to be heard at the time of this determination.
2. Any member society who willfully acts in violation of these bylaws or regulations made thereunder shall be liable for a fine, notwithstanding any other action that may be taken against it in accordance with Bylaws 8.1 and 8.2 and other applicable laws. The management board shall assess fines based on the policies of the union.
3. Any member society aggrieved by the decision of the management board may appeal to the general assembly, whose decision shall be final.

Article 7: Management Bodies

The management of the union shall be conducted by the following:

1. General Assembly;
2. Management Board;
3. Control Committee;
4. Loan Committee;
5. Education Committee; and
6. Other Committees and sub-committees as the union sees fit and in accordance with the bylaws.

Article 7.1: General Assembly

The general assembly is the supreme authority of the union comprised member societies with voting rights as set forth in Article 6.2.

Article 7.2: Meetings of the General Assembly

1. Meeting(s) of the General Assembly shall be held at least twice a year. However, emergency meetings can be held upon the request of the Management Board or the Control Committee.
2. Upon the request of not less than 1/3 of those entitled to vote at a meeting of the General Assembly, the Management Board shall call a meeting of the General Assembly upon 15 days prior notice.
3. If the Management Board fails to call a General Assembly meeting in accordance with Article 7.2 (1) and (2), the appropriate authority shall call the meeting. The meeting shall be deemed to have been called by the Management Board.
4. Notice of the time, place and agenda items shall be given to the member societies 15 days before any meeting of the General Assembly is held.
5. A meeting of the General Assembly can be convened if over 50 per cent of the voters from each member society are present. If the minimum are not present, another meeting shall be called after 15 days with appropriate notice as set forth in Article 7.2 (4). If again, the number of voters present is not over 50 per cent of the each society's voters, the meeting shall be conducted with those present, and any decisions made not requiring a special resolution shall be binding on the union.
6. All decisions require a majority vote with the exception of special resolutions.
7. Voting by proxy is forbidden.
8. Minutes of General Assembly meetings shall be recorded and kept by the secretary.

Article 7.3: Duties and Responsibilities of the General Assembly

The General Assembly of the union shall have the following duties and responsibilities:

1. To elect, supervise and dismiss members of the committees listed in Article 7.0 of this Bylaw.
2. To approve the annual work plan and budget.
3. To discuss the annual reports and the audit report and pass needed decisions.
4. To approve the maximum amount that the management board can borrow for the expansion of the union's activities. The amount shall not exceed _____ per cent of the total assets of the union.
5. To consider recommendations of the management board for the expulsion of member societies.
6. To approve and amend bylaws and internal regulations and policies of the union.
7. To approve the number of shares to be sold and their face value.
8. To approve the employment of the manager.
9. To settle disputes that may arise between committees and/or between committees and member societies.
10. To determine whether the union should be amalgamated with another union, dissolved, join a federation or be divided pursuant to Proclamation No. 147/1998.
11. To determine the number of shares the union will purchase in a federation.
12. To determine how the net surplus of the union is distributed.
13. To approve regulations regarding employment, promotion and maximum remuneration of employees;
14. To elect delegates and alternate delegates to represent the union in any federation of which this union is a member.
15. To carry out other necessary activities not prohibited by the bylaws or other applicable laws.

Article 7.4: Management Board

1. The management board members shall be elected from among the member societies. The number of board members shall be ______. At least ______ seats on the management board shall be reserved for women

to develop the social and economic culture of the union as encouraged by Proclamation No. 147/1998, part one, and sub-part 4.9.

2. The term of office of the members of the board shall be 3 years and no member may serve more than 2 consecutive terms.
3. ______ alternate board members shall also be elected from among the member societies' representatives. In the event of the death, resignation or termination of a board member, one of the alternate member societies' representatives shall be appointed by the board to serve as a full member of the board. The new member shall serve until the end of the original term.
4. The General Assembly should consider electing members of the board so that each area of operation of the union is represented on the board.
5. Women shall be actively encouraged to participate in every level of management.
6. Each member of the board has a duty to consider the interests of all member societies of the union.
7. Members of the board may be dismissed at any time by the General Assembly.
8. A member of the board who wants to resign shall give 15 days written notice to the board.
9. The schedule for ordinary meetings of the board shall be specified in the internal regulations of the union.
10. At least 50 per cent of the board members must be present to convene a regular meeting of the board.
11. Management board members have a both an individual and a common responsibility for the union's activities.
12. The management board may delegate duties and responsibilities as needed.
13. All decisions shall be approved by majority vote. In the case of a tie vote, the chairperson shall cast the deciding vote.

Article 7.5: Disclosure Prior to Election to Management Board or Committee

Before standing for election to a committee, a member must divulge to the General Assembly if any of the following are true:

1. He or she has been convicted for a crime of any kind committed against the union, another cooperative society or an institution of any kind.
2. He or she has committed any financial mismanagement in a professional capacity.

3. He or she has defaulted on a loan for over ______ month(s).
4. He or she has been expelled from the member society or dismissed from one of its committees.
5. His or her age is less than 18 years.
6. He or she is an employee of the union.
7. He or she is a committee member of a member society.
8. He or she is a close relative of the union employee.

Article 7.6: Duties and Responsibilities of the Management Board

The management board, subject to direction from the General Assembly, shall conduct the affairs of the union. In particular, it shall:

1. Execute the decisions of the General Assembly;
2. Ensure that the funds of the society shall be applied for the promotion of these stated objectives and purpose of the society.
3. Maintain the minutes of the General Assembly and the management board meetings.
4. Prepare balance sheets, income statements, cash-flow plans, budgets and any other relevant financial reports, and implement the plans and budgets upon approval by the general assembly.
5. Prepare draft bylaws, policies and internal regulations and implement them upon approval of the general assembly.
6. Ensure that the proper records of account are kept in the office.
7. Call meetings of the General Assembly pursuant to these bylaws.
8. Submit reports to the General Assembly on the activities of the union.
9. Supervise the work of sub-committees of the management board.
10. Ensure the collection of registration fees, the sale of shares and the receipt of loan repayments.
11. Prepare guidelines on the employment of staff and implement them upon approval by the General Assembly.
12. Facilitate the approval of employment of a manager by the General Assembly.
13. Settle disputes that may arise between member societies before they are sent to conciliators and arbitrators.
14. Propose policies to the General Assembly for pricing, purchasing and marketing of products to and from the member societies.

15. Propose procedures to the General Assembly for contracts between the union and its member societies and between the union and other parties, and execute the contracts on behalf of the union.
16. Authorize borrowing and lending operations of the union in accordance with the Proclamation No. 147/1998, regulations and the bylaws.
17. Approve the transfer of shares between member societies.
18. Perform or authorize any action consistent with the Proclamation No. 147/1998, regulations and these bylaws unless specifically reserved for the General Assembly or the Control Committee;
19. Delegate in writing such of its duties as it deems necessary to an officer, committee or employee of the union. Nothing in this sub-article shall discharge the board from its responsibility for running the affairs of the union in a proper and business-like manner. The board must accept full responsibility for its duties.
20. Ensure that the employees of the union have carried out their duties and responsibilities.
21. Recommend to the General Assembly lending policies and interest rates that cover relevant costs of lending to the union and reflect the level of risk involved.
22. Pursue the collection of delinquent accounts and otherwise protect the assets of the union.

Article 7.7: Control Committee

1. The Control Committee consists of ______ members and shall be elected by the General Assembly from among the elected representatives.
2. ______ alternate committee members shall also be elected from among the member societies' representatives. In the event of the death, resignation or termination of a committee member, one of the alternate member societies' representatives shall be appointed by the Control Committee to serve as a full member of the committee. The new member shall serve until the end of the original term.
3. The term of office of the members of the Control Committee shall be 3 years. No member may serve more than 2 consecutive terms.
4. The Control Committee shall have a chairperson and a secretary who shall be elected by the General Assembly.
5. The Union shall strive to ensure that all of the members of the Control Committee shall have book-keeping, accounting or auditing knowledge. If the members of the committee do not have this knowledge, the union shall take steps necessary to provide training to them.

6. The chairperson of the Control Committee may attend all management board meetings but has no voting rights.

Article 7.8: Duties of the Control Committee

The Control Committee shall have the following duties and responsibilities:

1. To inspect all documents and audit all functions of the union at least quarterly and more frequently as appropriate.
2. To ensure that the management board and all sub-committees carry out their duties and responsibilities properly.
3. To ensure that the funds and property of the Union are properly utilized.
4. To ensure that loans are prudently handled, collected and repaid in a timely manner.
5. To ensure that the various activities of the union are carried out pursuant to the bylaws and the internal regulations of the union.
6. To conduct an inventory of the Union's assets at least twice annually, and audit the inventory of the Union's stock at least monthly.
7. To prepare and present a report on its activities at least once per year to the General Assembly.
8. To ensure that the audit report is properly presented to the General Assembly at least once per year.
9. To call emergency meetings of the general assembly at its discretion.
10. The Control Committee shall perform other activities assigned by the General Assembly.

Article 7.9: Sub-committees

1. Sub-committees shall be elected by the General Assembly.
2. Sub-committees shall consist of **[1] ______ members.
3. The term of office of sub-committee members shall be ______ years not to exceed 3 years.
4. Sub-committee members shall not be elected to more than 2 consecutive terms. No more than 1/3 of the sub-committee members shall be elected in any given year.
5. A quorum for a meeting of the sub-committees shall be greater than 50 per cent of the sub-committee members.

---

1 ** 3 or a multiple of 3 (is required to make the election procedure work).

6. The sub-committees of this Union shall be the loan committee, the education committee and any other committees determined from time to time by the General Assembly or the management board.

Article 7.10: Duties of the Loan Committee

The Loan Committee shall have the following duties and responsibilities:

1. To inquire carefully and diligently into the reputation and financial condition of each applicant for a loan and the quality of its collateral, if any, to ascertain its ability to repay fully and promptly.
2. To recommend to the management board the approval or denial of all loan applications.
3. To maintain minutes of its meetings and records of its actions; and
4. To make such reports to the management board as it may require.

Article 7.11: Duties of the Education Committee

The Education Committee shall have the following duties:

1. To organize, facilitate and promote education and training of the member societies, committee members and staff.
2. To make reports on its activities to the management board.
3. To train the member societies on how to prepare a viable business plan with provisions for meeting repayment obligations to support loan applications.
4. To ensure the production and acquisition of literature including periodicals, and brochures.
5. To promote the distribution and understanding of the Proclamation No. 147/1998, these bylaws, and the internal regulations and policies of the union to the member societies.
6. To arrange for educational tours in conjunction with the management board.
7. To advise the management board and update member societies on matters of education and information.
8. To request funds for educational purposes and apply the funds for the benefit of the union.
9. To identify, collect, disseminate and/or publish cooperative news for the benefit of the union.
10. To identify educational needs of member societies and their members and propose work plans to address those needs.
11. To perform any other duties assigned by the management board.

Article 7.12: Minutes of Management Board and Committee Meetings

All business discussed or decided at management board or committee meetings shall be recorded in a minute book. Within one week of the meeting, the chairperson of the meeting, and either the secretary or at least one other management board or committee member who was present at the meeting shall sign the minutes. These signatures shall verify that the minutes are a true and complete record of all important matters that were discussed or decided at the meeting. At the next management board or committee meeting, changes to the minutes shall be noted below the signatures without altering the original record. The management board or committee shall then authorize the chairperson to sign and date the final record.

Article 7.13: Duties and Responsibilities of Union Officers

The officers of the union may be the chairperson, vice-chairperson, secretary, treasurer/cashier and/or chief accountant.

Chairperson

The Chairperson shall be elected by the General Assembly and have the following duties and responsibilities:

(a) To represent the union in all affairs;
(b) To preside at meetings of the General Assembly and meetings of the management board;
(c) To authorize payments and sign checks with other signatories;
(d) To perform other activities necessary as determined by the General Assembly or management board; and
(e) To delegate in writing and in accordance with union policies such tasks to the general manager as he or she determines.

Vice-Chairperson

The Vice-Chairperson shall be elected by the general assembly and shall perform the duties of the Chairperson during his/her absences, and shall perform such other duties as may be directed by the Chairperson.

Secretary

The Secretary shall be elected by the General Assembly and have the following duties and responsibilities:

(a) To ensure the proper recording of minutes of the management board meetings and General Assembly meetings.
(b) To prepare agendas for meetings of the General Assembly and the management board in consultation with the Chairperson and ensures the communication of notice of meetings.

(c) To delegate in writing and in accordance with union policies such tasks to the general manager as he or she determines.

(d) To keep properly all documents of the management board and General Assembly;

(e) To ensure that the union's correspondence is promptly and correctly attended to; and

(f) To perform such other duties as may from time to time be assigned by the Chairperson.

Chief Accountant

The chief accountant shall be elected by the General Assembly and should have accounting qualifications and experience necessary for the performance of his or her duties. The Union shall provide appropriate training to the Chief Accountant if needed. The powers and duties of the Chief Accountant shall be:

(a) To manage or cause to be managed the financial affairs of the union in a competent and efficient manner that corresponds to the union's bylaws.

(b) To maintain full and complete records of all assets, liabilities, income and expenses of the union.

(c) To ensure the safe-keeping of the union's money, securities, and books of account.

(d) To ensure that all payments and expenditures are duly authorized.

(e) To ensure compliance with all financial directives of the management board.

(f) To supervise staff accountants.

(g) To delegate in writing and in accordance with union policies such tasks to the staff accountants as he or she determines.

(h) To properly maintain and issue payment vouchers and any other supporting documents.

(i) To prepare, sign and submit to the management board within 15 days after the close of each month, a financial statement showing the condition of the union at the end of such month.

(j) To review and correct any problems with financial reports and procedures.

The Treasurer/Cashier

The Treasurer/Cashier shall be elected by the General Assembly and shall have the following duties and responsibilities:

[*Note:* In some unions this position will be a staff employee rather than an elected officer. In such case, this sub-article is unnecessary.]

(a) To make all payments and receive all incomes for the union with the appropriate receipts and vouchers;

(b) To sign checks with the chairperson;

(c) To properly hold cash, cash receipts, bank books and checks; and

(d) To perform any other duties assigned by the chief accountant and the chairperson.

Article 7.14: Board or Committee Member Leaving Office

Any member of the management board or a committee leaving office shall immediately return the property of the union.

1. Any member of the management board or a committee shall have the duty to train and guide any new member replacing him/her, whenever the need arises.

2. When a member of the management board or a committee resign his or her office or is expelled for any reason, he or she has the obligation to account for their service as a management board or a committee member, and to submit to an audit by the control committee and the appropriate authority.

Article 7.15: Payments

1. Internal regulations for the payment of per diem and transportation costs shall be presented by the management board for approval by the General Assembly.

2. The Union shall not pay any salary to its officers for their services. However, for the services they provide, the union may pay per diem and transportation costs upon approval of the management board.

Article 7.16: Staff

Subject to the approval of the General Assembly, the management board may hire a manager and such other staff as may be considered necessary for the proper and efficient administration of the work of the union.

Manager

The powers and duties of the manager shall be assigned by the management board and shall include the following:

(a) To manage the affairs of the union in a competent manner.

(b) To cause to be kept proper books of records and registers.

(c) To attend Management Board meetings and the General Assembly in an advisory capacity, but shall have no voting rights.

(d) To prepare and analyze on a quarterly basis the union's business plan and budget.

(e) To represent the Union in business transactions and any other transaction authorized by the Management Board including the execution of contracts for the Union as directed by the General Assembly or the Management Board.

(f) To provide information required by the Control Committee in a timely manner.

(g) To propose to the Management Board new positions needed by the union, and revisions to the salary schedule for the union's staff, when appropriate.

(h) To implement recommendations set forth in the audit reports and those issued by the Control Committee.

(i) To ensure on an ongoing basis that all cash of the union is handled and accounted for properly.

(j) To ensure on a monthly basis that the accounting records are in balance and the subsidiary accounts are up to date and the income statement, balance sheet, and delinquency list are complete and correct.

(k) To ensure that the account records are maintained in accordance with generally accepted accounting principles.

(l) To ensure that appropriate insurance is in place if available for all employees, officials, and the business premises.

(m) To recommend to the General Assembly, for its approval, an interest rate strategy that balances the needs of the member societies with the needs of the union. For this purpose the manager should consider costs, the union's capital needs and competitive pricing structures.

(n) To assist the Management Board with determining acceptable types of collateral that can be used to secure loans from the union.

(o) To ensure that there is adequate liquidity to meet loan demands and operating expenses.

(p) To ensure the creation, writing and regular updating of job descriptions for each employee and ensure that the union employees are profitably utilized.

(q) To supervise all staff members.

(r) To ensure prompt implementation of all decisions of the General Assembly.

(s) To keep the salaries of all employees confidential and divulge these only to the Management Board.

(t) To do other necessary tasks given to him or her by the Management Board.

Treasurer/Cashier

[*Note:* In some unions this position will be an elected officer rather than a staff position. In such case, this sub-article is unnecessary.]

(a) Make all payments and receive all incomes for the union with the appropriate receipts and vouchers.

(b) Sign checks with the chairperson.

(c) Properly hold cash, cash receipts, bank books and checks.

(d) Perform any other duties assigned by the chief accountant and the chairperson.

Professional Accountant

The powers and duties of the accountant shall be:

(a) To manage, under the general manager's supervision, the financial affairs of the union in a competent and efficient manner that corresponds to the union's bylaws.

(b) To maintain full and complete records of all assets, liabilities, income and expenses of the union.

(c) To keep safe the union's money, securities, and books of accounts.

(d) To seek appropriate authorization for all payments and expenditures.

(e) To comply with all financial directives of the management board.

(f) To properly maintain and issue payment vouchers and any other supporting documents.

(g) To prepare, sign and submit to the general manager within 15 days after the close of each month, a financial statement showing the condition of the union at the end of such month.

(h) To review and correct any problems with financial reports and procedures.

Article 7.17: Legal Standard of Care

In conducting the affairs of the union the members of the management board and the committees and officers of the union shall exercise the prudence and diligence of ordinary persons of business. Such persons who are guilty of any acts which are contrary to Proclamation No. 147/1998, regulations, these bylaws, and the directives of the General Assembly shall be held jointly and severally liable for any losses sustained by the union.

Article 7.18: Conflicts of Interest

1. Before taking part in any business transaction which the union may be about to discuss, every management board member, committee member and employee of the union shall be required to disclose any personal interest in the matter, and shall not take part in any discussion or vote upon that item of business. The management board member, committee member or employee shall physically absent himself or herself from the discussion unless it is determined that the individual has relevant information to provide. Failure to divulge this information or the personal interest shall result in removal from office or termination of employment.
2. No officer or employee of a member cooperative shall be party to a decision or influence a decision affecting the relationship, financial and otherwise, of the union to that person's organization.

Article 7.19: Confidentiality Oath

The officers, members of the committees and management board, and employees of the union shall hold in the strictest confidence all transactions of the union with its member societies, and all information respecting their confidential affairs, except to the extent deemed necessary by the Management Board for conducting and recording business of the union. In cases of breach of confidentially, besides the resulting action for damages, the responsible party shall be removed from office or their employment terminated.

Article 7.20: Books and Records

The union shall keep up to date and in a proper business-like manner such accounts and such books as Proclamation No.147/1998 and regulations may require from time to time.

1. The following books shall be kept by the union:
   (a) A register of member societies showing with respect to each member society:
      (i) The name, date of application for membership, address and business of the member society.
      (ii) The date on which it became a member or ceased to be a member.
      (iii) The amount of shares held and the registration fee paid by each member society.
   (b) A cash book showing the details of all payments received and expended or paid out by the union.

(c) A ledger containing such accounts as are necessary to properly record the transactions of the business of the union.

(d) A ledger for each member society showing its transactions with the union.

(e) A fixed assets register.

(f) A register of accounts payable including all loans and other obligations owed by the union.

(g) A register of accounts receivable including all loans and other obligations payable to the union.

(h) A guarantor's control register showing loan interest rates and obligated collateral.

(i) Copies of banking documents.

(j) Copies of all financial statements.

(k) Copies of audit reports.

2. Other union documents:

(a) Minutes of the General Assembly meetings, and meetings of the Management Board, Control Committee and all sub-committee meetings.

(b) A copy of the Cooperative Societies Proclamation (147/1998).

(c) A copy of any cooperative regulations issued by the appropriate authority.

(d) A copy of these bylaws.

(e) A copy of the federation's bylaws if this union is affiliated with a federation.

(f) Copies of member societies' bylaws.

(g) A copy of the internal regulations of the union.

(h) A certificate of registration of the union.

(i) Copies of all union policies.

(j) Copies of contracts entered into by the union such as insurance documents and others.

3. Such other books and records as the General Assembly may decide or the regulations may prescribe.

4. The following documents shall be made accessible to the member societies:

(a) The Cooperative Societies Proclamation No. 147/1998.

(b) These Bylaws.

(c) The internal regulations and policies of the union.

(d) The register of member societies.

(e) The annual audit reports.

(f) The annual work plan and budget.

(g) The minutes of general assembly and committee meetings.

(h) The operating statement and balance sheets of the union.

(i) The certificate of registration of the union.

(j) Other documents as determined by the General Assembly.

Article 8: Termination of Membership

Membership in the union shall be terminated upon:

1. The voluntary termination by the member society, which may be at any time;
2. The amalgamation or division of the member society;
3. The dissolution of the member society; or
4. The expulsion of the member society from membership.

Article 8.1: Expulsion

A member may be expelled for the following reasons:

1. Willfully failing or refusing to comply with the union's bylaws, policies and contracts and persisting in such refusal or failure.
2. Failing to repay loans due for a period exceeding ______ months.
3. Acting in any way detrimental or prejudicial to the union's interests.
4. Filing for bankruptcy or otherwise becoming insolvent.
5. Failing to participate in/patronize the union for ______ months.
6. Any other reason approved by the General Assembly.

Article 8.2: Expulsion Procedure

1. Upon the formal written accusation that a member has committed a violation punishable by expulsion as set forth in Article 8.1, the Management Board shall provide written notice to the member society stating the reason(s) for the proposed expulsion. The notice shall be provided to the member society at least 15 days prior to a hearing with

the Management Board. The accused member society shall sign a copy of the notice that shall be returned to and retained by the union.

2. The Management Board shall conduct a hearing in which the member society shall have the opportunity to be heard. If the member society fails to attend the hearing, the Management Board may nonetheless enter its recommendation.
3. At the conclusion of the meeting the Management Board shall make a written recommendation to the General Assembly whether or not to expel the member society.
4. At the next scheduled or special meeting of the General Assembly, the recommendation of the Management Board shall be heard. The member society shall also be entitled to be heard. After hearing the case, the General Assembly will vote whether or not to expel the member society. The decision of the General Assembly shall be final.

Article 8.3: Payments resulting from Termination of Membership

1. Withdrawal, expulsion, or termination of membership will not exonerate a member from any liability.
2. A member society that withdraws or is expelled shall be repaid the following amounts after deduction of any debts owed by it to the union as borrower, guarantor or otherwise:
   (a) The value of its shares, whose value will be determined by the next official audit.
   (b) Any dividends or interest due to it accrued to share value as of the end of the fiscal year, as determined by the next official audit.
   (c) Any deposits or other sums held by the union on the member society's behalf.
3. Notwithstanding the above, if a member society's membership in the union is terminated while a guarantor of the debt of another member society, such amounts shall not be repaid until the guaranteed loan is either repaid or a new guarantor is obtained.

Article 8.4: Readmission

Member societies who are terminated may re-apply for admission. In such circumstances, the approval of the General Assembly shall be required.

Article 9: Loans to Members

1. All member societies shall be entitled to apply for loans from the union subject to the availability of funds and the policies and regulations of the union.

2. All loans shall be subject to applicable laws, these bylaws and the policies and regulations of the union.
3. Loans may not be granted without the prior approval of the Management Board.
4. Security shall be required for all loans as outlined in the union's policies and regulations.
5. Applicant societies must complete and sign a loan application form and pay the fee for loan applications as established by the union's policies and regulations.
6. All approved loans must be supported by contracts signed between the union's representative, the member society and the guarantors, if any.
7. Loans may be repaid prior to maturity without penalty.
8. The union shall disclose to member societies the availability of loan funds during scheduled meetings of the union.
9. The types of eligible loans shall be determined by the General Assembly.
10. The union shall not extend loans other than to its member societies or to a cooperative established under Proclamation No. 147/1998.
11. All joint loan applications by member societies or applications by cooperatives shall be treated as if submitted by one client.
12. The guarantor or the borrower may request a change of guarantors for compelling reasons.
13. The union shall develop borrowing and lending policies based on sources of capital, lenders' policies, needs of the union and competitive markets. Such policies shall be approved by the General Assembly.
14. Except in cases where it is not financially prudent, repayments of loans from member societies shall be allocated first to expenses to collect the loan, second to interest on the loan and third to loan principal.

Article 10: Cash Management

1. The cash-in-hand requirements of the union will be determined on a monthly basis by the management board, based on the expected expenses during the month under consideration.
2. The union shall maintain bank accounts only in the name of the union.
3. Signatories for bank accounts will be the chairperson and the treasurer/cashier as per Article 7.13 (1)(c) and (5)(c) or to the general manager if so delegated.

Article 11: Net Surplus

1. At least annually, the union shall allocate 30 per cent of the net surplus for the following purposes:

   (a) __________ per cent for reserves until the reserves reach __________ Birr.

   (b) __________ per cent for expansion of activities.

   (c) __________ per cent for social services.

2. After the amount prescribed in sub-article (1) is deducted, the remaining 70 per cent of the net surplus shall be divided among the member societies on the basis of the member societies' shares and the member societies' patronage in accordance with the decision of the General Assembly.

3. The union may, with the decision of the General Assembly, opt to increase the number of member societies' shares rather than compensating with an immediate payment of dividends in cash.

4. Any funds set aside for general reserves, expansion and social services as provided for in sub-article (1) may not be distributed to member societies unless the union is dissolved.

Article 12: Auditing of the Union

1. The union shall submit to an audit by the appropriate authority or by an independent auditor appointed by the appropriate authority at least once a year. The union will share with the auditors all relevant books and accounts of the union and cooperate fully with the audit.

2. The audit report shall be presented to the General Assembly for approval.

Article 13: Fiscal Year

The fiscal year of the union shall be from ______ to ______.

Article 14: Amendments

1. These bylaws shall be amended by a special resolution.
2. Any amendment made by the General Assembly shall be communicated to the appropriate authority within 30 days.
3. Any amendment shall be effective after approval of the appropriate authority.

Article 15: Internal Regulations

Based on the bylaws of the union, internal regulations shall be recommended by the Management Board for approval by the General Assembly.

Article 16: Interpretation

Any ambiguity in the interpretation of these bylaws shall be resolved by the General Assembly.

Article 17: Settlement of Disputes

1. The Management Board will attempt to resolve any disputes that may arise within the union prior to referral of such disputes to conciliation and arbitration pursuant to Proclamation No. 147/1998. However, the General Assembly shall appoint a special mediation committee or other appropriate body that shall attempt to resolve any disputes that may arise between:
   (a) the union and the management;
   (b) a member society and the union; or
   (c) the union's board and/or committees.
2. Disputes not revolved within the union shall be conciliated or arbitrated pursuant to Proclamation No. 147/1998.

Article 18: Dissolution of the Union

1. The union shall be dissolved upon a two-thirds (2/3) majority vote of the member societies' representatives, or when the number of member societies falls below two (2).
2. The union may be dissolved when the union ceases activities for more than ______ years, or when the union becomes insolvent or bankrupt. Whenever the union is bankrupt, the provisions of Article 970(1) and (2) of the Commercial Law and other applicable laws shall apply.
3. In the case of a decision to dissolve the union, the appropriate authority shall be notified within seven days.
4. Upon the liquidation of the union due to bankruptcy, if the member society does not have a loan with an outstanding balance owed to the union, the liability of the member society shall be limited to the value of its shares in the union. If a member society has a loan from the union outstanding, its liability includes the value of the outstanding balance of the loan.
5. In the event of liquidation, where available funds are insufficient to pay the value of the shares held by the member societies, the funds shall be distributed pro-rata among the shareholders according to the amount of shares held by each.
6. In the event of dissolution of the union, notice to creditors shall be given in the following manner:

(a) Notice by registered letter shall be sent to all creditors known to the union.

(b) Notice to other creditors shall be given by publishing notice in two successive monthly issues of a newspaper published in the area of operation of the union and by posting notice on the union's notice board.

7. The procedure for formal liquidation of the union shall be as set forth in Proclamation No. 147/1998 and other applicable laws.

Article 19: Official Seal

The union may adopt and use an official seal bearing the words "______ Cooperative Union Limited Liability" and shall be kept securely under lock and key by a duly designated officer of the union and shall be used only by officers authorized to sign documents on behalf of the union.

Article 20: Borrowing by the Union

The union shall not borrow for any reason or from any source without the approval of the General Assembly.

Article 21: Validity and Effectiveness of these Bylaws

These Bylaws shall be valid and effective when approved by the General Assembly and registered by the appropriate authority. These Bylaws shall be effective beginning from the date of their registration.

Date ________	Year ________
Signature ________	Signature ________
Signature ________	Signature ________
Signature ________	Signature ________

BYLAWS OF SAVINGS AND CREDIT COOPERATIVE SOCIETY LIMITED LIABILITY

Bylaws of ________ Savings and Credit Cooperative Society Limited Liability.

Article 1: Name and Address

1. The name of the society shall be ________ Savings and Credit Cooperative Society Limited Liability.

2. The address of the society shall be

________ Regional State.

________ Zone

________ District

________ Kebele

P.O. Box ________

Tel. #: ________

The society shall notify the appropriate authority (as defined in the relevant law) of any change of address within 30 days of the change.

Article 2: Objectives and Activities

Article 2.1: Objectives

1. The objectives of the society shall be as follows:
   - (a) To encourage thrift among its members by affording them an opportunity for accumulating savings.
   - (b) To provide members with the opportunity to receive credit.
   - (c) To offer members the use of banking services.
   - (d) To improve members' awareness and participation by providing continuous education on savings and credit.
   - (e) To improve the standard of living of members.
   - (f) To contribute to the development ofcommunity.
   - (g) To provide the members access to insurance coverage.

The funds of the society shall be applied for the promotion of these stated objectives and purposes.

Article 2.2: Activities

2. The activities of the society shall be as follows:
   - (a) To collect compulsory and voluntary savings from members;
   - (b) To collect voluntary saving from non-members;
   - (c) To provide loans to members;
   - (d) To collect loans and interest from members;
   - (e) To pay interest on savings;
   - (f) To sell shares to members;
   - (g) To deposit liquid funds at commercial banks in savings accounts;
   - (h) To pay out voluntary savings upon the request of the savers;
   - (i) To collect registration fees, service fees, and other fees; and
   - (j) To perform other necessary activities in furtherance of the objectives of the society.

Article 3: Area of Operation

The area of operation of the society shall be ....

Article 4: Guiding Principles of this Society

The society shall be guided by the following principles:

1. The society is a voluntary organization open to all persons able to use its services and willing to accept the responsibilities of membership without gender, social, racial, political or religious discrimination.
2. The society is a democratic organization controlled by its members who actively participate in setting its policies and making decisions. Every member regardless of shares has only one vote.
3. Members shall receive dividends from the society's net surplus according to the calculation made on their savings and investments with the society and the purchased number of shares after deducting and setting aside amounts for contingencies, expansion and social services.
4. The society is an autonomous self-help organization controlled by its members and if it enters into agreements with other organizations, including the government, or raises capital from external sources, it shall do so in terms that ensure democratic control by its members and maintain its autonomy.
5. The society shall provide education and training for its members, elected representatives, managers of the society and employees so as to enable them to contribute effectively to the development of their society. It shall inform the general public, particularly the youth, about the nature and benefit of cooperatives.
6. The society serves its members most effectively and strengthens the society's movement by working together through local, regional, national, and international structures.
7. The society shall work for the sustainable development of local communities through policies approved by it.

Article 5: Membership

Article 5.1: Eligibility

A person of either sex or a cooperative shall be eligible for membership:

1. Who has attained 14 years of age and is emancipated in accordance with the Civil Code of 1960, or which is a cooperative registered under Proclamation No. 147/1998.
2. Who is not directly or indirectly a money-lender or carrying out any activity which is contrary to the society's objectives.
3. Who is not an employee of the society.

4. Who is able to pay the share capital and registration fee required by the Society.
5. Who is not a member of another saving and credit cooperative.
6. Who is resident within or occupies land within the society area of operation.
7. Who can save the amount decided by the society in the manner decided by the society.
8. Who is willing to honor his or her obligations and observe the objectives and bylaws of the society and the directives issued for the implementation of Proclamation No. 147/1998.
9. Which is a cooperative registered under the Proclamation No. 147/1998.
10. Who is a spouse or family member of an existing member.
11. Who has not been expelled from membership from another saving and credit cooperative in the last 4 years.
12. Who is not otherwise prevented by law from performing juridical acts.

Article 5.2: Membership Application

1. Every applicant for membership shall fill out an application form.
2. Upon the receipt of the application form, the management committee shall check the submitted application form against Article 5.1 and forward its decision to accept or reject the application within one month of the date that the application form is received.
3. Applicants not satisfied with the decision of the management committee may appeal to the General Assembly at the next scheduled meeting, whose decision shall be final.

Article 5.3: Member Register

The society shall assign each member a unique number and keep the members register with the following details:

1. Name, address, age, sex and occupation of the member.
2. Date, registered as a member.
3. Date, membership is terminated.
4. The amount of shares held and the registration fee paid by each member.
5. The name and address of the heir.

Article 5.4: Member Shares

1. The society may sell ________ shares having the face value of ________ Birr.

2. The number and face value of shares to be sold may be increased by the General Assembly.
3. Each member shall be required to buy at least one share.
4. Where the General Assembly requires members to purchase additional shares, other than in the ordinary course of business of the society, those members who cannot pay in full the value of additional share(s) at once shall pay within ________ months.
5. No member shall hold more than 10 per cent of the total paid-up share capital of such society.
6. Each member shall be given a share certificate or receipt for shares purchased.
7. Dividends shall be paid on share capital and patronage pursuant to Article 11.
8. No transfer by a member of the member's shares in the society shall be valid unless the member has held those shares for at least one year before the transfer and the transfer is approved by the management committee.
9. All transfers of shares must be registered with the management committee, and no transfer shall be valid unless so registered.
10. A member shall be required to give ________ days written notice of the intention to withdraw shares, in whole or in part.
11. The shares or benefits of any member may be set off for debts due to the society from the member.

Article 6: Rights and Duties of Members

Article 6.1: Rights

Each member shall have the following rights:

1. To attend, participate and vote at General Assembly meetings. Each member shall have one vote irrespective of the member's total share holding.
2. To elect or be elected to committees of the society.
3. To submit initiatives to the General Assembly or to the committees of the society.
4. To use the society's services according to the policies and procedures approved by the society.
5. To be issued a passbook that can be audited against books of account.

6. To receive periodically or upon request, and at least once a year, a statement of accounts containing the individualized record of his or her credit and debit transactions.
7. To be repaid voluntary saving upon his or her request in line with the bylaws.
8. To withdraw membership voluntarily with payment of benefits in accordance with the policies and procedures of the society.

Article 6.2: Duties

Members of the society shall be obliged to:

1. Comply with applicable laws, the bylaws, General Assembly resolutions, and the policies and procedures of the society.
2. Buy shares and pay the fees decided by the General Assembly.
3. Make use of the services of the society as stated in the objectives of the society.
4. Attend meetings and take part in decision-making.
5. Appropriately protect and safeguard the common property of the society.
6. Participate in projects undertaken by the society both physically and financially.
7. Participate in educational activities of the society.
8. Contribute to solving any problems affecting the society.
9. Promote the society to non-members.
10. Abide by all contracts between the member and the society.
11. Save in accordance with the saving policy of the society.

Article 6.3: Shares or Benefits not Liable to Attachment or Sale

The shares or benefits of a member in this society shall not be liable to attachment or sale except as provided for in Article 5.4 (11) of these Bylaws.

Article 6.4: Right of Hearing and Appeal

1. The management committee shall hear and determine matters relating to any alleged violation of the bylaws or internal regulations of the society by a member. The member has the right to be heard at the time of this determination.
2. Any member who willfully acts in violation of these bylaws or regulations made thereunder shall be liable for a fine, notwithstanding any other action that may be taken against him in accordance with Bylaws 8.1 and 8.2 and other applicable laws. The management committee shall assess fines based on the policies of the society.

3. Any member aggrieved by the decision of the management committee may appeal to the General Assembly, whose decision shall be final.

Article 7: Society Management Bodies

The management of the society shall be conducted by the following:

1. General Assembly;
2. Management Committee;
3. Control Committee;
4. Loan Committee;
5. Saving Committee;
6. Education Committee; and
7. other committees and sub-committees as the society sees fit and in accordance with the bylaws.

Article 7.1: General Assembly

1. The General Assembly is the supreme authority of the society comprised of individual members with one vote each.
2. A member that is a cooperative shall be represented in the General Assembly by the chairperson, secretary, and treasurer and by one representative for _____ members of that cooperative. While the cooperative may have multiple representatives, it shall have only one vote. Further, the member that is a cooperative will abide by Article 7.19 covering "Conflicts of Interest".

Article 7.2: Meetings of the General Assembly

1. Meeting(s) of the General Assembly shall be held at least once a year. However emergency meetings can be held upon the request of the Management Committee or the Control Committee.
2. Upon the request of not less than 1/3 of the members, the Management Committee shall call a meeting of the General Assembly upon 15 days notice.
3 If the Management Committee fails to call a General Assembly meeting in accordance with Article 7.2 (1) and (2), the appropriate authority shall call the meeting. The meeting shall be deemed to have been called by the Management Committee.
4. Notice of the time, place and agenda items shall be given to the members 15 days before any meeting of the General Assembly is held.
5. A meeting of the General Assembly can be convene if over 50 per cent of the members are present. If the minimum 50 per cent are not present,

another meeting shall be called after 15 days with appropriate notice as set forth in Article 7.2 (4). If again, the number of members present is not over 50 per cent of the membership, the meeting shall be conducted with the members present, and any decisions made not requiring a special resolution shall be binding on the society.

6. All decisions require a majority vote with the exception of special resolutions. Special resolutions being voted upon by the General Assembly must be passed by a minimum of 2/3 of the membership.
7. Voting by proxy is forbidden.
8. Minutes of General Assembly meetings shall be recorded by the secretary.

Article 7.3: Duties and Responsibilities of the General Assembly

The General Assembly of the society shall have the following duties and responsibilities:

1. To elect, supervise and dismiss members of the committees listed in Article 7.0 of these Bylaws.
2. To approve the annual work plan and budget.
3. To discuss the annual reports and the audit report and pass needed decisions.
4. To approve the maximum amount that the management committee can borrow for the expansion of the society's activities. The amount shall not exceed ________ per cent of the total assets of the society.
5. To consider recommendations of the management committee for the expulsion of members.
6. To approve and amend bylaws and internal regulations and policies of the society.
7. To approve the number of shares to be sold and their face value.
8. To approve the employment of the manager.
9. To settle disputes that may arise between committees and/or between committees and members.
10. To determine whether the society should be amalgamated with another society, dissolved, join a cooperative union or be divided pursuant to Proclamation No. 147/1998.
11. To determine how the net surplus of the society is distributed.
12. To approve regulations regarding employment, promotion and maximum remuneration of employees.

13. To determine annually, the saving policy of the society will be determined annually by the General Assembly.
14. To elect delegates and alternate delegates to represent the society in any cooperative union of which this society is a member.
15. To determine the number of shares the society will purchase in a cooperative union.
16. To carry out other necessary activities not prohibited by the bylaws or other applicable laws.

Article 7.4: Disclosure Prior to Election to Committees

Before standing for election, a member must divulge to the general assembly if any of the following are true:

1. He or she has been convicted of a crime of any kind committed against the society, another society or an institution of any kind.
2. He or she has committed any financial mismanagement in a professional capacity.
3. He or she has defaulted on a loan for over ________ month(s).
4. He or she has been dismissed from the society or from one of its committees.
5. He or she cannot take responsibility for Birr ________ by signing.
6. His or her age is less than 18 years.
7. He or she is an employee of the cooperative.
8. He or she is a board member of a member cooperative.

Article 7.5: Management Committee

1. The Management Committee members shall be elected from among the members. The number of committee members shall be ________. At least ________ seats on the Management Committee shall be reserved for women members to develop the social and economic culture of the society as encouraged by the Proclamation 147/1998, part one, 4.9.
2. The term of office of the members of the Management Committee shall be three years, and no member may serve more than two consecutive terms.
3. ________ alternate committee members shall also be elected from among the members. In the event of the death, resignation or termination of a committee member, one of the alternate committee members shall be appointed by the Management Committee to serve as a full member of the committee. The new member shall serve until the end of the original term.

4. The General Assembly should consider electing members of the Management Committee so that each area of operation of the society is represented on the committee.
5. Women members of the society shall be actively encouraged to participate in every level of management.
6. Each member of the Management Committee has a duty to consider the interests of all members of the society.
7. Members of the Management Committee may be dismissed at any time by the General Assembly.
8. A member of the committee who wants to resign shall give 15 days written notice to the committee.
9. The schedule for ordinary meetings of the committee shall be specified in the internal regulations of the society.
10. At least 50 per cent of the committee members must be present to convene a regular meeting of the committee.
11. Management Committee members have both a common and an individual responsibility for the society's activities.
12. The Management Committee may delegate duties and responsibilities as needed.
13. All decisions shall be approved by majority vote. In the case of a tie vote, the chairperson shall cast the deciding vote.

Article 7.6: Duties and Responsibilities of the Management Committee

The Management Committee, subject to direction from the General Assembly, shall conduct the affairs of the society. In particular, it shall have the following rights, duties and responsibilities:

1. To maintain the minutes of the General Assembly and the Management Committee meetings.
2. To ensure that the funds of the society are utilized for the stated objectives of the society.
3. To prepare balance sheets, income statements, portfolio reports, cash-flow plans, budgets and any other relevant financial reports, and implement the plans and budgets upon approval by the General Assembly.
4. To prepare draft bylaws and internal regulation and implement same upon approval of the General Assembly.
5. To ensure that the proper records of account are kept in the office.
6. To call meetings of the General Assembly pursuant to these bylaws.
7. To submit reports to the General Assembly on the activities of the society.

8. To supervise the work of sub-committees.
9. To ensure the collection of registration fees, the sale of shares, the receipt of loan repayments and the collection of savings.
10. To prepare guidelines on the employment of staff and implement the same upon approval by the General Assembly.
11. To recommend the approval of employment of a manager by the General Assembly.
12. To supervise the general manager.
13. To settle disputes that may arise between members before they are sent to arbitrators.
14. To authorize borrowing and lending operations of the society in accordance with the Proclamation No. 147/1998, regulations and the bylaws.
15. To approve the transfer of shares between members.
16. To perform or authorize any action consistent with the Proclamation No. 147/1998, regulations and these bylaws unless specifically reserved for the General Assembly or Control Committee.
17. To delegate in writing such of its duties as it deems necessary to an officer, committee or employee of the society. Nothing in this sub-article shall discharge the committee from its responsibility for running the affairs of the society in a proper and business-like manner. The Management Committee must accept full responsibility for its duties.
18. To ensure that the employees of the society have carried out their duties and responsibilities.
19. To recommend to the General Assembly lending policies and interest rates that cover relevant costs of lending to the society and reflect the level of risk involved.
20. To pursue the collection of delinquent accounts and otherwise protect the assets of the society.

Article 7.7: Control Committee

1. The Control Committee consists of ________ members and shall be elected by the General Assembly.
2. ________ alternate committee members shall also be elected from among the members. In the event of the death, resignation or termination of a member, one of the alternate committee members shall be appointed by the Control Committee to serve as a full member of the committee. The new member shall serve until the end of the original term.

3. The term of office of the members of the Control Committee shall be 3 years. No member may serve more than two consecutive terms.
4. The committee shall have a chairperson and a secretary who shall be elected by the General Assembly.
5. The society shall strive to ensure that at least one of the members of the committee shall have either book-keeping, accounting or auditing knowledge. If none of the members of the committee has this knowledge, the society shall take steps necessary to provide training.
6. The chairperson of the Control Committee may attend all Management Committee meetings but has no voting rights.

Article 7.8: Duties of the Control Committee

The duties of the Control Committee shall be as follows:

1. To audit and inspect all documents of the society at least monthly.
2. To check member and non-member passbooks against existing ledgers at least once per year.
3. To ensure that the management committee and all sub-committees carry out their responsibilities properly.
4. To ensure that the funds and property of the society are properly utilized.
5. To ensure that the various activities of the society are carried out pursuant to the bylaws and the internal regulations of the society.
6. To prepare and presents a report at least once per year to the General Assembly.
7. To call emergency meetings of the General Assembly at its discretion; and
8. To perform other activities assigned by the General Assembly.

Article 7.9: Sub-committees

1. Sub-committees shall be elected by the General Assembly.
2. Sub-committees shall consist of **[2] ________ members.
3. The term of office of sub-committee members shall be ________ years not to exceed 3 years.
4. Sub-committee members shall not be elected to more than two (2) consecutive terms. Not more than 1/3 of the sub-committee members shall be elected in any given year.
5. A quorum for a meeting of the sub-committees shall be greater than 50 per cent of the sub-committee members.

---

2 ** 3 or a multiple of 3 (is required to make the election procedure work).

6. The sub-committees of this society shall be: the Loan Committee, the Savings Committee, the Education Committee and any other committees determined from time to time by the General Assembly or the Management Committee.

Article 7.10: Duties of the Loan Committee

The duties of the Loan Committee shall be:

1. To inquire carefully and diligently into the character and financial condition of each applicant for a loan and his or her guarantors if any, to ascertain their ability to repay fully and promptly.
2. To recommend to the management committee the approval or denial of all loan applications.
3. To maintain minutes of its meetings and records of its actions.
4. To make such reports to the Management Committee as it may require.

Article 7.11: Duties of the Savings Committee

The Savings Committee shall have the following duties and responsibilities:

1. To account for deposits to and withdrawals from member savings accounts and ensure maintenance of accurate and up to date member savings account records.
2. To ensure that the members save in accordance with the internal regulations of the society and shall encourage members to increase savings.
3. To recommend to the Management Committee the terms and conditions of savings.
4. To prepare and present financial reports of the savings accounts each month to the Management Committee as well as other reports requested by the Management Committee.
5. To conduct research on new products that may be provided to members.
6. To perform other duties as assigned by the Management Committee.

Article 7.12: Duties of the Education Committee

The Education Committee shall have the following duties and responsibilities:

1. To organize, facilitate and promote education and training of the members, committee members and staff.
2. To make reports on its activities to the Management Committee.

3. To train the members on how to prepare a viable business plan with provisions for meeting repayment obligations to support loan applications.
4. To ensure the production and acquisition of literature including periodicals and brochures.
5. To promote the distribution and understanding of these bylaws to members.
6. To arrange for educational tours in conjunction with the Management Committee.
7. To advise the Management Committee and update members on matters of education and information.
8. To request funds for educational purposes and apply the funds for the benefit of the society.
9. To identify, collect, disseminate and/or publish cooperative news for the benefit of the society.
10. To perform any other duties assigned by the Management Committee.

Article 7.13: Minutes of Committee Meetings

1. All business discussed or decided at committee meetings shall be recorded in a committee minute book. Within one week of the meeting, the chairperson of the meeting, and either the secretary or at least one other committee member who was present at the meeting shall sign the minutes document. The signatures shall verify that the minutes are a true and complete record of all important matters that were discussed or decided at the meeting. At the next committee meeting, changes to the minutes shall be noted below the signatures without altering the original record. The committee shall then authorize the chairperson to sign and date the final record.
2. Confidential or private details of member transactions and employee files shall not be included in committee minutes.
3. Members have the right to review these minute books upon 24 hours request.

Article 7.14: Duties and Responsibilities of Society Officers

The officers of the society may be the Chairperson, Vice-Chairperson, Secretary, Treasurer/Cashier and/or Chief Accountant.

Chairperson

The Chairperson shall be elected by the General Assembly and shall have the following duties and responsibilities:

(a) To represent the society in all affairs.
(b) To preside at meetings of the general assembly, and meetings of the Management Committee.
(c) To authorize payments and sign checks with other signatories.
(d) To perform other activities necessary as determined by the General Assembly or Management committee.

Vice-Chairperson

The Vice-Chairperson shall be elected by the General Assembly and shall perform the duties of the chairperson during his/her absence, and shall perform such other duties as may be directed by the chairperson.

Secretary

The Secretary shall be elected by the General Assembly and shall have the following duties and responsibilities:

(a) To ensure the proper recording of minutes of the management Committee meetings and General Assembly meetings;
(b) To prepare agendas for meetings of the General Assembly and the Management Committee in consultation with the chairperson, and ensure the communication of notice of meetings.
(c) To ensure that the society's correspondence is promptly and correctly attended to.
(d) To perform such other duties as may from time to time be assigned by the chairperson.

Chief Accountant

The Chief Accountant shall be elected by the General Assembly and should have reasonable accounting qualifications and experience necessary for the performance of his or her duties. The society shall provide appropriate training to the chief accountant if needed. The powers and duties of the chief accountant shall be:

1. To manage or cause to be managed the financial affairs of the society in a competent and efficient manner.
2. To maintain full and complete records of all assets, liabilities, income and expenses of the society.
3. To ensure the safe-keeping of the society's money, securities, and books of account.
4. To ensure that all payments and expenditures are duly authorized.
5. To ensure compliance with all directives of the Management Committee.
6. To supervise staff accountants.

7. To properly maintain and issue payment vouchers and any other supporting documents.
8. To prepare, sign and submit to the management committee within 15 days after the close of each month, a financial statement showing the condition of the society at the end of such month.
9. To review and correct any problems with financial reports and procedures.

Treasurer/Cashier

The treasurer/cashier shall be elected by the General Assembly and shall have the following duties and responsibilities:

1. To make all payments and receives all incomes for the society with the appropriate receipts and vouchers.
2. To sign checks with the chairperson.
3. To properly hold all cash, checks, savings books, and cash receipts.
4. To perform any other duties assigned by the chief accountant or chairperson.

Article 7.15: Committee Member Leaving Office

1. Any member of a committee leaving office shall immediately return the property of the society.
2. Any member of a committee shall have the duty to train and guide any new member replacing him or her, whenever the need arises.
3. When a member of a committee resigns his or her office or is expelled for any reason, he or she has the obligation to account for the service as a committee member, and to submit to an audit by the Control Committee and the appropriate authority.

Article 7.16: Payments

1. The Management Committee shall present for approval by the General Assembly internal regulations for the payment of per diem and transportation costs.
2. The society shall not pay any salary to its officers for their services. However, for the services they provide, the society may pay per diem and transportation costs upon approval of the Management Committee.

Article 7.17: Staff

Subject to the approval of the General Assembly the Management Committee may hire a manager and such other staff as may be considered necessary for the proper and efficient administration of the work of the society.

Manager

The powers and duties of the manager shall be assigned by the management committee and shall include the following:

1. To manage the affairs of the society in a competent manner.
2. To cause to be kept proper books of records and registers.
3. To attend Management Committee meetings and the General Assembly in an advisory capacity, but shall have no voting rights.
4. To prepare and analyze on a quarterly basis the society's business plan and budget.
5. To represent the society in business transactions and any other transaction authorized by the Management Committee.
6. To provide information required by the Control Committee in a timely manner.
7. To propose to the Management Committee new positions needed by the society, and revisions to the salary schedule for the society's staff, when appropriate.
8. To implement recommendations set forth in the audit reports and those issued by the Control Committee.
9. To ensure on an ongoing basis that all cash of the society is handled and accounted for properly.
10. To ensure on a monthly basis that the accounting records are in balance and the subsidiary accounts are up to date and the income statement, balance sheet, and delinquency list are complete and correct.
11. To ensure that the account records are maintained in accordance with generally accepted accounting principles.
12. To ensure that adequate insurance is in place if available for all employees, officials, and the business premises.
13. To recommend to the General Assembly, for its approval, an interest rate strategy that balances the needs of the members with the needs of the society. For this purpose the manager should consider costs, the society's capital needs and competitive pricing structures.
14. To assist the Management Committee with determining acceptable types of collateral that can be used to secure loans from the society.
15. To ensure there is adequate liquidity to meet loan demands, savings withdrawal, and operating expenses.
16. To ensure the creation, writing and regular updating of job descriptions for each employee.

17. To ensure prompt implementation of all decisions of the General Assembly.
18. To keep the salaries of all employees confidential and divulge these only to the management committee.
19. To do other necessary tasks given to him or her by the management committee.

Article 7.18: Legal Standard of Care

In conducting the affairs of the society the members of the committees and officers of the society shall exercise the prudence and diligence of ordinary persons of business. Such persons who are guilty of any acts which are contrary to Proclamation No. 147/1998, regulations, these bylaws, and the directives of the General Assembly shall be held jointly and severally liable for any losses sustained by the society.

Article 7.19: Conflicts of Interest

1. Before taking part in any business transaction which the society may be about to discuss, every committee member and employee of the society shall be required to disclose any personal interest in the matter, and shall not take part in any discussion or vote upon that item of business. The committee member or employee shall physically absent himself or herself from the discussion unless it is determined that the individual has relevant information to provide. Failure to divulge this information or the personal interest shall result in removal from office or termination of employment.
2. No officer or employee of a member cooperative shall be a party to a decision or influence a decision affecting the relationship, financial and otherwise, of the society to that person's organization.

Article 7.20: Confidentiality Oath

The officers, members of committees, and employees of the society shall hold in the strictest confidence all transactions of the society with its members, and all information respecting their personal affairs, except to the extent deemed necessary by the management committee for conducting and recording the business of the society. In cases of breach of confidentiality, besides the resulting action for damages, the responsible party shall be removed from office or their employment terminated.

Article 7.21: Books and Records

The society shall keep up to date and in a proper business-like manner such accounts and such books as Proclamation No. 147/1998 and regulations may require from time to time.

1. The following books shall be kept by the society:
   (a) A register of members showing with respect to each member:
      (i) The name, age, sex, date of application for membership, address and occupation.
      (ii) The date on which he or she became a member or ceased to be a member.
      (iii) The amount of shares held and the registration fee paid by each member.
      (iv) The name and address of the heir of the member.
   (b) A cash book showing the details of all monies received and all monies expended or paid out by the society.
   (c) A ledger containing such accounts as are necessary to properly record the transactions of the business of the society.
   (d) A personal ledger for each member showing his or her transactions with the society.
   (e) A fixed assets register.
   (f) A register of accounts payable including all savings deposits, loans and other obligations owed by the society.
   (g) A register of accounts receivable including all loans and other obligations payable to the society.
   (h) A ledger showing deposits and withdrawals made by members.
   (i) A guarantor's control register showing loan interest rates and obligated collateral.
   (j) Copies of banking documents.
   (k) Copies of all financial statements.
   (l) Copies of audit reports.
2. Other cooperative documents:
   (a) Minutes of the general assembly meetings, and meetings of the management, control and all subcommittee meetings.
   (b) A copy of the Cooperative Proclamation No. 147/1998.
   (c) A copy of any cooperative regulations issued by the appropriate authority.
   (d) A copy of these Bylaws.
   (e) A copy of the union's bylaws if this society is affiliated with a union.

(f) A copy of the internal regulations and policies of the society.

(g) A certificate of registration of the society.

(h) Copies of contracts entered into by the society such as insurance documents and others.

3. Such other books and records as the General Assembly may decide or the regulations may prescribe.

4. The following documents shall be made accessible to the members:

   (a) The Cooperative Societies Proclamation No. 147/1998;

   (b) These Bylaws;

   (c) The internal regulations and policies of the society;

   (d) The register of members;

   (e) The annual audit;

   (f) The annual work plan and budget;

   (g) The minutes of the General Assembly and committee meetings;

   (h) The certificate of registration of the society;

   (i) The operating statement and balance sheet of the society; and

   (j) Others as determined by the General Assembly.

Article 8: Termination of Membership

Membership in the society shall be terminated upon:

1. The voluntary resignation by the member, which may be at any time;
2. The death of the member; or
3. Expulsion from membership.

Article 8.1: Expulsion

A member may be expelled for the following reasons:

1. Willfully failing or refusing to comply with the society's bylaws, policies and contracts and persisting in such refusal or failure.
2. Defaulting in the repayment of loans due for a period exceeding ________ months.
3. Failure to save in accordance with the society's approved saving regulations.
4. Acting in any way detrimental or prejudicial to the society's interests.
5. Any other reason approved by the general assembly.

Article 8.2: Expulsion Procedure

1. Upon the formal written accusation that a member has committed a violation punishable by expulsion as set forth in Article 8.1, the management committee shall provide written notice to the member stating the reason(s) for the proposed expulsion. The notice shall be provided to the member at least 15 days prior to a hearing with the Management Committee. The accused member shall sign a copy of the notice that shall be returned to and retained by the society.
2. The committee shall conduct a hearing in which the member shall have the opportunity to be heard. If the member fails to attend the hearing, the committee may nonetheless enter its recommendation.
3. At the conclusion of the meeting the Management Committee shall make a written recommendation to the General Assembly whether or not to expel the member.
4. At the next scheduled meeting or a special meeting of the General Assembly, the recommendation of the Management Committee shall be heard. The member shall also be entitled to be heard. After hearing the case, the General Assembly will vote whether or not to expel the member. The decision of the General Assembly shall be final.

Article 8.3: Payments resulting from Termination of Membership

1. Withdrawal, expulsion, or termination of membership will not exonerate a member from any personal or membership liability.
2. A member who withdraws or is expelled shall be repaid the following amounts after deduction of any debts owed by him/her to the society as borrower, guarantor or otherwise:
   (a) The value of their shares, whose value will be determined by the next official audit;
   (b) Any dividends or interest due to him or her accrued to share value as of the end of the fiscal year, as determined by the next official audit;
   (c) Any interest due to him or her on savings as of the date of payment; and
   (d) Any deposits or other sums held by the society on the member's behalf.
3. Notwithstanding the above, if a member's membership in the society is terminated while a guarantor of the debt of another member, such amounts shall not be repaid until the guaranteed loan is either repaid or a new member-guarantor is obtained.

Article 8.4: Readmission

Members who are terminated may re-apply for admission. In such circumstances, the approval of the general assembly shall be required.

Article 9: Loans to Members

1. All members shall be entitled to apply for loans from the society subject to the availability of funds and the policies and regulations of the society.
2. All loans shall be subject to applicable laws, these bylaws and the policies and regulations of the society.
3. Loans may not be granted without the prior approval of the Management Committee.
4. Security shall be required for all loans as outlined in the society's policies and regulations.
5. Applicants must complete and sign a loan application form and pay the fee for loan applications as established by the society's policies and regulations.
6. All approved loans must be supported by contracts signed between the society's representative, the member and the guarantors, if any.
7. Loans may be repaid prior to maturity without penalty.
8. The society shall disclose to members the availability of loan funds during scheduled meetings of the society.
9. The types of eligible loans shall be determined by the General Assembly.
10. The society shall not extend loans other than to its members or to a cooperative established under the Proclamation No. 147/1998.
11. The total amount of members' savings utilized for loans shall not at any time exceed ________ per cent of the total liability of compulsory savings.
12. All joint loan applications by members or applications by member cooperatives shall be treated as if submitted by one individual client.
13. The guarantor or the borrower may request a change of guarantors for compelling reasons.

Article 10: Cash Management

The funds of the society will be invested in the following manner:

1. Loans to members shall not exceed ________ per cent of the liabilities of the cooperative;
2. The cash-in-hand requirements of the society will be determined on a monthly basis, based on the expected withdrawals during the month under consideration.

Article 11: Net Surplus

1. At least annually, the society shall allocate 30 per cent of the net surplus for the following purposes:

   (a) ________ per cent for reserves until the reserves reach ________ Birr;

   (b) ________ per cent for expansion of activities; and

   (c) ________ per cent for social services.

2. After the amount prescribed in sub-article (1) is deducted, the remaining 70 per cent of the net surplus shall be divided among the members on the basis of the members' shares and members' savings in accordance with the decision of the General Assembly.

3. The society may, with the decision of the General Assembly, opt to increase the value of members' shares rather than compensating with an immediate payment of dividends in cash.

4. Any funds set aside for general reserves, expansion and social services as provided for in sub-article (1) may not be distributed to members unless the society is dissolved.

Article 12: Auditing of the Society

1. The society shall submit to an audit by the appropriate authority at least once a year. The society will share with the auditors all relevant books and accounts of the society and cooperate fully with the audit.

2. The audit report shall be presented to the General Assembly for approval.

Article 13: Fiscal Year

The fiscal year of the society shall be from ________ to ________.

Article 14: Amendments

1. These Bylaws shall be amended by a two-thirds (2/3) majority vote of the General Assembly.

2. Any amendment made by the General Assembly shall be communicated to the appropriate authority within 30 days.

3. Any amendment shall be effective after approval of the appropriate authority.

Article 15: Internal Regulations

Based on the bylaws of the society, internal regulations shall be recommended by the Management Committee for approval by the general assembly.

Article 16: Interpretation

Any ambiguity in the interpretation of these bylaws shall be resolved by the General Assembly.

Article 17: Settlement of Disputes

(a) The Management Committee will attempt to resolve any disputes that may arise within the society prior to referral of such disputes to conciliation and arbitration pursuant to the Proclamation No. 147/1998.

(b) However, the General Assembly shall appoint a special mediation committee or other appropriate body that shall attempt to resolve any disputes that may arise between:

(i) the society and the management;

(ii) a member and the society; and

(iii) the society's committees.

(c) Disputes not resolved within the society shall be conciliated or arbitrated pursuant to the Proclamation No. 147/1998.

Article 18: Dissolution of the Society

1. The society shall be dissolved upon two-thirds (2/3) majority vote of the membership, or when the number of members falls below 10.
2. The society may be dissolved when the society ceases activities for more than ________ years, or when the society becomes insolvent or bankrupt. Whenever the society is bankrupt, the provisions of Article 970(1) and (2) of the Commercial Law and other applicable laws shall apply.
3. In the case of a decision to dissolve the society, the appropriate authority shall be notified within seven days.
4. Upon the liquidation of the society due to bankruptcy, if the member does not have a loan with an outstanding balance owed to the society, the liability of the member shall be limited to the value of his or her shares in the society. If a member has a loan from the society outstanding, his or her liability includes the value of the outstanding balance of the loan.
5. In the event of liquidation, where available funds are insufficient to pay the value of the shares held by the members, the funds shall be distributed pro-rata among the shareholders according to the amount of shares held by each.
6. In the event of dissolution of the society, notice to creditors shall be given in the following manner:

(a) Notice by registered letter shall be sent to all creditors known to the society;

(b) Notice to other creditors shall be given by publishing notice in two successive monthly issues of a newspaper published in the area of operation of the cooperative and by posting notice on the society's notice board.

7. The procedure for formal liquidation of the society shall be as set forth in Proclamation No. 147/1998 and other applicable laws.

Article 19: Official Seal

The society may adopt and use an official seal bearing the words "________ Savings and Credit Cooperative Society Limited Liability". The seal shall be kept securely under lock and key by a duly designated officer of the society and shall be used only by officers authorized to sign documents on behalf of the society.

Article 20: Borrowing by the Society

The society shall not borrow for any reason or from any source without the approval of the General Assembly.

Article 21: Validity and Effectiveness of these Bylaws

These bylaws shall be valid and effective when approved by the General Assembly and registered by the appropriate authority. These Bylaws shall be effective beginning from the date of their registration.

Date ________	Year ________
Signature________	Signature ________
Signature ________	Signature ________
Signature ________	Signature ________
Signature ________	Signature ________
Signature ________	Signature ________

Summary

- The major objectives of the union shall be to solve problems collectively that member societies cannot individually solve, and to facilitate direct relationships between member societies and financial institutions.
- The activities of the union shall include bulk purchase of agricultural produce, supply of agricultural inputs, provision of education and training, marketing facilities, provision of consumer goods and inculcating the habits of savings among member societies.

- Any registered cooperative that satisfies the criteria set by the union shall be eligible for membership in the union.
- Membership application form has to be approved by the management body of the union.
- Union should maintain a membership register which contains details of all the member societies.
- Provision has been made on restriction on holding shares by member societies.
- Member societies do have their rights and duties as prescribed in the bylaw.
- The management of the union shall be conducted by the general assembly; management board; control committee; loan committee; education committee; and other committees and sub-committees as the union sees fit and in accordance with the bylaws.
- All business discussed or decided at management board or committee meetings shall be recorded in a minute book.
- The union shall not pay any salary to its officers for their services. However, for the services they provide, the union may pay per diem and transportation costs upon approval of the management board.
- No officer or employee of a member cooperative shall be party to a decision or influence a decision affecting the relationship, financial and otherwise, of the union to that person's organization.
- The officers, members of the committees and management board, and employees of the union shall hold in the strictest confidence all transactions of the union with its member societies, and all information respecting their confidential affairs, except to the extent deemed necessary by the management board for conducting and recording business of the union.
- The union shall keep up to date and in a proper business-like manner such accounts and such books as the Proclamation No. 147/1998 and regulations may require from time to time.
- Membership in the union shall be terminated upon the voluntary termination by the member society, which may be at any time; the amalgamation or division of the member society; the dissolution of the member society; or the expulsion of the member society from membership.
- Member societies who are terminated may re-apply for admission. In such circumstances, the approval of the general assembly shall be required.

- All member societies shall be entitled to apply for loans from the union subject to the availability of funds and the policies and regulations of the union.
- The cash-in-hand requirements of the union will be determined on a monthly basis by the management board, based on the expected expenses during the month under consideration.
- 30 per cent of the net surplus shall be distributed for reserves, expansion of activities and social services and 70 per cent shall be distributed to member societies as dividend.
- The union shall submit to an audit by the appropriate authority or by an independent auditor appointed by the appropriate authority at least once a year.
- The management board will attempt to resolve any disputes that may arise within the union prior to referral of such disputes to conciliation and arbitration pursuant to Proclamation No. 147/1998.
- The union shall be dissolved upon a two-thirds (2/3) majority vote of the member societies' representatives, or when the number of member societies falls below two (2).
- The union shall not borrow for any reason or from any source without the approval of the General Assembly.
- The main objectives of the SACCO shall be to encourage thrift among its members by affording them an opportunity for accumulating savings; to provide members with the opportunity to receive credit; and to offer members the use of banking services.
- The main activities of the SACCO shall be to collect compulsory and voluntary savings from members; to collect voluntary saving from non-members; to provide loans to members; to collect loans and interest from members; and to pay interest on savings.
- A person of either sex or a cooperative shall be eligible for membership provided that they should fulfill the conditions set forth in the bylaw.
- Every member shall have rights and duties as prescribed in the bylaw.
- The Management Committee shall hear and determine matters relating to any alleged violation of the bylaws or internal regulations of the society by a member. The member has the right to be heard at the time of this determination.
- The management of the society shall be conducted by the General Assembly; Management Committee; Control Committee; Loan Committee; Saving Committee; Education Committee; and other committees and subcommittees as the society sees fit and in accordance with the bylaws.

- ❖ All business discussed or decided at committee meetings shall be recorded in a committee minute book.
- ❖ Any member of a committee leaving office shall immediately return the property of the society.
- ❖ In conducting the affairs of the society the members of the committees and officers of the society shall exercise the prudence and diligence of ordinary persons of business.
- ❖ Before taking part in any business transaction which the society may be about to discuss, every committee member and employee of the society shall be required to disclose any personal interest in the matter, and shall not take part in any discussion or vote upon that item of business.
- ❖ The officers, members of committees, and employees of the society shall hold in the strictest confidence all transactions of the society with its members, and all information respecting their personal affairs, except to the extent deemed necessary by the Management Committee for conducting and recording the business of the society.
- ❖ The society shall keep up to date and in a proper business-like manner such accounts and such books as the Proclamation No. 147/1998 and regulations may require from time to time.
- ❖ Membership in the society shall be terminated upon the voluntary resignation by the member, which may be at any time; the death of the member; or Expulsion from membership.
- ❖ Members who are terminated may re-apply for admission. In such circumstances, the approval of the General Assembly shall be required.
- ❖ All members shall be entitled to apply for loans from the society subject to the availability of funds and the policies and regulations of the society.
- ❖ All loans shall be subject to applicable laws, these bylaws and the policies and regulations of the society.
- ❖ The society shall submit to an audit by the appropriate authority at least once a year. The society will share with the auditors all relevant books and accounts of the society and cooperate fully with the audit.
- ❖ The Management Committee will attempt to resolve any disputes that may arise within the society prior to referral of such disputes to conciliation and arbitration pursuant to Proclamation No. 147/1998.
- ❖ The society shall be dissolved upon two-thirds (2/3) majority vote of the membership, or when the number of members falls below 10.
- ❖ The society shall not borrow for any reason or from any source without the approval of the General Assembly.

- These bylaws shall be valid and effective when approved by the general assembly and registered by the appropriate authority. These bylaws shall be effective beginning from the date of their registration.

Self-Learning Activity

1. List down the activities of the Farmers Cooperative Union as prescribed in the bylaw.
2. Discuss the duties of members of Farmers Cooperative Union as prescribed in the bylaw.
3. Explain the duties of Education Committee of the union as prescribed in the bylaw.
4. What do you understand by the article "Confidentiality Oath".
5. Explain the procedures to be followed for expulsion of members?
6. What are the objectives of SACCO as per bylaw provisions?
7. What do you understand about disclosure prior to election to committees?
8. Explain the duties of Loan Committee of SACCO?
9. Explain the duties of Savings Committee of SACCO?
10. What do you understand by Legal Standard of care?

ANNEX 1
DRAFT COOPERATIVE POLICY OF ETHIOPIA

One of the important steps taken by the Federal Government of Ethiopia is to introduce a draft cooperative policy of Ethiopia. This draft policy is yet to be implemented, but it is under the process of implementation.

Features of Draft Cooperative Policy of Ethiopia

A Policy is defined as statement of a government as to what it intends to do with, for and about something of national importance and significance.

Goal of the Cooperative Policy

Ethiopia has been managing the affairs of cooperatives without having any definite cooperative policy for the past decades. At present the Federal Cooperative Commission has issued a draft of such policy. It is stated in the draft policy that the goal of the cooperative policy is to create conducive socio-economic environment, legal and institutional framework both for the rural and urban dwellers of the population so that they can voluntarily organize cooperative societies by coordinating their knowledge, labour and wealth with which they can be the direct participants and users of the fruits of their movement.

Details of the Policy Objectives

The details of the policy objectives are:

1. Transformation of subsistence farming into modern commercial farming.
2. To create conditions for cooperatives to properly discharge their responsibilities in poverty reduction.
3. To coordinate government, private and cooperative efforts in providing for example, rural electricity and telephone services.
4. To enact cooperative legislations and regulations to assist the cooperative movement.
5. To establish the sustainable working relationship between cooperative movement and government, and non-government institutions.
6. Assist and support women, the youth and the physically disabled segment of the population to organize cooperatives to improve their lives.
7. To organize cooperatives fitting to the peculiar characteristics of the values and customs of the pastoralists to enable them properly utilize the resources of their respective region.
8. To conduct various studies and researches that can help hammer operational and implementation weaknesses and suggest future directions and solutions.

9. To create conducive environment for the relationship to be establish between the national cooperative movements and in other parts of the world and international organizations.

The draft cooperative policy includes the following major issues in order to transform the country's cooperative movement to an elevated level.

(a) Expansion and development of cooperatives;
(b) Cooperative organizational structure – primary, union, federation;
(c) Cooperative finance;
(d) Cooperative education and training;
(e) Cooperative audit and inspection system;
(f) Social participation by cooperatives;
(g) Role and support of the government;
(h) The relationship between cooperatives and other institutions;
(i) Policy implementation.

Expansion and Development of Cooperatives

1. Cooperative shall be established in any socio-economic sector of the economy without contradicting values and principles of cooperatives.
2. Cooperatives shall be encouraged to improve both rural and urban marketing systems by supplying inputs to enhance the production and productivity of the farmers; they will arrange both local and foreign markets for the produces of the farmers so that the farmers could receive better price and efforts shall be made to prevail efficient credit system.
3. Cooperatives shall be encouraged to curb the shortage of houses in cities in collaboration with the private sector and the government.
4. Through continuous education and awareness traditional associations shall be encouraged to organize into cooperatives.
5. To create a link between the consumers and the producers, consumer cooperatives shall be organised.
6. Producers, traders and service providers in rural as well as urban areas shall organize cooperatives to enhance their economic capacity.
7. To enrich the saving culture of the people, saving and credit cooperatives shall be established both in rural and urban areas.
8. In the regions where livestock husbandry is the main stay, cooperatives shall be organised and involved in the production of exportable products, foodgrains, in the mineral and extraction and collection of wild adhesives.

9. Cooperatives shall contribute towards establishing of agro-ecological based diversification and specialization production methods.
10. Efforts shall be made to establish a national network of market information system to help cooperatives in all regions to assist each other in sharing experiences.
11. The government shall offer its maximum support for cooperatives to have their own managers to effectively operate their business.
12. In connection with the making use of appropriate technologies in the fields of artisanship and cottage industries, cooperatives shall be established in urban and rural areas.
13. Notwithstanding international cooperative ceremonies that are celebrated by cooperative movements, "Ethiopian Cooperative Day" shall be celebrated annually on Sunday the first week of July.

Cooperative Organization and Structure

Cooperatives can be established at different levels depending on the type and functions performed by individual cooperatives, usually known as three-tier structure which include primary, union and federation cooperative structures. Primary and union cooperatives are particularly encouraged to be established to participate in the provisions of marketing and credit services. Primary cooperatives, unions and federations may establish a cooperative league.

The operational area of the cooperative societies established at different levels would be based on their economic benefits. The organisation of cooperatives from primary to the national level shall be free from duplication and competition but rather to obtain a better result.

Cooperative Finance

1. In cooperatives, because of the fact that members share capital is the primary source of finance, members shall be encouraged to invest in their cooperatives by buying additional shares. In line with this, members payments and other forms of participation shall be registered and maintained in an appropriate manner and system.
2. Cooperatives shall be encouraged to save and allocate some of their earnings for the expansion of investments.
3. The cooperative fund shall be established in order to let cooperatives access and obtain credit services from commercial banks.
4. Cooperatives shall be encouraged to insure their properties against risks and uncertainties.

5. Cooperatives shall contribute towards building investment capacity by providing additional saving and credit services.
6. Cooperative banks shall be formed when cooperatives have gained financial strength through internal savings.

Cooperative Education and Training

1. Basic cooperative education and benefits shall be included into curriculum of primary education. Further, regular cooperative programme shall be offered in higher education institutions.
2. Programmes in cooperatives shall be disseminated through mass media both at regional and federal levels.
3. With a view to enhance and assure the competitiveness of cooperatives in the free market economy, management, book-keeping, business administration and other related skills improving training shall be offered in the short term and in the long term.
4. Domestic and international experience sharing programmes shall be prepared to produce sufficient manpower trained in the cooperative profession. Capable cooperatives shall be motivated via different mechanisms.
5. Cooperative Training Institutions shall be established at regional as well as federal levels.
6. To support cooperatives to attain efficient operation and to make their products competitive in the world market, studies and researches shall be conducted in the field of cooperation.

Cooperative Audit and Inspection

1. The government shall provide audit services until cooperatives have become self sufficient in affording to pay such services.
2. A system of operation and management peculiar to one type of cooperatives shall be established. To support this effort various operational manuals shall be developed and implemented.

Community Service by Cooperatives

1. Cooperatives shall participate and would play their role based on the regulations in the effort to solve the problems of their community. Particularly cooperatives would contribute in expanding rural electrical activities, education and environmental health care, clean water supply, natural resource conservation, protection and inharmonizing cultural and traditional lives of the people with technological advancements.
2. Cooperatives shall not be a forum for promoting political or religious objects. However, a member is entitled to follow or not any political or religious outlook on his/her own.

3. The sustainability of cooperation is measured by the participation of younger generation in cooperative societies. In this regard cooperatives shall create job opportunities with the objective of refraining the youth from spending their time and energy inappropriately and to instill in them good attitude towards diligent by establishing youth clubs and formulating various income generating schemes.

The Role and Support of the Government

1. The government will enhance the capacity of the rural cooperatives to help them transform subsistence farming into modern one through capacity building.
2. The government shall play positive intervention role in organizing and expanding cooperatives in different sectors of the economy. It shall transfer this role to cooperative federations and league to be established in the future.
3. Cooperatives shall participate in the rural, urban and industrial development and capacity building, and other development policies, strategies and programmes to bring about enhanced overall development.
4. The government shall issue cooperative legislations, it provides technical supports and carries out appropriate supervision.
5. Land shall be given free for cooperatives to carry out production, distribution and service provision and house construction.
6. Cooperatives shall be encouraged to be involved in real estate development to alleviate shortage of housing.
7. Cooperatives shall be entitled to participate in the marketing activities without additional permit requirement once they are legally certified and registered.
8. The government shall provide legal protection to ensure that cooperative properties are not exposed for misappropriation.

Cooperative Relations with other Institutions

1. The relationship between cooperatives and other private and governmental organizations shall be based on members approval and consent.
2. NGOs can financially and materially support cooperatives in carrying out integrated development activities and in human resource development.
3. Cooperatives can participate in development activities with private organisations either in concessions or in partnership.

4. These relationships with other institutions shall be checked that cooperative values and principles are maintained and the spirit of societies self help and autonomy are not violated.

Policy Implementation

1. The ultimate beneficiary of cooperative policy is the people and without active participation of it, the implementation of this policy is unconceivable.
2. Thus, based on the constitutional right given under Article 31 of the Federal Constitution, conducive conditions shall be prevailed to enable the people to benefit from this right.
3. Different government structures at all level shall create conducive condition to ensure that this policy is appropriately implemented and to let the people make use of rights granted in the constitution.
4. Federal and Regional governments shall render appropriate support in the endeavour to expand cooperatives in Ethiopia.
5. Cooperatives that are organized from primary to federation shall mobilize their members in implementing this policy, they shall also generate policy improving ideas by carrying out studies and researches.
6. All concerned cooperatives at all levels, government bodies and others involved in the sector shall meet and evaluate and discuss on performance and problems encountered.
7. The Federal Cooperative Commission shall be responsible for presenting and getting it approved on policy improvements in collaboration with others involved in the sector and based on comments obtained from the people.
8. An advisory board shall be established comprising members from the Federal Council of representatives, Rural Development Committee, Cooperative Institutes, mass media and from NGOs to oversee the implementation.of the policy on established criteria.

References

Baldwin, Van P., "*A Legal Guide to Co-op Administration,*" A Reference to those who work with cooperative administration and the legalities encountered, Seventy Pages, Center for Cooperatives, University of California.

Cooperative Development Center, "Cooperative Development Center." Four Pages. Gives their purpose, services, contact name, critical organization steps, and "why incorporate". Available: *http://gw.pol.org/Agriculture_Resources/Cooperative_Development_Cente.htm,*

Guenzel, Robert. "Liability of Directors." Original presented at the annual meeting of the Nebraska Cooperative Council, 1975, revised 1992, 1993. Discusses the Directors' Duties. "Legal Precautions for Cooperative Directors." A one-page handout without a source includes main points such as insurance.

Minnesota Association of Cooperatives, "Legal." One Page. States that there was a recodification of Minnesota's Cooperative Laws in 1993, you can download Chapter 308A from this site. Available: *http://www.mncoop.org/issues-legal.htm,*

Negarit Gazeta, "A Proclamation (Proclamation No.138/1978) to Provide for Establishment of Cooperative Societies", The Provisional Military Administration Council, Addis Ababa.

Negarit Gazeta, "A Proclamation (Proclamation No.274/2002) to Provide for Establishment of Cooperatives Commission", Addis Ababa.

Negarit Gazeta, "Cooperative Societies Proclamation No. 147/1998", Addis Ababa.

Negarit Gazeta, "Cooperative Societies Proclamation No. 241/1966", Addis Ababa.

Negarit Gazeta, "Council of Ministers Regulation No. 106/2004 of FDRE", Addis Ababa.

Negarit Gazeta, "Cooperative Societies (Amendment) Proclamation No. 402 / 2004", Addis Ababa.

Negarit Gazeta, "Farm Workers' Cooperative Decree No. 44/1960", Addis Ababa.

Negarit Gazeta, "Proclamation No. 85/1995, Agricultural Cooperative Societies Proclamation", Addis Ababa. Roy, E.P. (1964).

Negarit Gazeta, "Proclamation No. 85/1994, Agricultural Cooperative Societies Proclamation", Addis Ababa.

Sippel, William L., "Marketing Agencies in Common, It Takes Two (or more) to Tango." Three pages. It discusses the antitrust immunity for marketing agencies in common. Available: *http://www.mncoop.org/publications-marketing.htm.*

United States, Department of Agriculture, Agricultural Cooperative Service, "*Cooperative Principles and Legal Foundations*" Cooperative Information Report 1, section 1, issued 1977, reprinted 1988, reviewed and approved for reprinting July 1990. *It gives basic features, objectives and structure, and legal foundations.*

University of Wisconsin Center for Cooperatives, "Articles of Incorporation for Cooperatives, including a sample outline."Two pages. A fill in the blank sample of articles of incorporation. Available: *http://www.uwcc.wisc.edu/info/anicles.html.*

University of Wisconsin Center for Cooperatives, "Bylaws for Cooperatives, including a sample outline." Three Pages. A sample outline for bylaws for a cooperative. Available: *http://www.uwcc.wisc.edu/info/bylawus.html.*

University of Wisconsin Center for Cooperatives, "Guidelines for Cooperative Bylaws." Two pages. Gives a list of twenty guidelines for cooperative bylaws. Available: *http://www%20wise%20edu/uwcc/info/bylaw%20html*

University of Wisconsin Center for Cooperatives, "Membership Application for Cooperatives, including a sample outline." Three Pages. A sample membership contract for a cooperative. Available: *http://www.uwcc.wisc.edu/info/memapp.html.*

Index